IMAGES
of America

Walnut Street YMCA and YWCA

On the Cover: This early-1940s photograph illustrates the collaboration between the YMCA and YWCA in an activity for both male and female adults. It takes place in one of the meeting rooms in the new building, which was completed in September 1940. The adult standing in the three-piece suit is Earl Bruce Tate, secretary of Boys' Work from 1940 to 1945. (Courtesy of the Delaware Historical Society.)

IMAGES
of America

WALNUT STREET YMCA AND YWCA

Jeanne D. Nutter, PhD

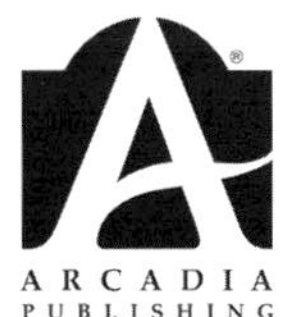
ARCADIA PUBLISHING

ISBN 978-1-4671-6160-2

Published by Arcadia Publishing
Charleston, South Carolina

Printed in the United States of America

Library of Congress Control Number: 2024932066

For all general information, please contact Arcadia Publishing:
Telephone 843-853-2070
Fax 843-853-0044
E-mail sales@arcadiapublishing.com

Visit us on the Internet at www.arcadiapublishing.com

To William Young Sr., whose documentation of the early history provided a context for the book, and to Barbara Washam, who preserved many of the photographs that illustrate the rich experiences enjoyed at the Walnut Street YMCA and YWCA.

Contents

ACKNOWLEDGMENTS

The majority of the photographs in this book have been contributed by the Walnut Street YMCA, the Delaware Historical Society (DHS), and the Washam family collection. I would like to thank Anesha Laws, executive director of the Walnut Street YMCA, for graciously allowing me access to the archives of the organization. For over 20 years, I have worked with the archives at the Delaware Historical Society for both book and documentary film projects. I would like to thank Leigh Rifenburg, Bill Robinson, and Ed Richi for their assistance in finding both photographs and documents in the DHS collections. Dolores Washam and Lynn Clayton Jones generously allowed me to use the many photographs and documents Barbara Washam had collected over her years as the physical education director at the YWCA. I would also like to thank Linda Gross, reference librarian at Hagley Library; Valerie Stenner, library assistant II at the University of Delaware; and Margaret Winslow, curator of the Delaware Art Museum, for providing me with images. Gerald Piotrowski at Colourworks did an excellent job providing photography and digital services. I could not have completed this project without the assistance of so many in the Wilmington community and beyond, including these individuals: Spencer Henry, Jamie Loper, Ernest Jackson, Clara Hollis, Beverly Evans, Pattie Harris, Addie Mae Cole, Judith Gupton Wiley, Sheryll Jackson Slade, Gilbert Jackson III, Doris Cannon, Charity Patton, Canon Lloyd S. Casson, Thomas Roberts, Jacqueline Roberts, Patricia Sadler Griffin, Patricia Hackett Hampton, William S. Young, Anita Young, Enid Wallace-Haley, Christopher M. Ryan and Andrew Foy of the YMCA of Delaware, Mary Young, Buck Simpers, Thorpe Moeckel, Cynthia Oates, Madeline Bolden Johnson , Linda Woodard, Alphonso Brock, Stephanie Hunt Evans, Marvin Thomas, Debra Campagnari Martin of the City of Wilmington, Charles B. Ryan from Homsey Studio, Florence Collins Hardy, Gladys Brister Spikes, Marion Brister, Beatrice Coker, Juanita Pritchett, Ernest, 'Sammy" Congo, Niki Ingram, Donald Brown, Willard Cephas Sr., Willard Cephas Jr., John Barnes, Charles Hayward, Julius Jackson, Victor Morgan, Evelyn Poe Jr., Mark Sills, Lucille LaFate, Claire Lamar Carey, Harmon Carey, Dr. Roderick Carey, Ned Brown, Kathleen Williams, Dawn Stevenson, William Wallace, Pearl Wallace, Lafayette Jackson, Sharon Bryant, Retha Fisher, Edward Johnson, George Washington, and Tim Fisher.

Introduction

Excitement grew on November 19, 1939, as 3,000 people assembled at the cornerstone laying for the much anticipated Walnut Street YMCA and YWCA. The program included dignitaries from both the African American and white communities. The following year, this magnificent edifice, a gift from philanthropist H. Fletcher Brown and his wife, Florence Hammett Brown, was opened to a throng of over 1,000. Little did the Browns realize how the institution would make such an imprint on the African American community. It was the physical structure, the programs, the staff, and volunteers that changed the lives of so many. The Browns had expressed their wish to have space for both the YMCA and YWCA. In doing so, they created the only YMCA building in the country that accommodated both a YMCA and YWCA. During the 1940s, 1950s, and 1960s, because of segregation, there were no facilities for African Americans in Wilmington except the schools and churches. The Walnut Street YMCA and YWCA, therefore, became the de facto center of African American culture. It was the "heartbeat" of the African American community and a center of Black excellence. Outside organizations such as the NAACP, fraternities, sororities, and social clubs also held their activities there.

The building was designed by G. Morris Whiteside, a well-known architect in the area. Ten years earlier, he had designed the Central YMCA which was the branch for white men. The Walnut Street building was fabricated in a contemporary style and incorporated African American sculptural elements on the exterior. The six friezes were designed by architectural sculptural artist S.H. Bass. Many thought the artist was African American but Bass was a Russian immigrant from Philadelphia. He must have studied African American culture thoroughly because the friezes depicted many notable African Americans of the 1930s. These architectural friezes created a welcoming motif for members and visitors. The importance of these images cannot be overstated, because they were probably the only public art of African Americans in the city of Wilmington at that time. The friezes were a source of pride for the community. One of the defining features of the structure was the lighted clock tower. Members looked at the light as a beacon of welcome. When the building was renovated in the 1990s, the clock tower was the only structure that was retained. The light, however, is no longer lit. Whiteside took care to include original artwork in most of the rooms. Two paintings were created by African American artist Edward Loper Sr., who later became a major artist in the United States. The rooms were decorated with fine furniture and beautiful drapery. It was a very pleasant place to enter.

The staff created programs and activities that expanded the worlds of both children and adults. Many of the executive officers came from other YMCA and YWCA positions and had considerable experience operating a facility and developing programs. As a result, when the building opened there were significant programs in place. Both the YMCA and YWCA were in full operation. The volunteers were leaders in the broader community and their expansive network provided support for Walnut Street. Many of the male board members were also members of the Monday Club and the Masons. Both male and female volunteers belonged to the numerous African American churches, fraternities, and sororities. Many were teachers, administrators, and business and medical professionals. The volunteer leadership drew from a pool of highly skilled individuals. The reach of the YMCA and the YWCA was immense.

The programs were varied and many provided expertise that members often utilized later in life. This was not a facility that functioned as a "drop in" center, but a place where children, especially African American boys, "lived." They did everything at Walnut Street. One man said that in the summer and on the weekends he would go to the YMCA at 8:00 a.m. in the morning and leave at 9:00 p.m. in the evening. He stayed all day as did many other youngsters. When they grew older, it was not uncommon for boys to earn money by working as "pin boys" in the bowling alley. Youth programs such as the Hi-Y and the Y Teens provided valuable leadership skills. There were also activities such as dance, gymnastics, bowling, charm, chess, golf, drama, art, and choir. The most significant program, however, was swimming and lifesaving.

During the 1940s, 1950s, and 1960s, African Americans in most states were forbidden to swim at public beaches and swimming pools. The pool at Walnut Street was, therefore, a significant part of the building, because it was the only indoor pool available to African Americans. Kruse Pool was available, but it was an outdoor pool. Through the swimming program, hundreds of children and adults learned swimming and lifesaving skills. A July 26, 1947, article in the *Morning News* reported that Forrester Lee had organized 350 boys in a swimming course. The article even mentioned water polo. The following month, the newspaper reported on a water safety course Lee was offering. Boys were not the only ones learning to swim. Barbara Washam, a physical education director of the YWCA, conducted numerous swimming and lifesaving classes for women and girls. An interesting phenomenon was that the program helped many young people become award-winning swimmers and divers. They competed in the larger community and beat their competitors. This is important because it was often believed that African Americans could not or did not swim, let alone compete. Lafayette Jackson, James Lewellyn Bell, Willard Cephas, Barbara Washam, Betty Ann Naylor, and Yvonne Bratcher were some of those award-winning aquatic athletes. There was even a swim team. Another program called Gym/Swim had young people participate in gymnastic activities and then had them swim. It was difficult to participate in Walnut Street YMCA and YWCA programs without spending considerable time in the pool. In recent years, there has been much concern about the disproportionate number of African American children drowning because of a lack of swimming skills. The national YMCA has even initiated a program called *Safety Around Water.* Over 70 years ago, the Walnut Street YMCA and YWCA found a solution to this issue.

The YWCA was highly organized before they moved to the Walnut Street facility. In fact, they had their own building on Tatnall Street. As with the men, the women were leaders in their communities. Some of the leaders of the YMCA had spouses who were equally active in the YWCA. The organization often coordinated activities with the YMCA. A major difference between the YWCA and the YMCA is that one of the aims of the national YWCA organization was to eliminate racial discrimination so there were many joint activities with the white King Street YWCA and the Walnut Street YWCA. During segregation, African American professional women who moved to Wilmington often stayed at the King Street YWCA dormitory, because they could not find adequate housing elsewhere.

Walnut Street also held public forums relevant to the African American community through its Public Affairs programming. Educating the community was a key component of the institution. The Walnut Street YMCA and YWCA offered something for all.

One

The Cornerstone Laying

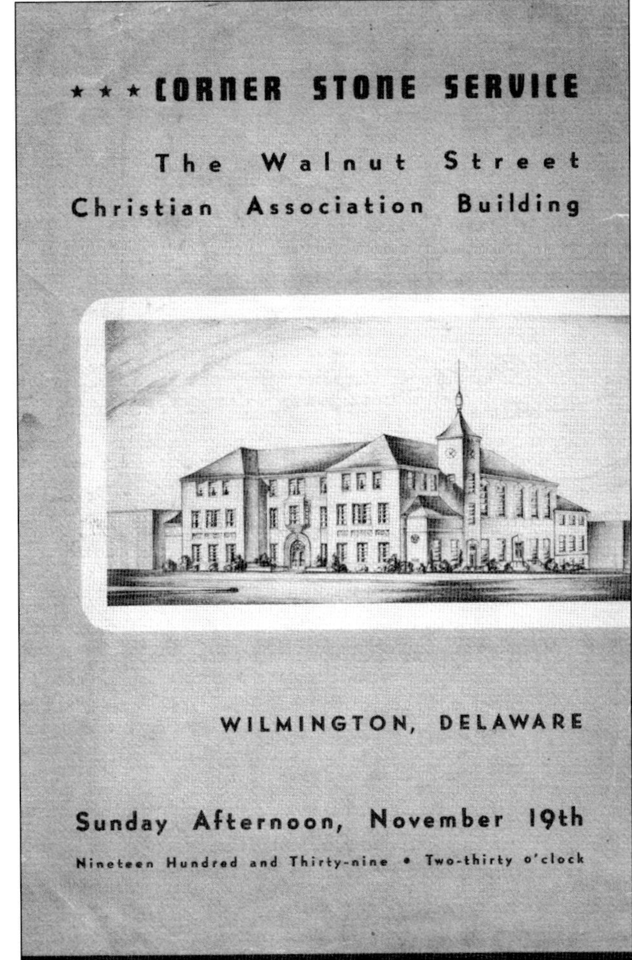
★ ★ ★ CORNER STONE SERVICE

The Walnut Street
Christian Association Building

WILMINGTON, DELAWARE

Sunday Afternoon, November 19th

Nineteen Hundred and Thirty-nine • Two-thirty o'clock

This is the program cover for the cornerstone laying in 1939. This event was attended by 3,000 people and included speeches and performances by local elected officials, religious leaders, Masonic officials, and YMCA and YWCA staff and volunteer leadership. It was one of the most notable events of the year. (Courtesy of the Delaware Historical Society.)

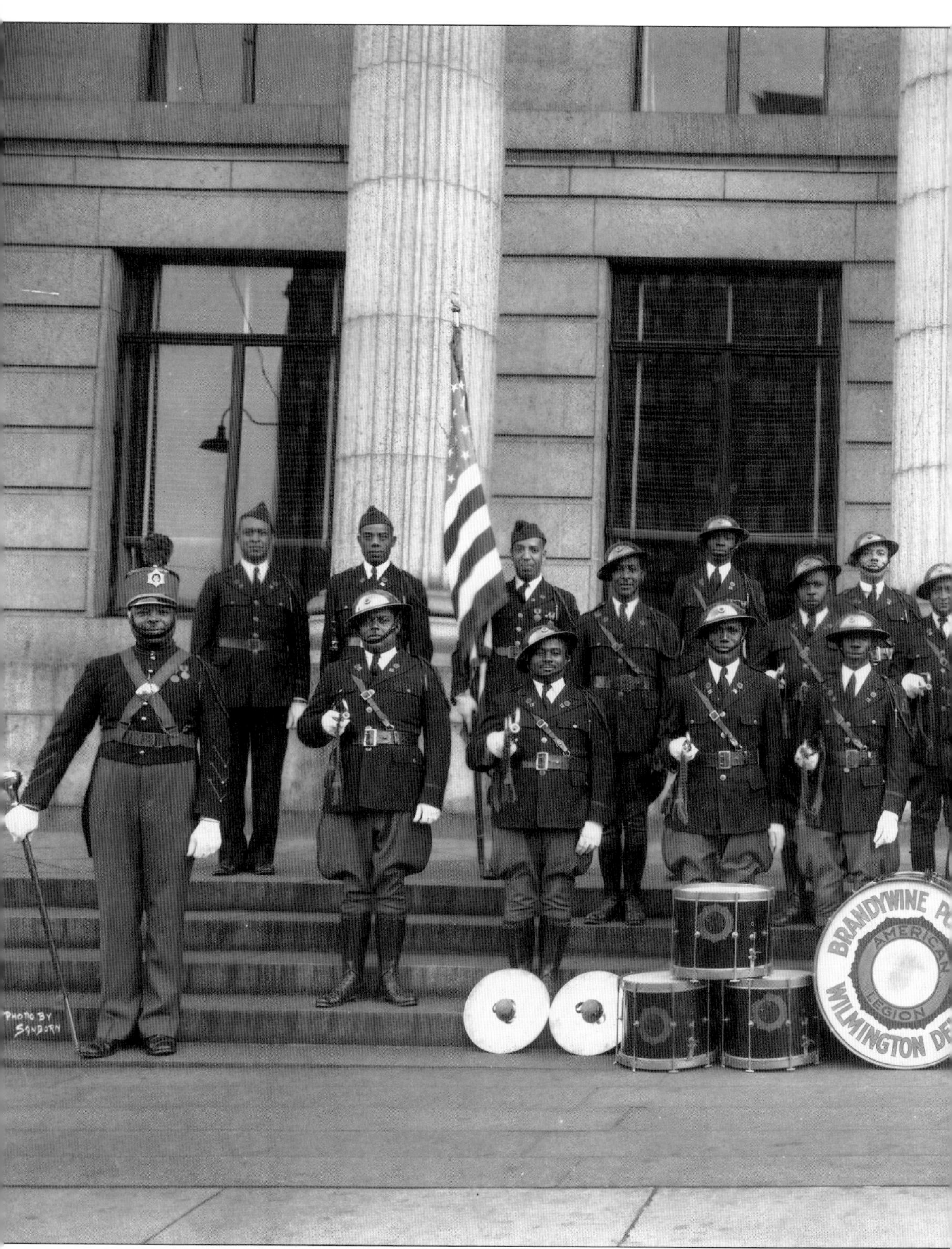

Prior to the cornerstone laying program, there was an impressive parade composed of African American bands from the Paul Laurence Dunbar Elks Lodge, the John A. Watts Band, the Hiram

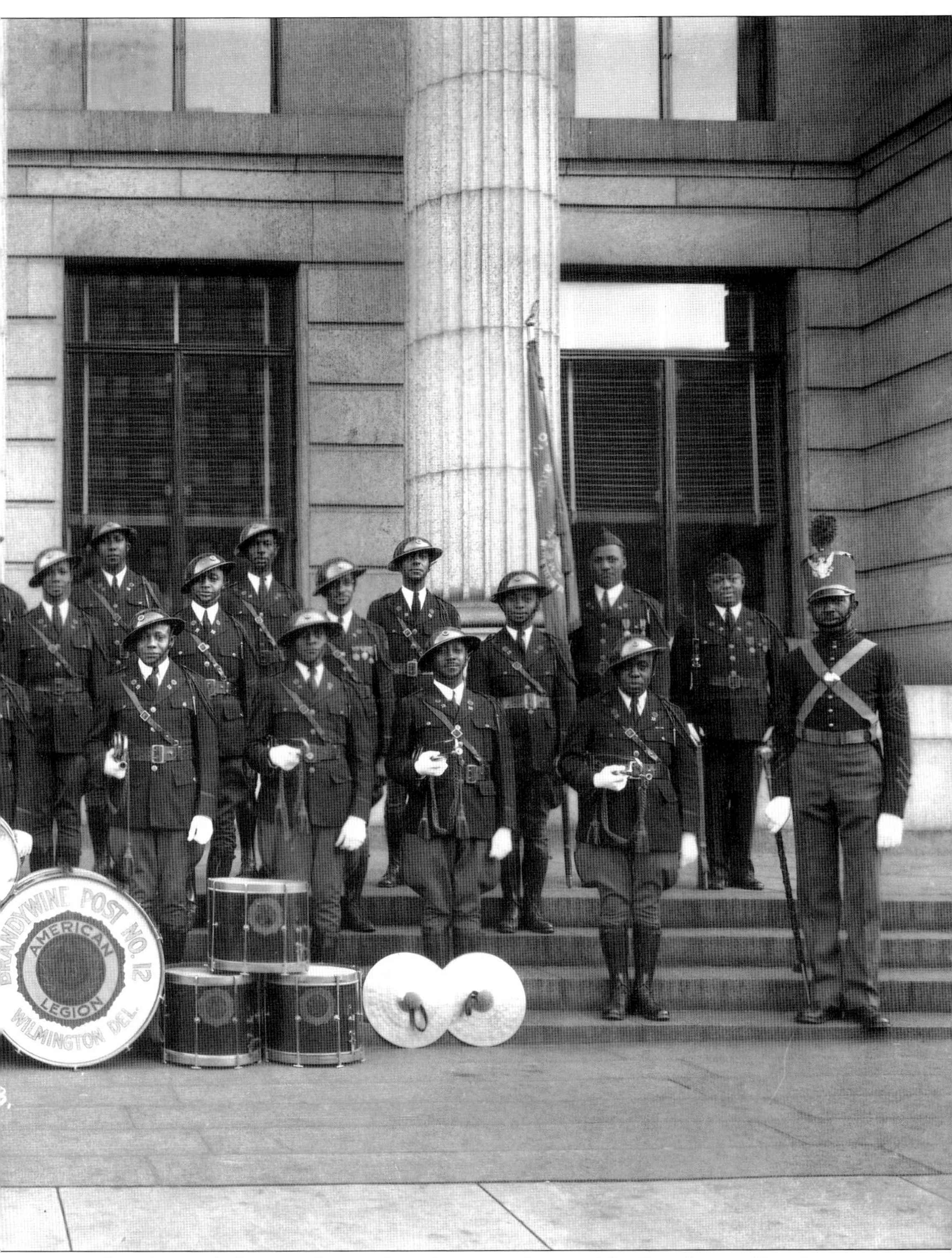

Grand Lodge, and the Brandywine Post American Legion. The Brandywine Post American Legion Drum and Bugle Corps is pictured here. (Courtesy of the Delaware Historical Society.)

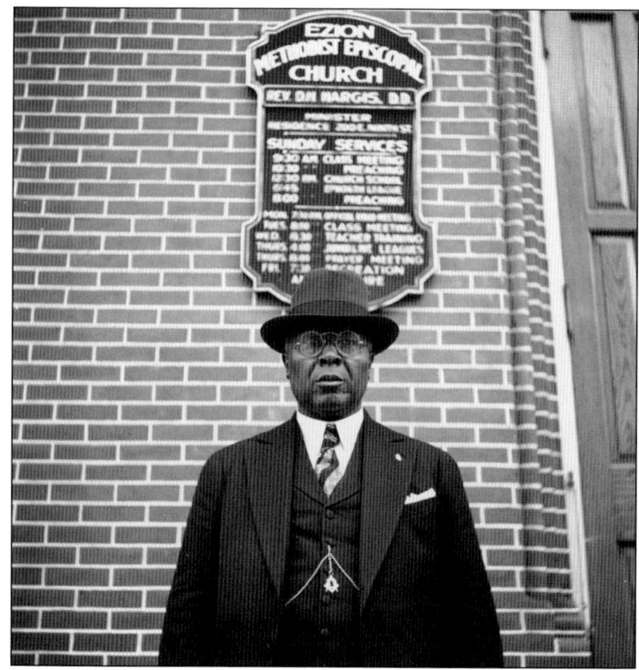

Pictured here is the senior minister of Ezion Church, Rev. David Hargis, who provided the scripture reading. He also became very involved with the YMCA over the years. Notice the medallion on his vest. It is a Masonic symbol. The Masons were a major part of the ceremony and members were later active in YMCA leadership. Rev. S.H. Barker, minister of Bethel AME Church participated in the program by offering the invocation and the benediction. He also became very involved in the activities of the YMCA. (Courtesy of the Delaware Historical Society.)

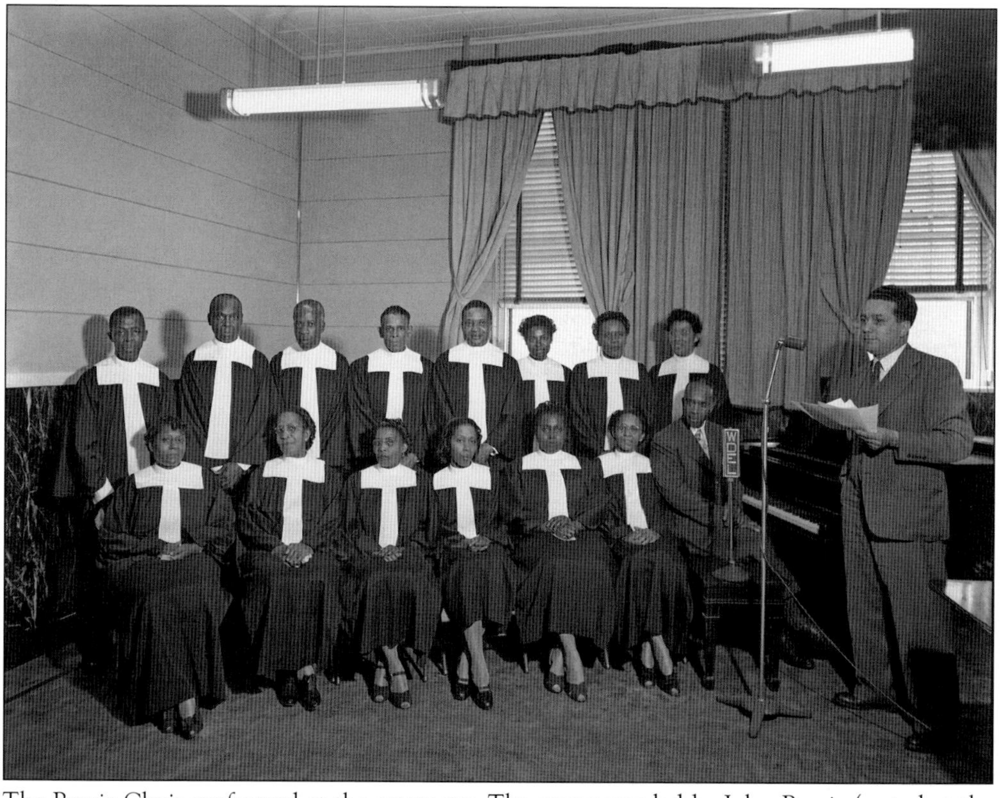

The Bowie Choir performed at the ceremony. The group was led by John Bowie (seated at the piano), who was also the choir director of Bethel AME Church. (Courtesy of the Delaware Historical Society.)

C. Oscar Carrington, pictured on the right, coordinated the entire cornerstone-laying event. He managed all of the correspondence and arrangements. For most of his life, Carrington was an active member of the YMCA Board of Managers. He was the longest-serving chair of the board. Carrington was employed as a counselor at Bancroft School. Among his many activities, he was a Grand Master of the Masons, volunteered with the Boy Scouts, and received the Silver Beaver Award. Highly revered in Wilmington, when he died, the flags in the city were lowered to half-mast. His wife, Florence Carrington, was a very active volunteer with the YWCA and was also employed at the Y. (Courtesy of the Walnut Street YMCA.)

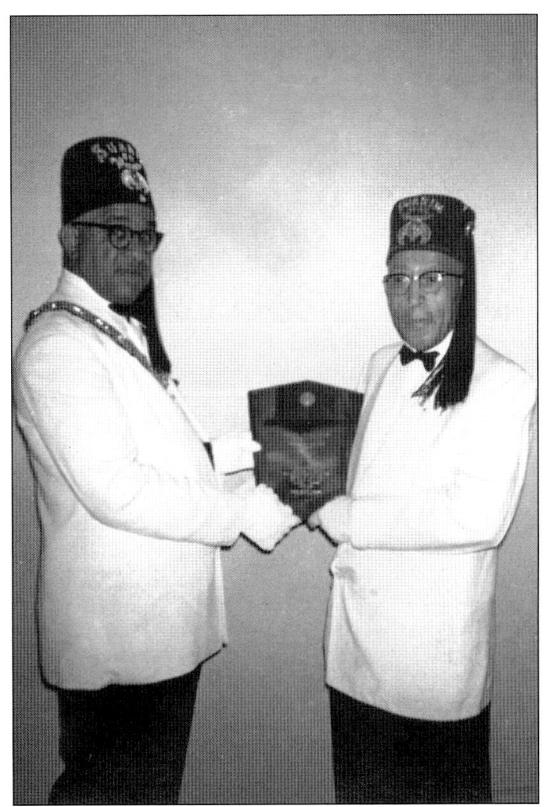

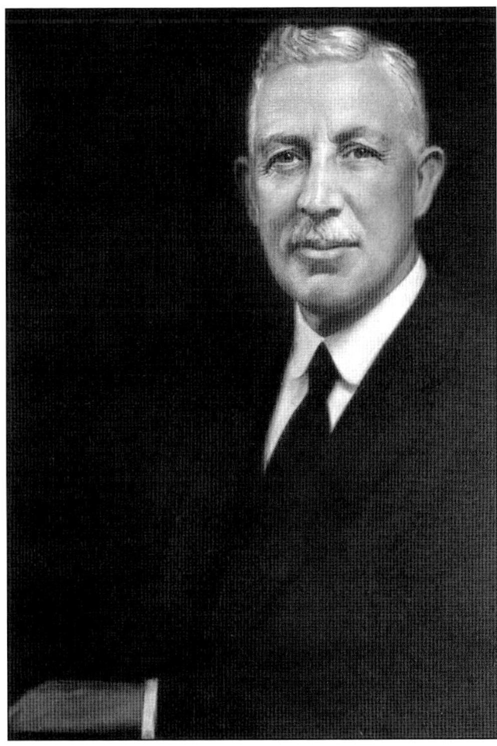

Gov. Richard Cann McMullen was the highest elected official to participate in the event. He served as governor of the state from 1937 to 1941. (Courtesy of the Delaware Historical Society.)

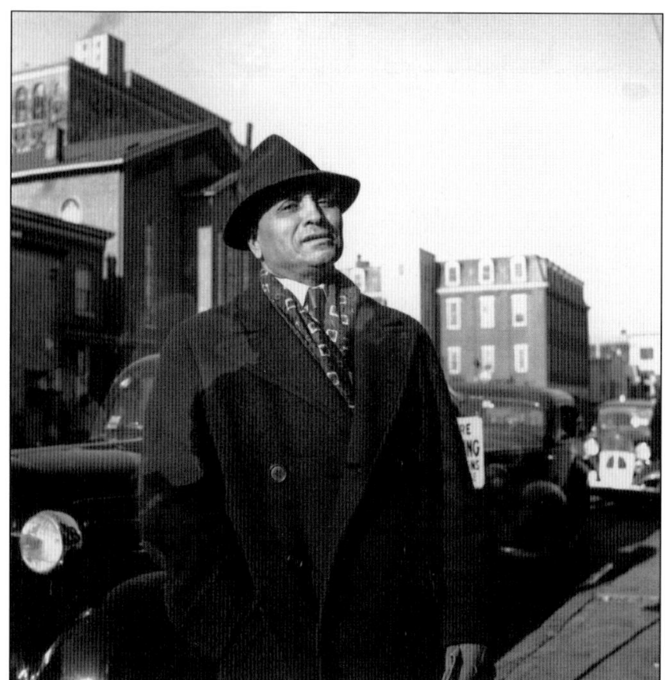

John Hopkins represented the City Council of Wilmington. Hopkins was one of the first African Americans to be elected to the city council serving from 1913 to 1945. He was also a prominent entrepreneur who owned the only African American movie theater in Wilmington. Hopkins actively participated in the YMCA. (Courtesy of the Delaware Historical Society.)

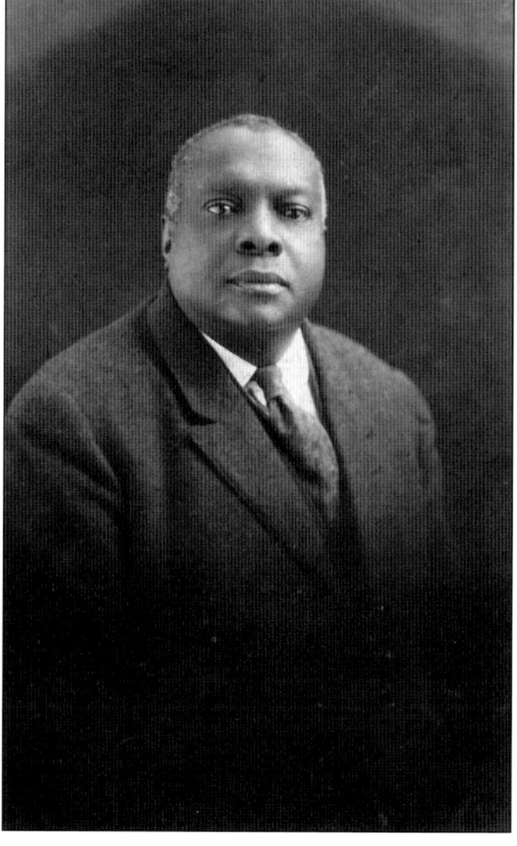

William Winchester also represented the City Council of Wilmington. He, too was one of the early African Americans to serve on city council serving from 1925 to 1941. In 1948, he became the first African American elected to the Delaware House of Representatives. The William Winchester Bridge was named in his honor. (Courtesy of Beverly Evans.)

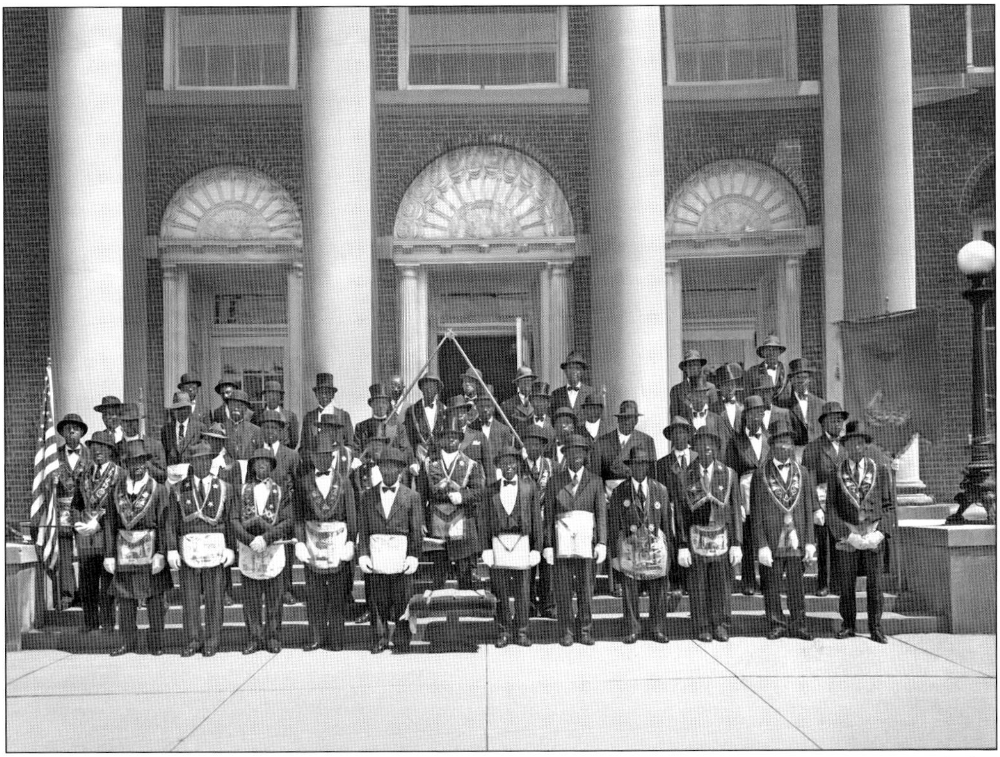

Hiram Grand Lodge participated in the ceremony, led by John Hubert, Grand Master. The lodge was officially organized in 1849. In 1880, it acquired property on Twelfth Street in Wilmington. The building not only served the lodge but also provided temporary space for other organizations such as Shiloh Church and Howard High School. (Courtesy of the Delaware Historical Society.)

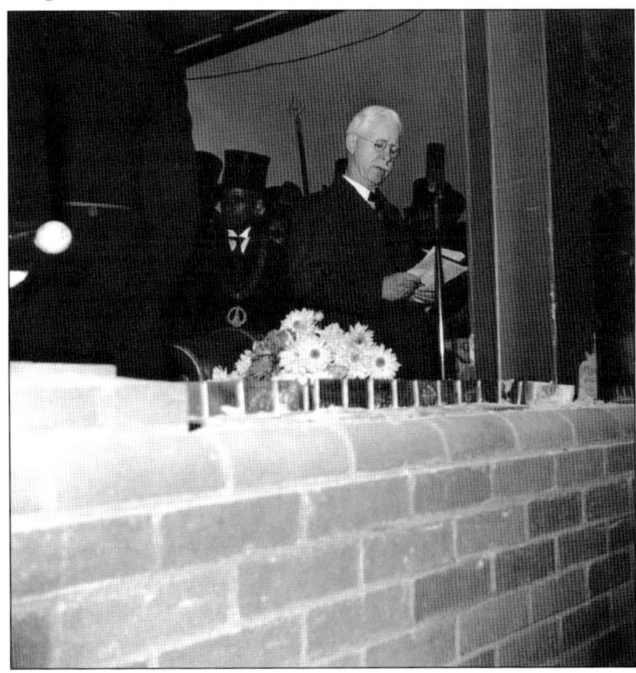

Pictured here is Walter Livingston Wright, president of Lincoln University who provided the keynote address. Wright served as president of Lincoln from 1936 to 1945. During World War I, he worked in France doing educational work with the YMCA. The president following him was Horace Mann Bond, the first African American president of Lincoln. After Bond, all of the presidents of the college were African American. Bond was the father of H. Julian Bond, a civil rights activist who served on both the Georgia House of Representatives and Georgia State Senate. (Courtesy of the Delaware Historical Society.)

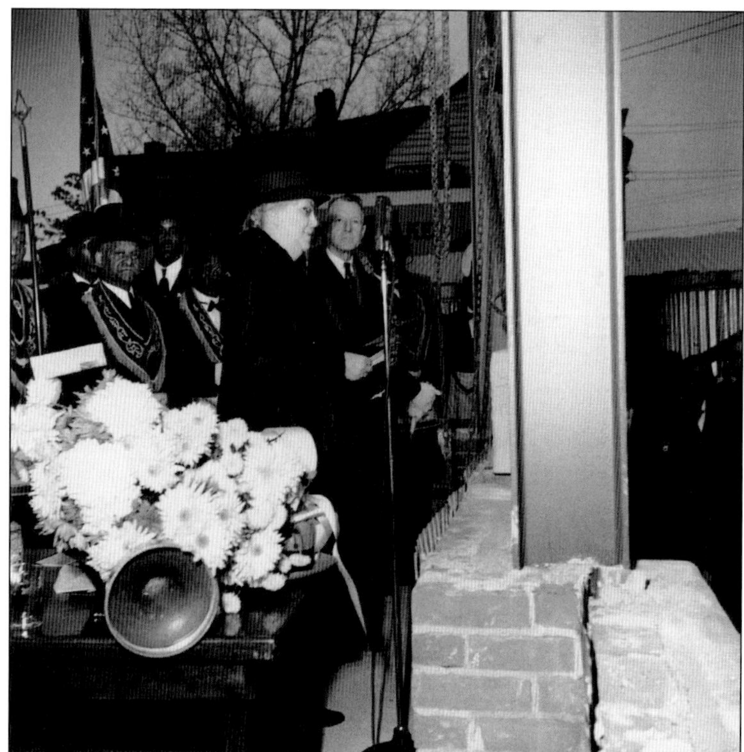

The woman in the photograph is Matilda Horn, president of the YWCA of Wilmington. She remained active with the Walnut Street YMCA. (Courtesy of the Delaware Historical Society.)

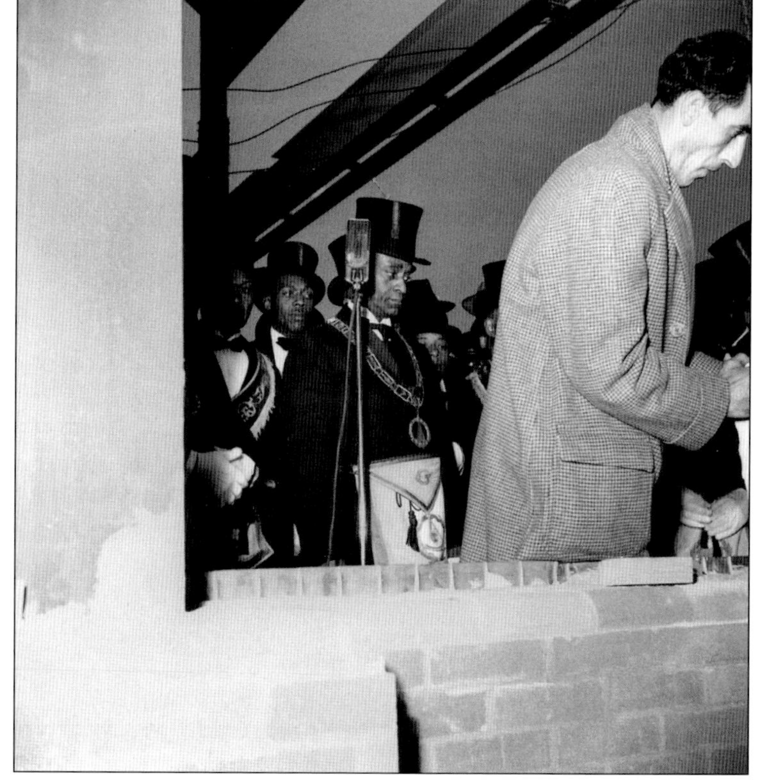

This is a picture of the actual cornerstone ceremony. John Hubert, Grand Master of the Hiram Grand Lodge, is prominent in the photograph wearing the top hat. His rank in the organization is represented by the medallion around his neck. He helped place the mortar on the stone. (Courtesy of the Delaware Historical Society.)

In this picture, one can see the actual cornerstone being placed. A time capsule which included letters from African American organizations and dignitaries was placed in the cornertsone. (Courtesy of the Delaware Historical Society.)

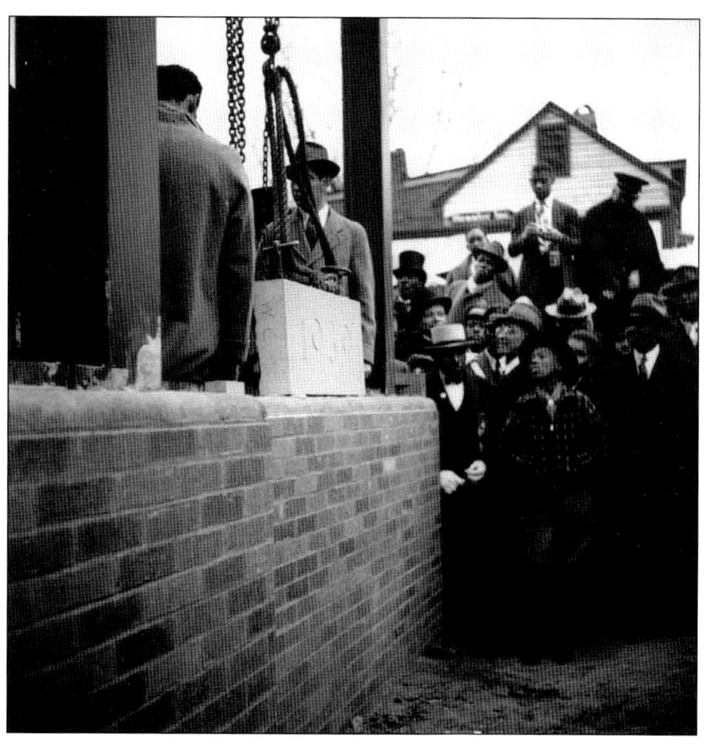

Monday Club, Inc.

917 FRENCH STREET

BELL PHONE, 2-9755

WILMINGTON, DELAWARE

November I9. I939

We as a civic body in the community wish to show our appreciation to Mr. H. Fletcher BROWN for having made it possible for our people to enjoy what promises to be a very splended Y. M. C. A. building and we hope all our people will fully realize the need of this building and rally to its support at all times so that in many many years to come those related to Mr. Brown can say; Well; Fletcher's gift must have been appreciated.

To the Committee on the laying of the corner stone we congratulate. and to the world we want it known that; The Monday Club Inc. is always one hundred percent in support all simular movements.

Signed;

Dr. John H. W. Ayers
President

Patrick J. Harris (Secretary)

H. Roland Milbury Treas.

This is a letter from the Monday Club, which is believed to be the oldest African American male club in the nation. It dates back to 1893. Originally, it was composed of men who worked in wealthy white homes as butlers and chauffeurs. Later, it became a club for professional men too. Many of the leaders in the YMCA were members. This letter is significant because it was one of the letters in the time capsule placed in the cornerstone. (Courtesy of the Delaware Historical Society.)

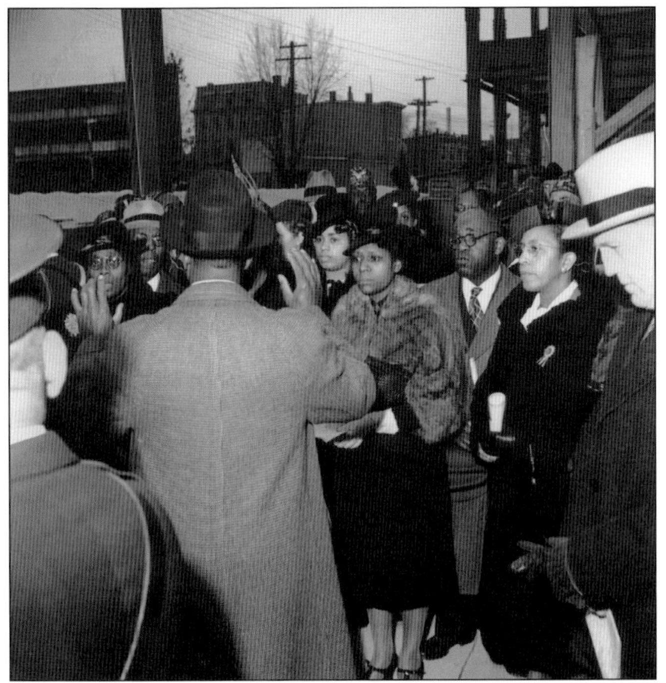

This group of people appears to be the Bowie Choir actually performing at the event. The man in the hat with hands raised appears to be John Bowie conducting the choir. The woman on the far right is a well-known Howard High School teacher, Allie Holley. (Courtesy of the Delaware Historical Society.)

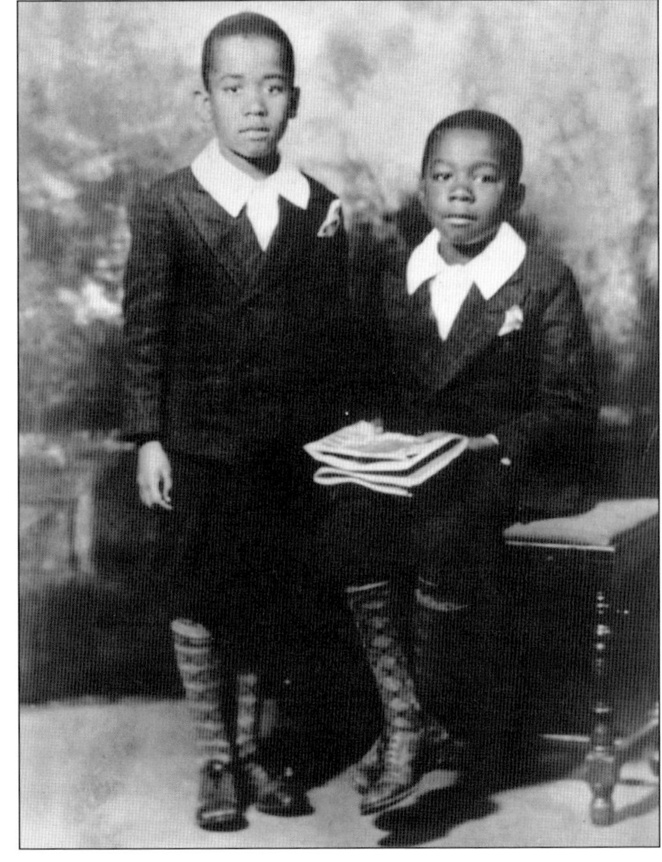

Adults were not the only people attending the event—five-year-old twins Floyd and Lloyd Casson were there too. Lloyd Casson fondly remembers the ceremony. Floyd and Lloyd were placed in foster care and lived in many different homes. The Walnut Street YMCA became the one constant in their lives. They participated in the Hi-Y, learned to swim, and attended Camp Brown and Camp Tockwogh. They had their first paying job as pin boys in the Y bowling alley. Later, as adults, they became volunteer leaders. (Courtesy of Canon Lloyd S. Casson.)

Two

The New Building

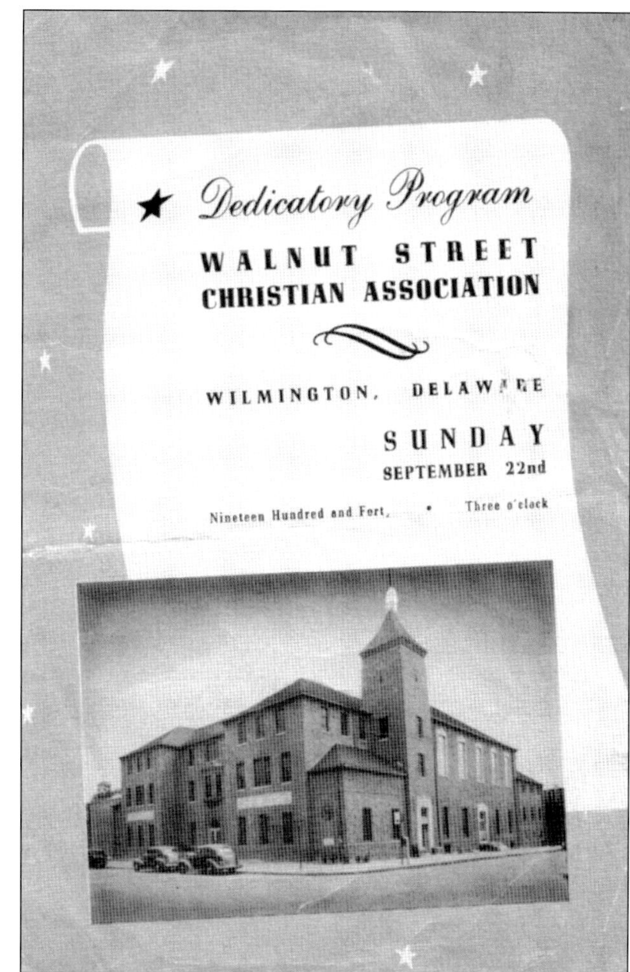

The official dedication of the building was held on September 22, 1940. There were 1,000 people in attendance. The auditorium seated 600 and the gymnasium seated 400. Many people had to listen to the festivities through speakers posted on the outside of the building. (Courtesy of Ora Belcher.)

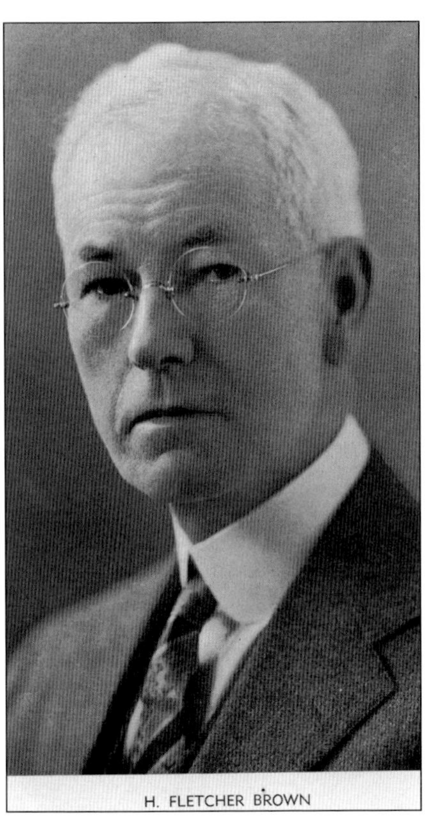
H. FLETCHER BROWN

H. Fletcher Brown was a retired DuPont Company executive and a major philanthropist in Delaware. He and his wife provided $1 million for the construction of the building and an endowment to assist with the maintenance of the facility. Brown participated in the opening ceremony (Courtesy of Hagley Museum and Library.)

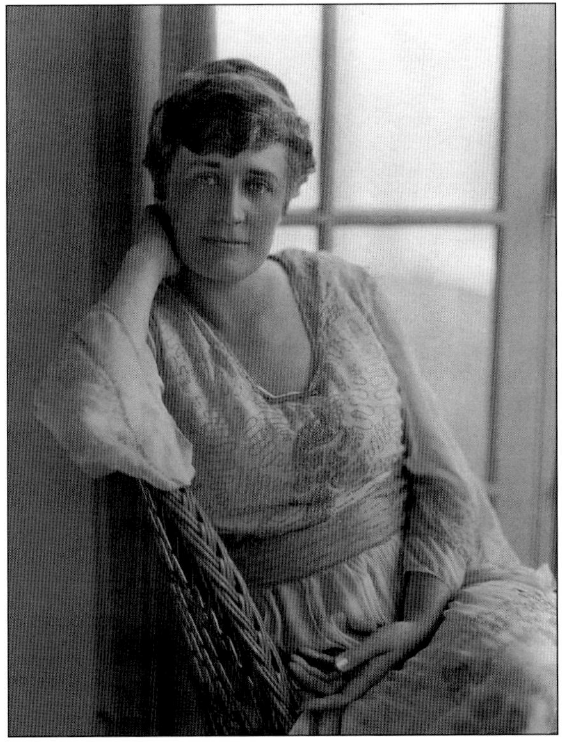

Florence Hammett Brown was a partner with her husband in donating the building. She may have been the influence to ensure that the YWCA was part of the building. The Browns encouraged the YMCA to include the women's branch in the endeavor. As a result, the Walnut Street YMCA/YWCA became the only building in the country to accommodate both men and women. (Courtesy of the Delaware Historical Society.)

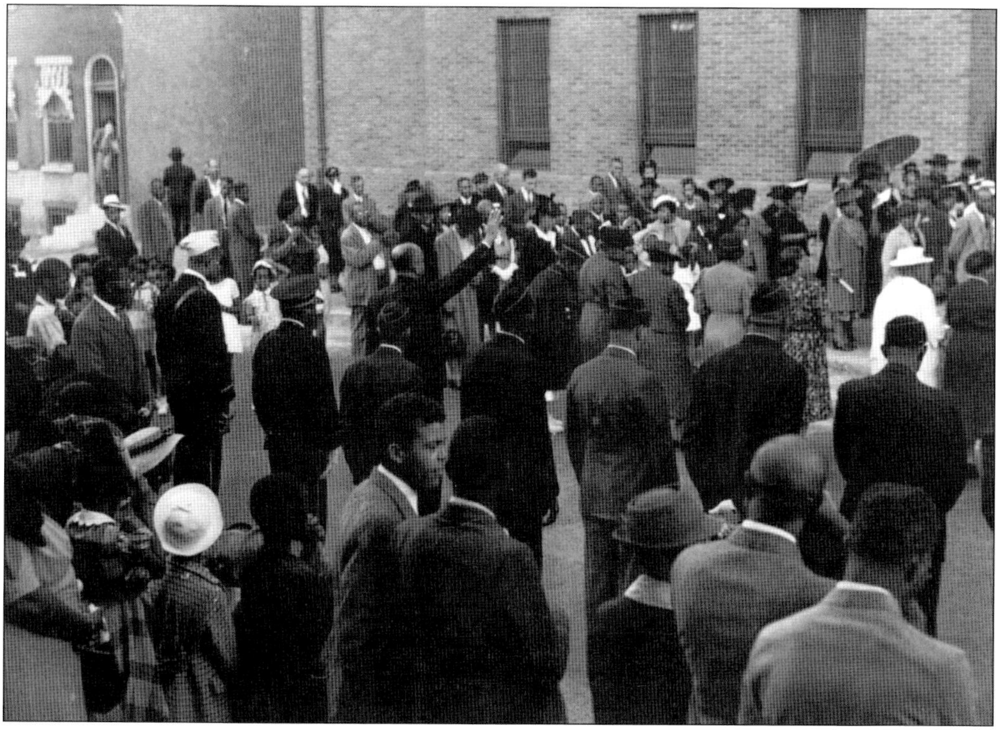

This photograph of people assembled outside the building during the opening were probably those who were not able to obtain seats inside. (Courtesy of the Walnut Street YMCA.)

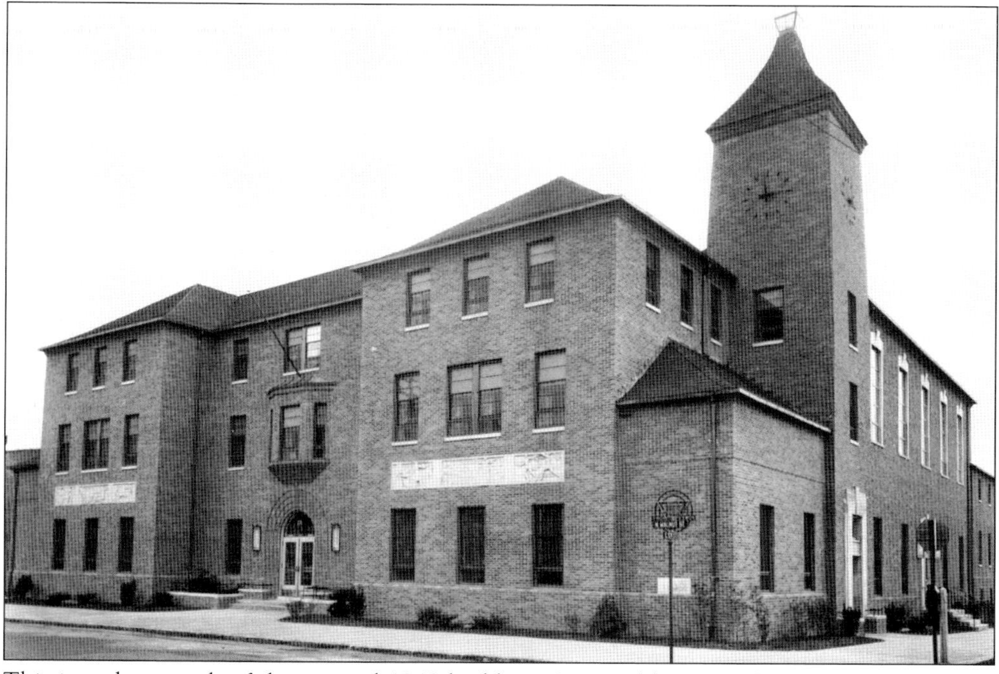

This is a photograph of the original 1940 building. One is able to see the six friezes across the front of the building and the ironwork over the main door and on the symbol located on the right side facing the building. (Courtesy of the Walnut Street YMCA.)

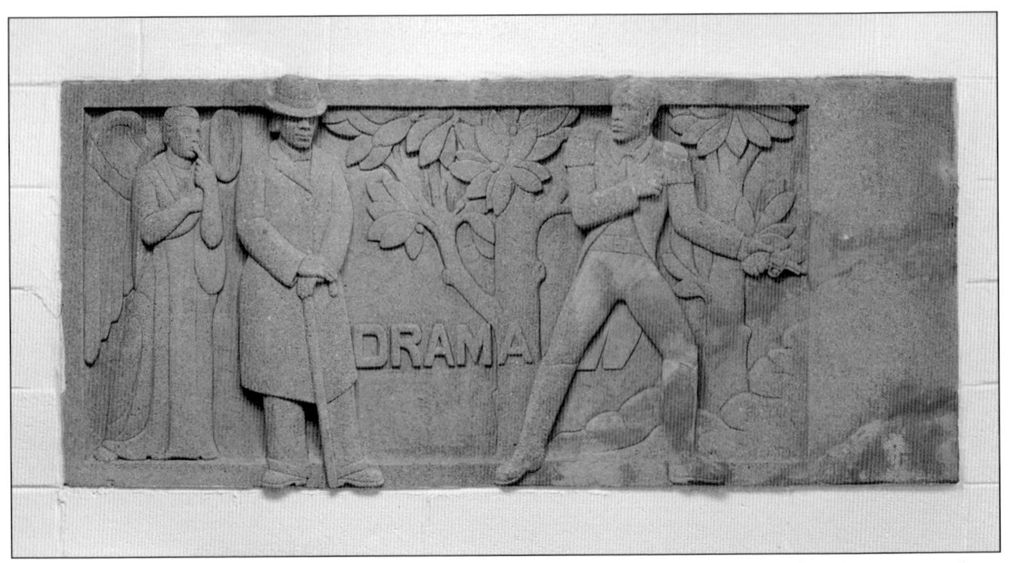

This panel is entitled "Drama." On the left Richard B. Harrison is depicted as he appeared on Broadway as "de Lawd" in the 1930 play *Green Pastures*. He was featured on the cover of *Time* magazine 10 days before he died. On the right side of the frieze is Paul Robeson depicted in the 1935 play *The Emperor Jones*. Robeson was a well-known actor, singer, athlete, and activist. (Courtesy of the author.)

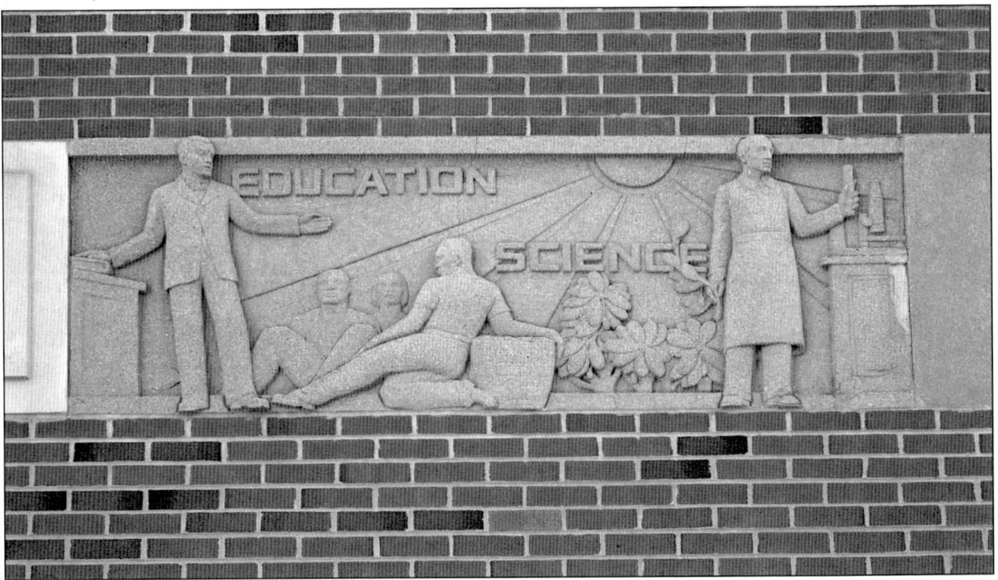

This panel reads "Education" and "Science." On the left is educator Booker T. Washington, who founded the Tuskegee Institute. Washington was a well-known African American leader who believed in the value of manual education in sharp contrast with W.E.B. Dubois, who favored a more academic approach. On the right is the scientist George Washington Carver, who was born enslaved but became one of the most prominent African American scientists. Carver taught and worked at Tuskegee Institute so it was fitting that he and Washington were positioned on the same panel. He is noted for discovering numerous uses for the sweet potato, almond, and peanut. It was timely that he was honored on this panel in 1940 because he died in 1943. (Courtesy of the author.)

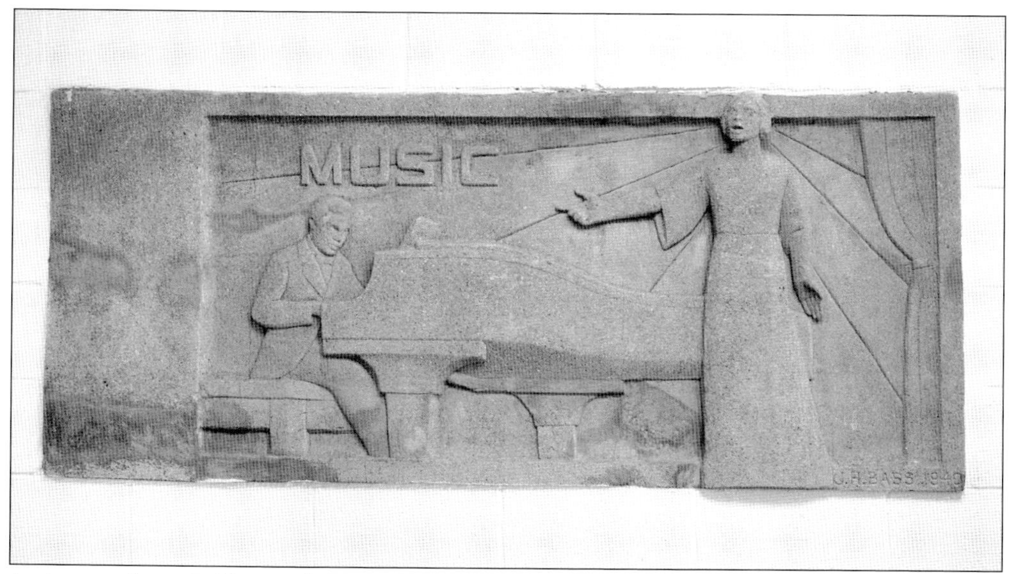

In this panel entitled "Music," the world-famous contralto Marian Anderson is portrayed standing next to a piano. In 1939, the Daughters of the American Revolution refused to allow Anderson to appear in their concert hall. First Lady Eleanor Roosevelt took up the cause and arranged for Anderson to appear at the Lincoln Memorial. The concert became a historical event. Anderson was also the first African American female to sing at the Metropolitan Opera. Even though Bass would not have known, Anderson would eventually have a Wilmington connection. Her husband, architect Orpheus Fisher, lived in Wilmington as a child. During their marriage, the Fishers would often visit his relatives in Wilmington. (Author's collection.)

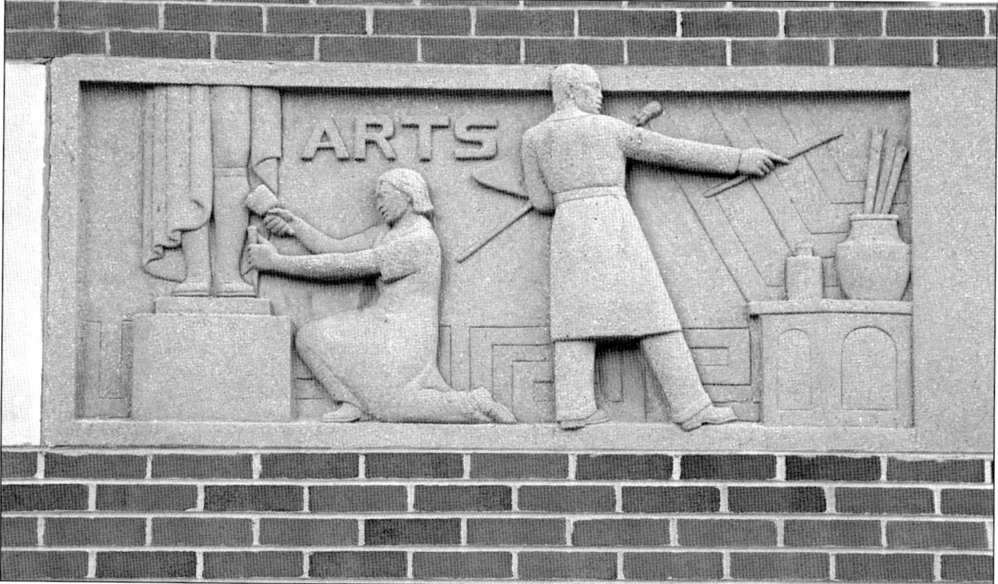

In the "Arts" panel, one can see a female sculptor and a male painter. Even though these figures are not identified with any particular individual, the woman may have been modeled after sculptor Augusta Savage. At the time she was known for creating a sculpture for the 1939 World's Fair, entitled *Lift Every Voice and Sing*. Meta Warrick Fuller was also an active African American female sculptor at the time, but the figure favors Savage. (Author's collection.)

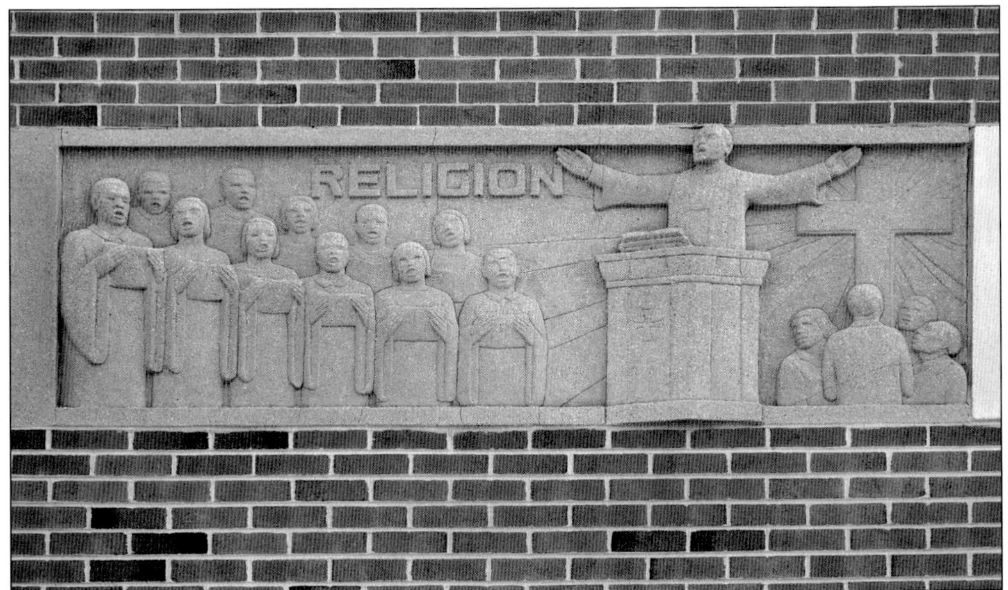

This panel, entitled "Religion," shows an African American minister and a choir. This panel is significant because the "C" in YMCA and YWCA stands for "Christian." The organizations have a religious foundation. (Author's collection.)

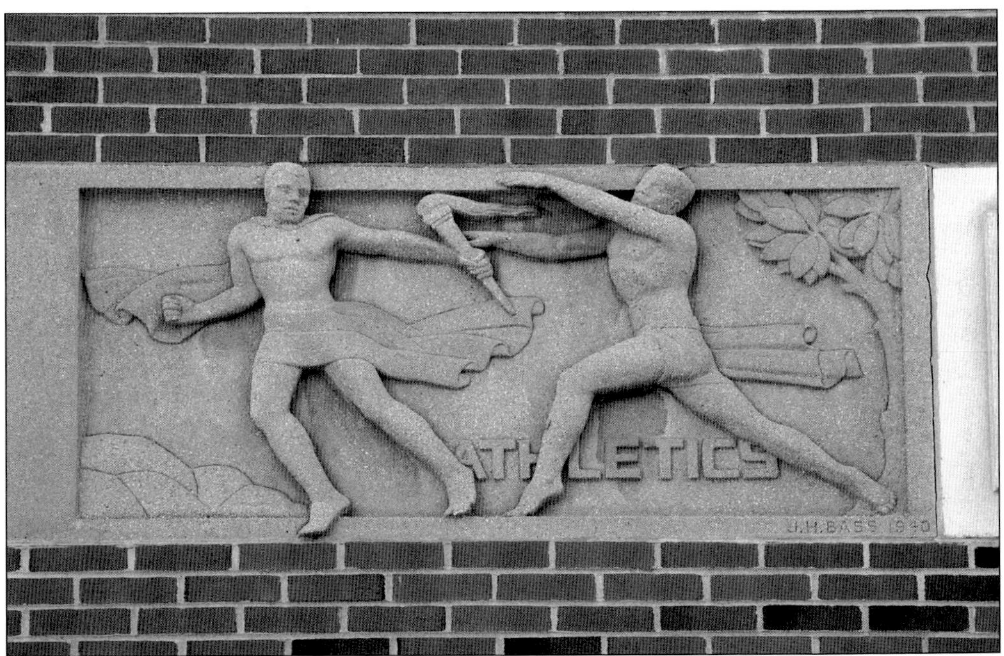

This final panel, "Athletics," shows runners in a relay race. Again, the individuals were not identified but this was the era when Jesse Owens broke the world record for track at the 1936 Berlin Olympics and won four gold medals. (Author's collection.)

In addition to sculptural art, the building was enhanced with decorative ironwork by a well-known company in Wilmington, Victor, and Frank. The depiction of a sailing ship graced the doorway of the building. Groups often took photographs at the entrance of the Y, and the ship is prominent in the pictures. Victor and Frank were known for their ironwork, and it could be found at the gates of Grace Lawn Memorial Park and the railings at First Presbyterian Church. (Author's collection.)

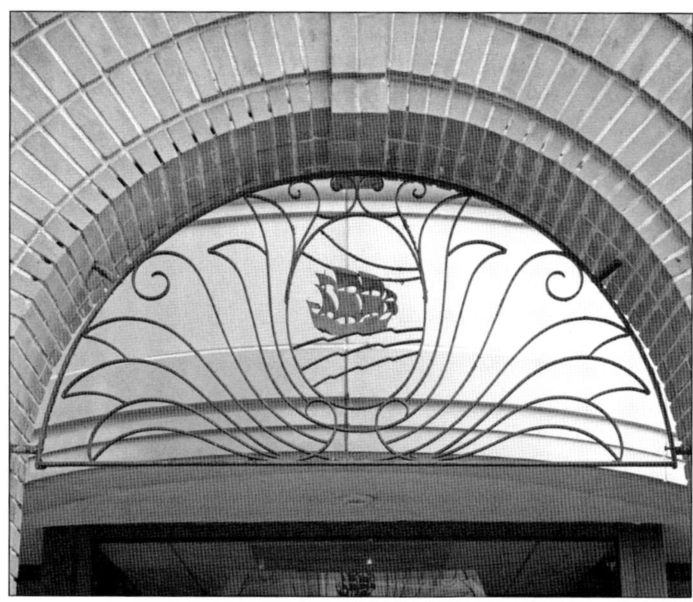

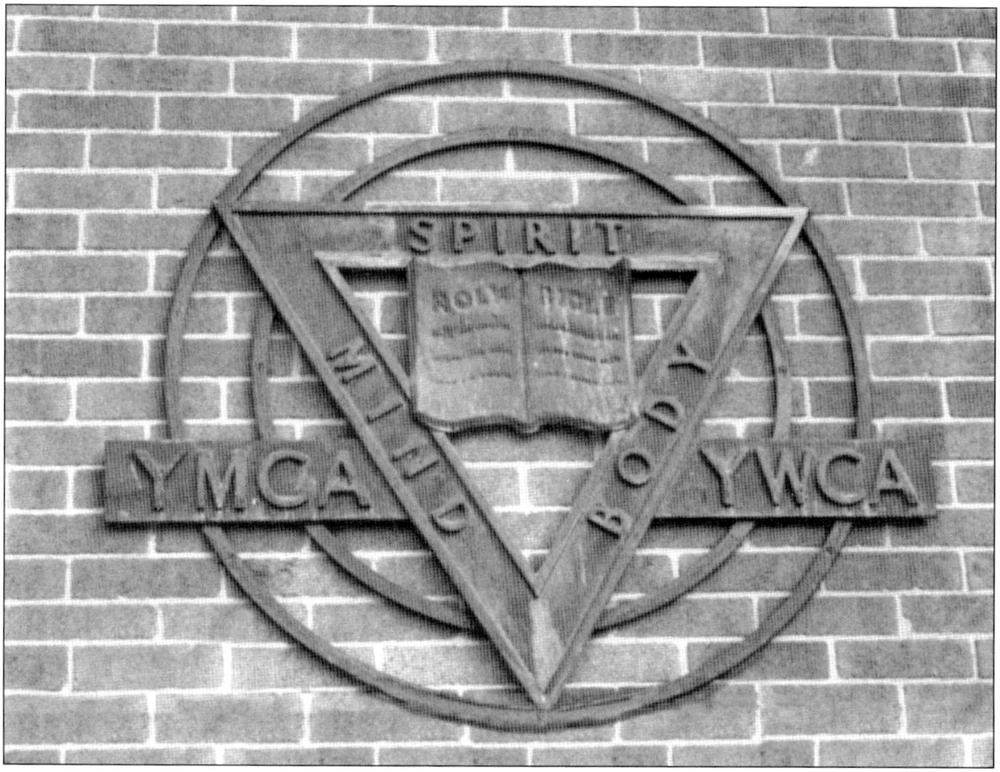

On the left corner of the building was the symbol of the YMCA. The words "spirit," "mind," and "body" were the motto of the organization. These attributes formed the foundation for the programming. Local photographer Devere Patton took this photograph before the original building was demolished. Patton was one of the first African American professional photographer at the DuPont Company. He also had his own business as a freelance photographer and documented many African American events. (Courtesy of Charity Patton.)

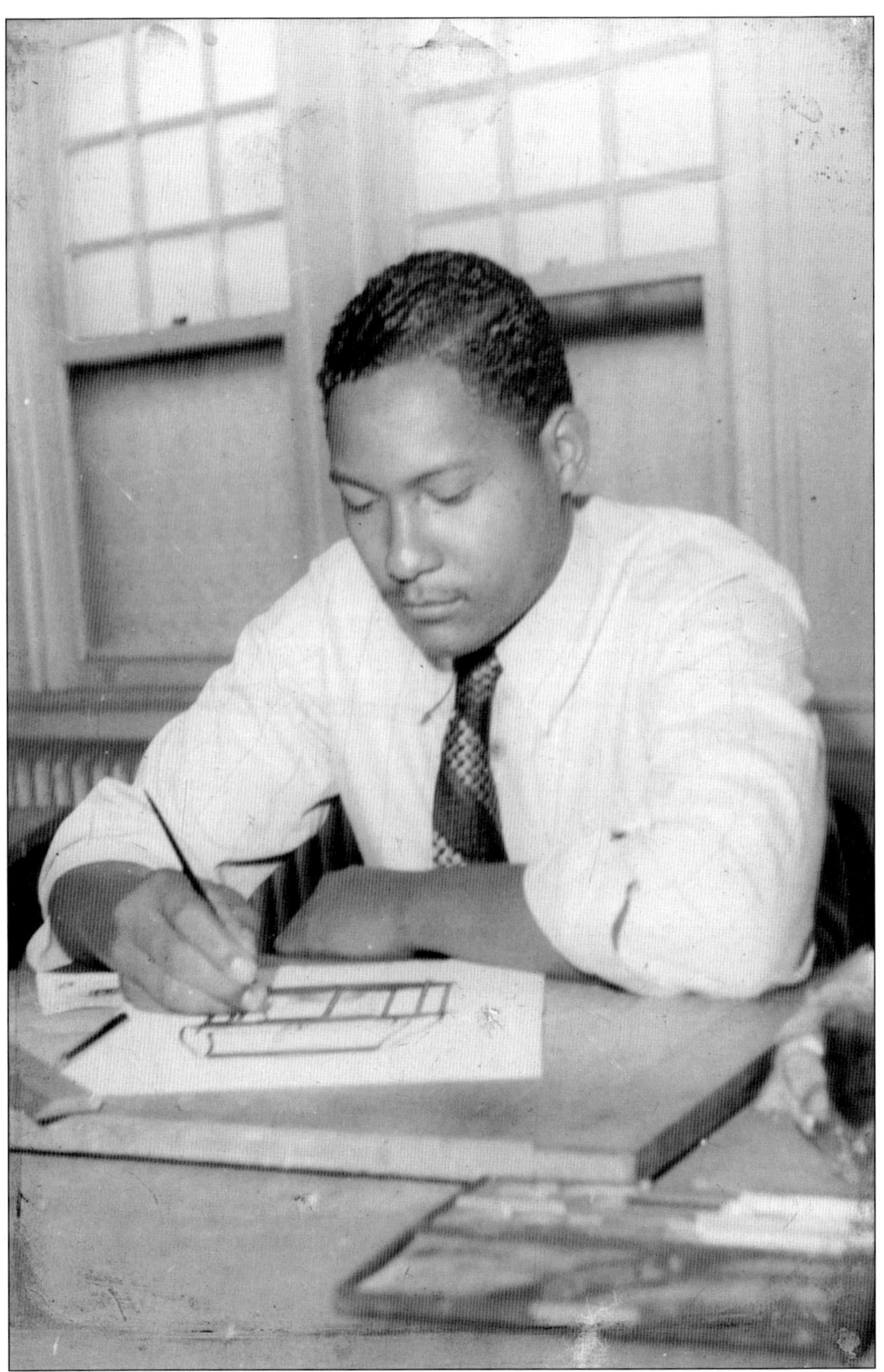

Edward Loper Sr. was a native of Wilmington and a product of the public schools. He developed artistic talents as a young man and became a nationally recognized artist. During the 1930s, he was just embarking on his career, and during the time the building was constructed, Loper was part of the WPA doing illustrations of folk arts and crafts. Two of his paintings were hung in the new Walnut Street building. Loper is also credited for stenciling some of the beams in the rooms. (Courtesy of the Delaware Historical Society.)

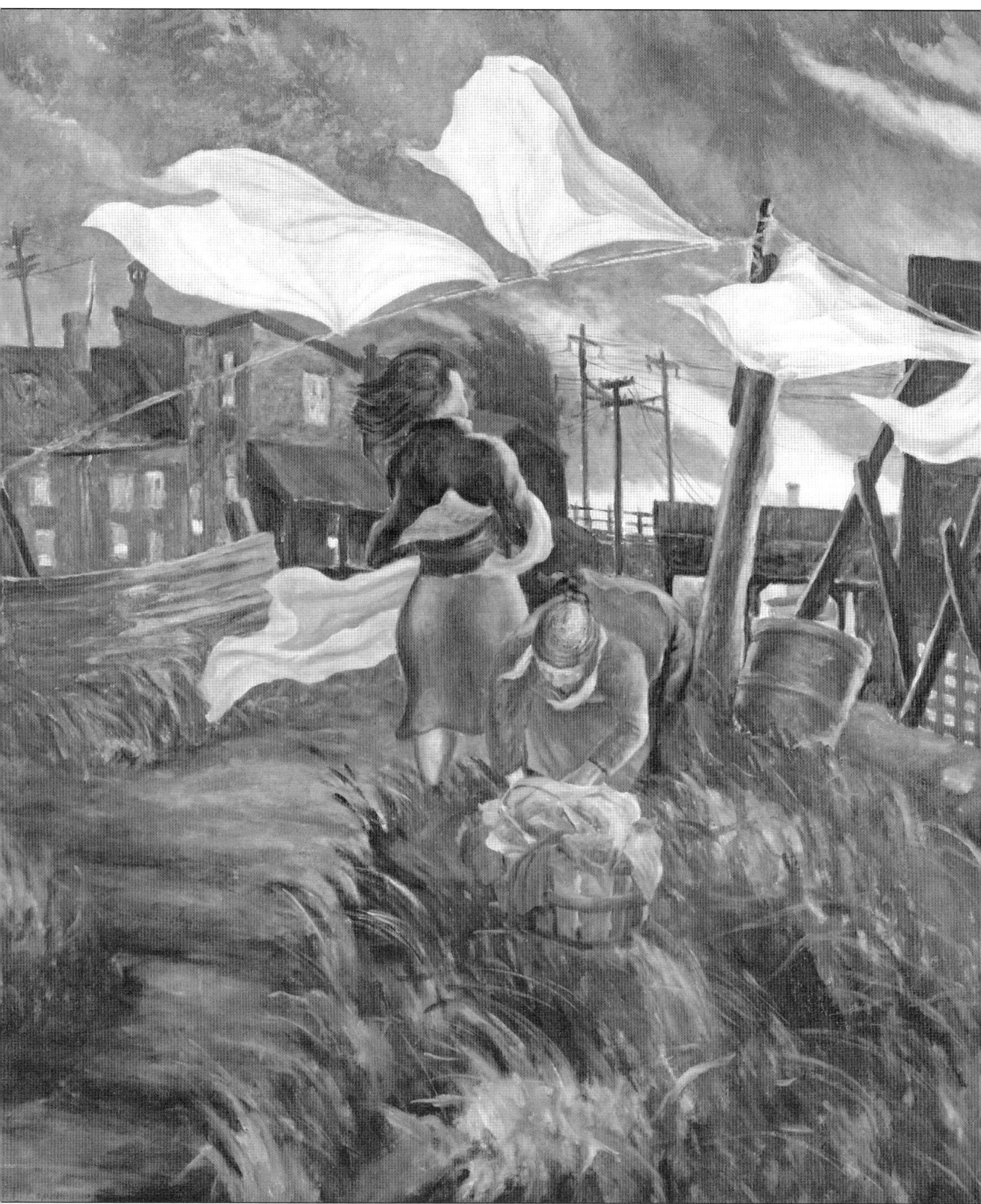

Hanging Up Clothes is the title of this painting. This was a work that was entered into an exhibit at the Delaware Art Center (now the Delaware Art Museum). The painting won an honorable mention in 1939. It is one of Loper's earliest paintings and has historical significance. (Photograph by Carson Zullinger, courtesy of the Walnut Street YMCA.)

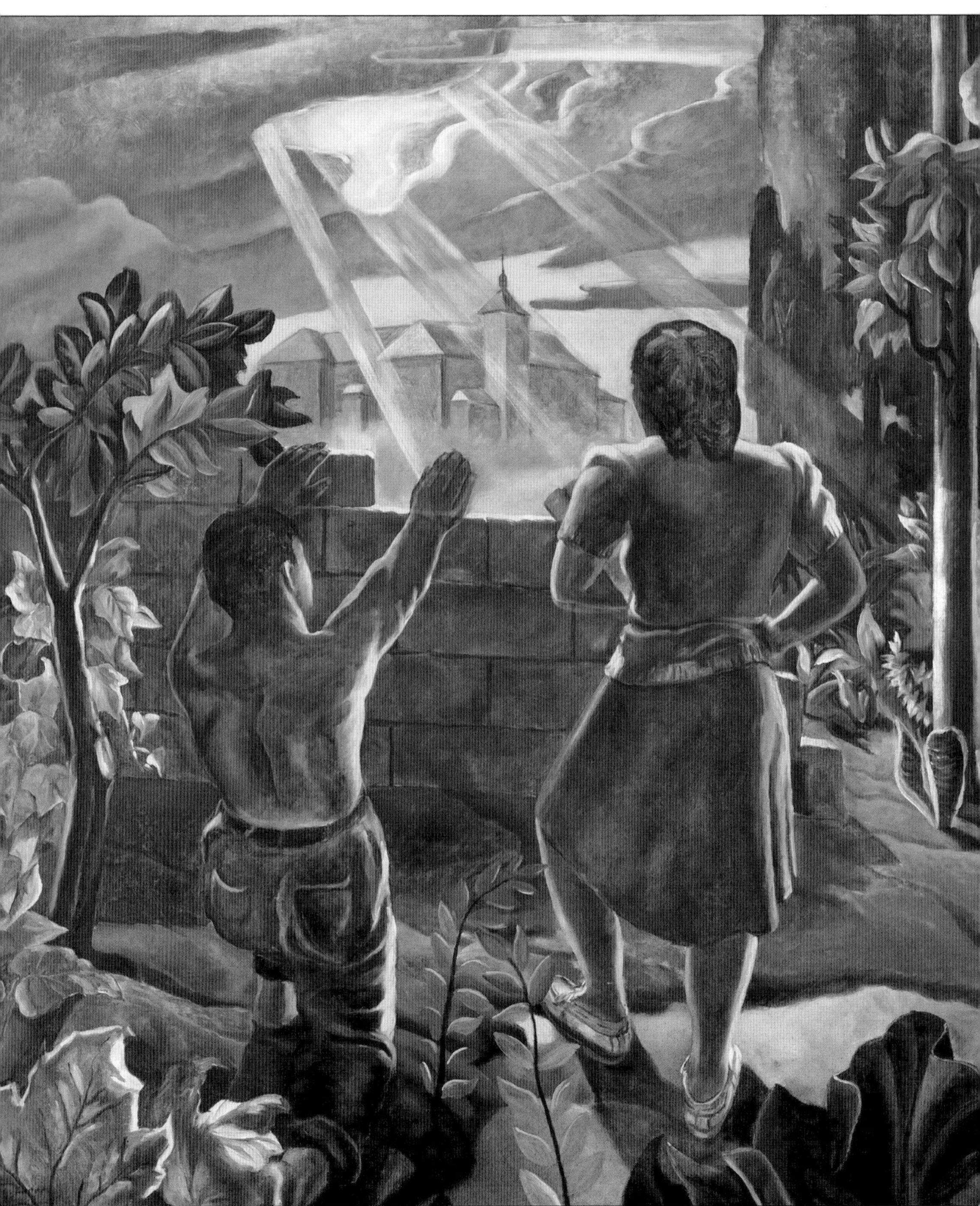

This painting is entitled *The Dream* and appears to have been commissioned for the YMCA because the two figures are reaching toward a building that looks familiarly like the Y. The building indeed was a dream come true for many in the African American community. (Photograph by Carson Zullinger, courtesy of the Walnut Street YMCA.)

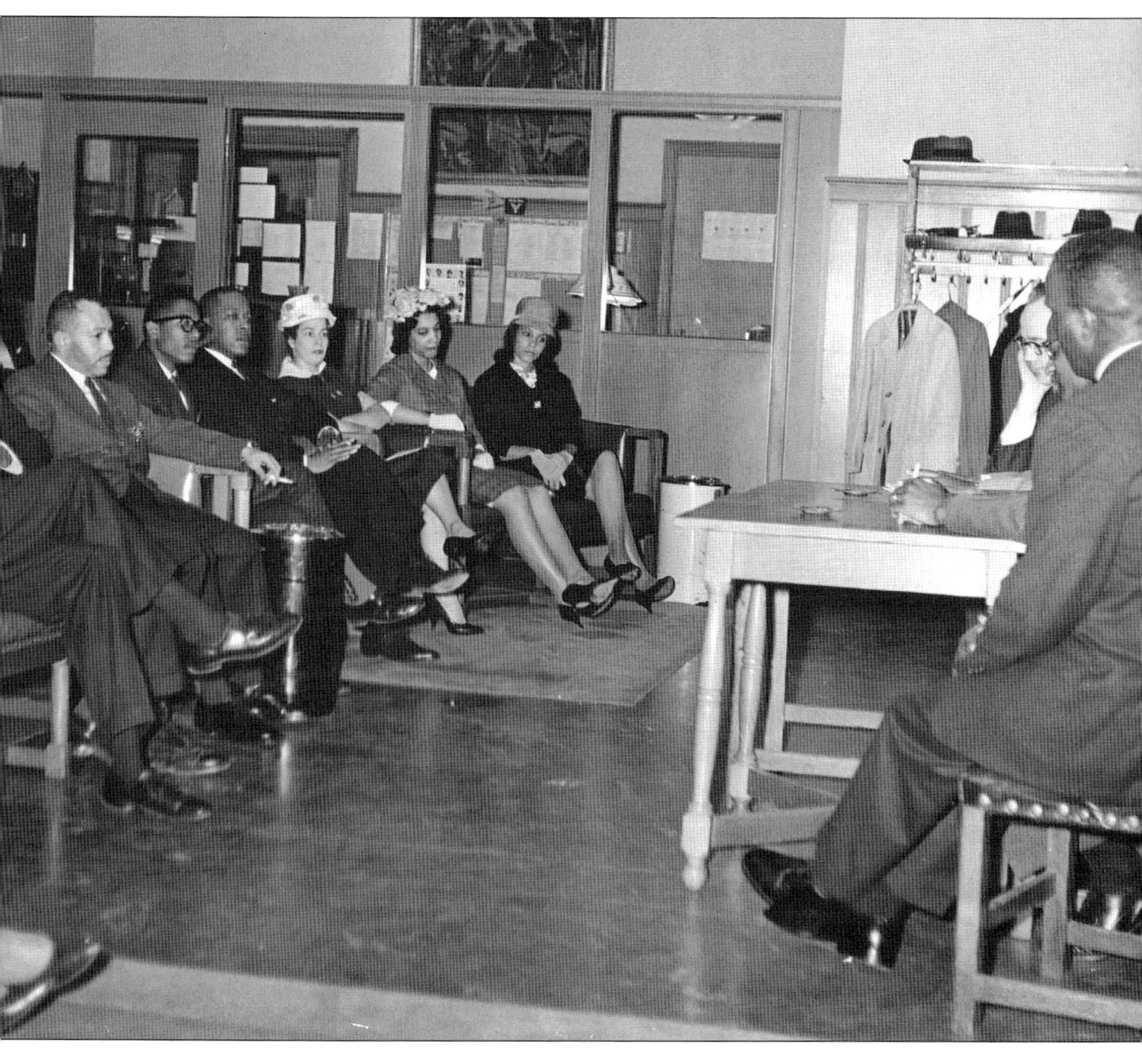

Even though the placement of *Hanging Up Clothes* is unknown, *The Dream* was hung prominently outside of the members' lounge. In this meeting of the Y-Phalanx, one is able to see the painting in the top center of the photograph located outside of the room. Lloyd Casson, third from the left, was pictured earlier as a young child attending the cornerstone laying. In this photograph, he is a professional adult still participating in YMCA activities. The only other identified individual is Anthony Williams, first from the left. (Courtesy of the Walnut Street YMCA.)

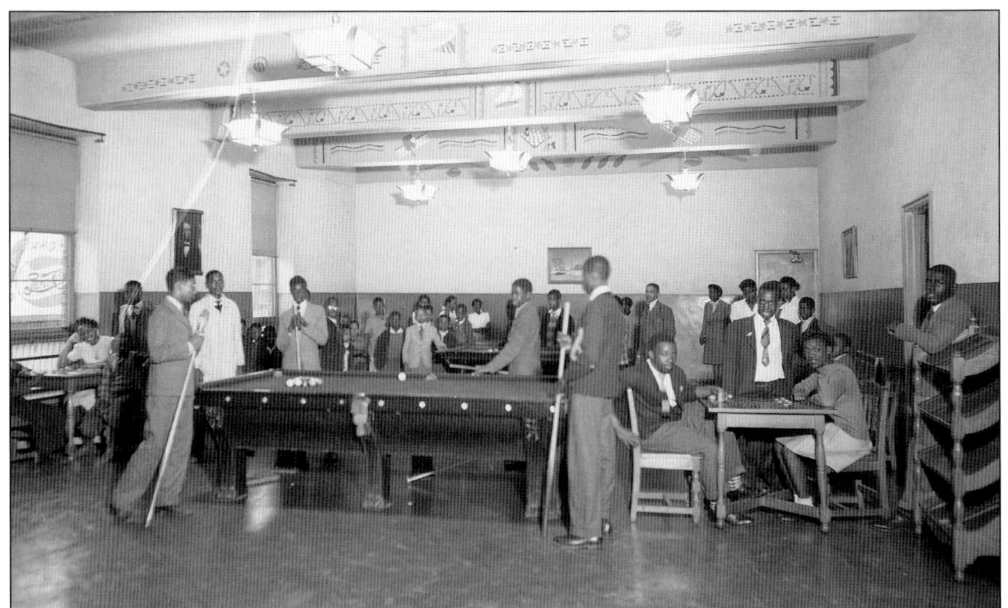

This 1940s photograph is of the game room, which was located on a lower floor. This facility was used by both men and women. The beams in the room are stenciled and may be the work of Edward Loper Sr. (Courtesy of the Delaware Historical Society.)

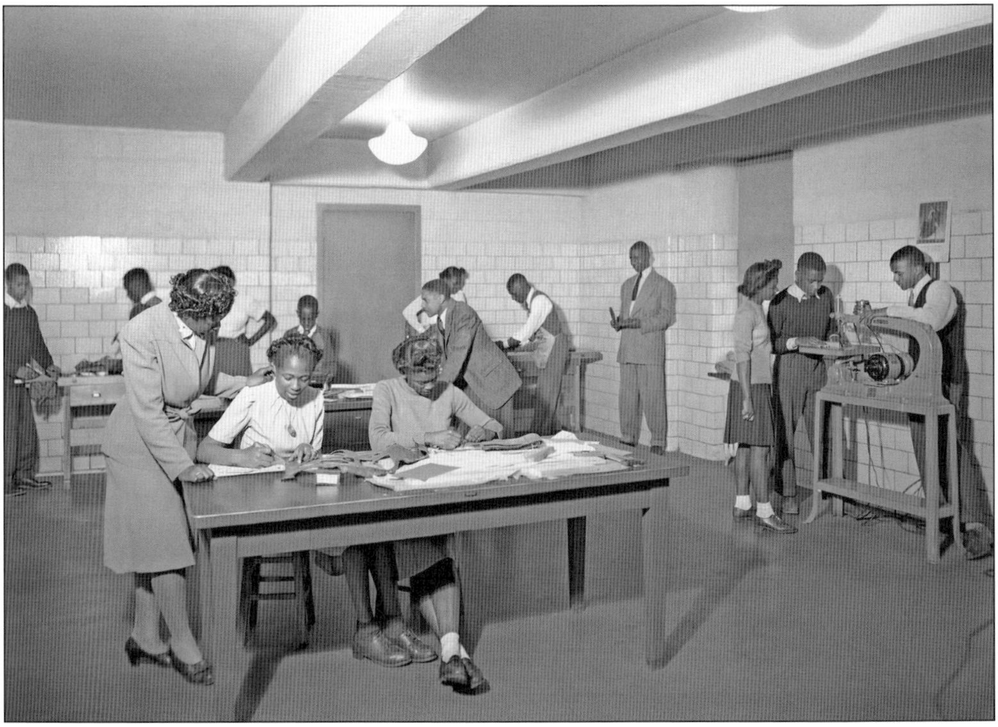

This 1940s photograph is a view of the wood shop. It is interesting to note that both men and women are working in the room. Throughout the years, the wood shop became a place where many young people learned to create beautiful wood objects and to learn the skill of woodworking. (Courtesy of the Delaware Historical Society.)

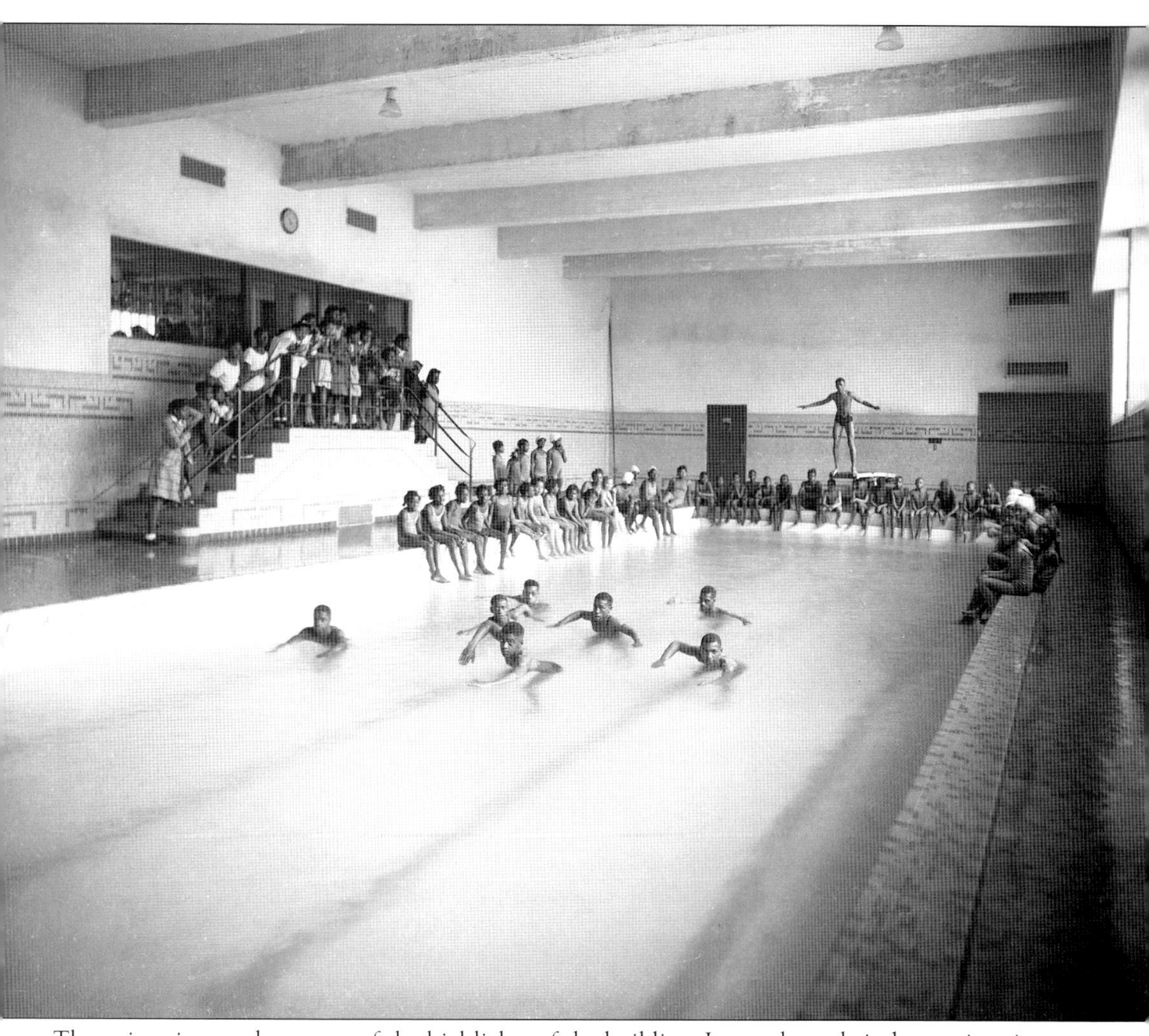

The swimming pool was one of the highlights of the building. It was the only indoor swimming pool for African Americans in Wilmington. (Courtesy of the Delaware Historical Society.)

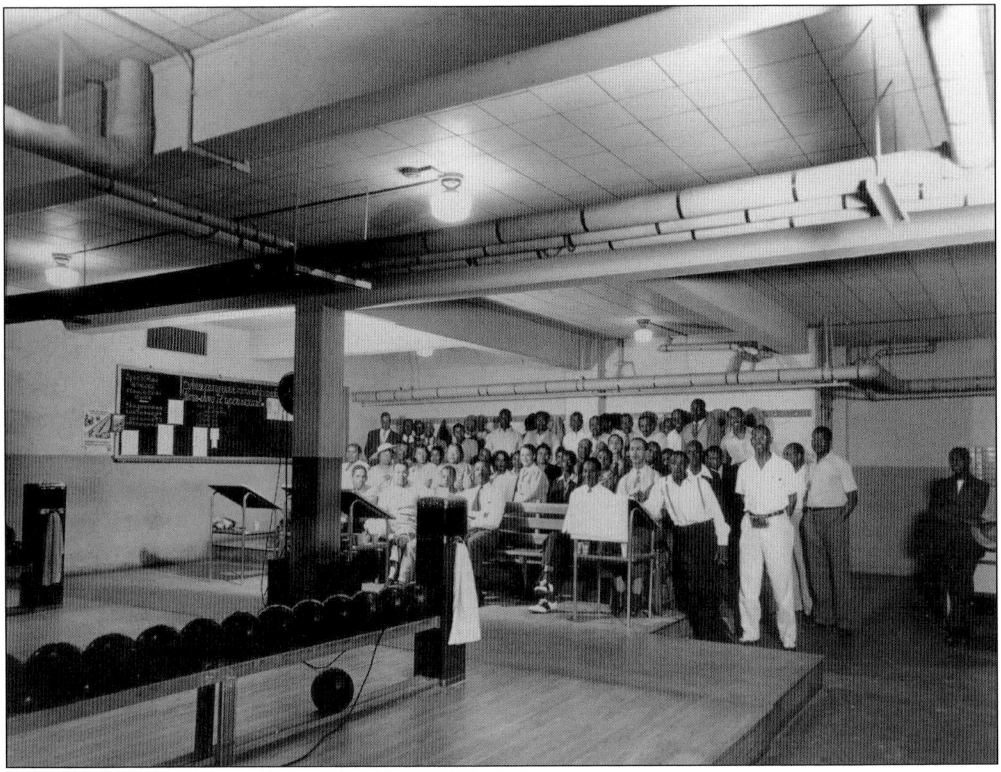

The bowling alley was used by young and old alike. Again, it was the only such facility for African Americans. There were bowling teams for men, women, and youth. Bowling was a very popular activity. H. Sylvester Clark, building supervisor is pictured on the far right in white. Ms. Wilson, not pictured here, is remembered for managing the bowling alley. (Courtesy of the Delaware Historical Society.)

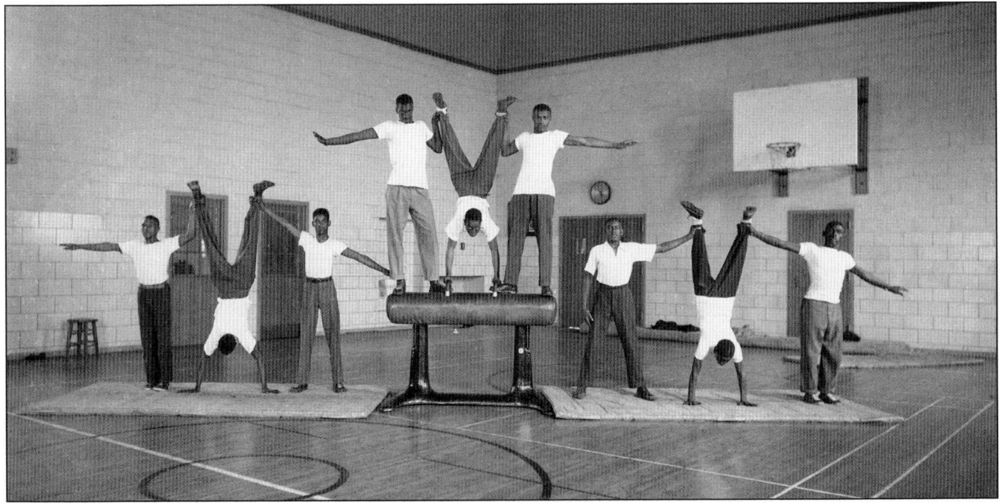

The gymnasium was another major facility in the building. It was where young people did gymnastics, practiced ballet lessons, and learned the rules of basketball and other sports. Annually, the circus was held in this room. The gym was well-equipped with horses, parallel bars, rings, and trampolines. (Courtesy of the Delaware Historical Society.)

The auditorium was where dance recitals, banquets, teas, lectures, dances, and other cultural events were held. There was a stage and a dressing room. It was able to accommodate at least 400 people in auditorium-style seating. (Courtesy of Dolores Washam and Lynn Clayton Jones.)

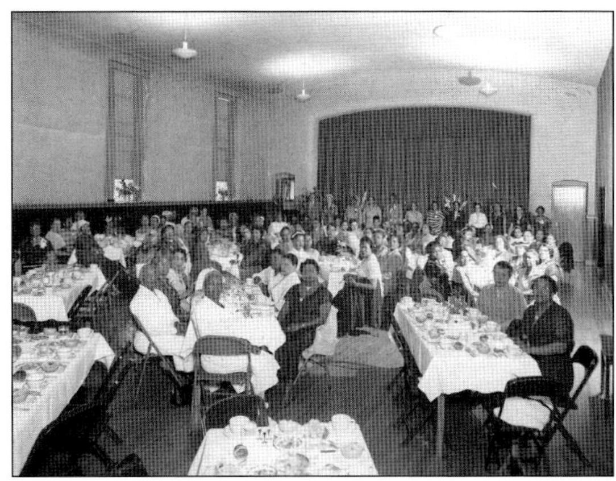

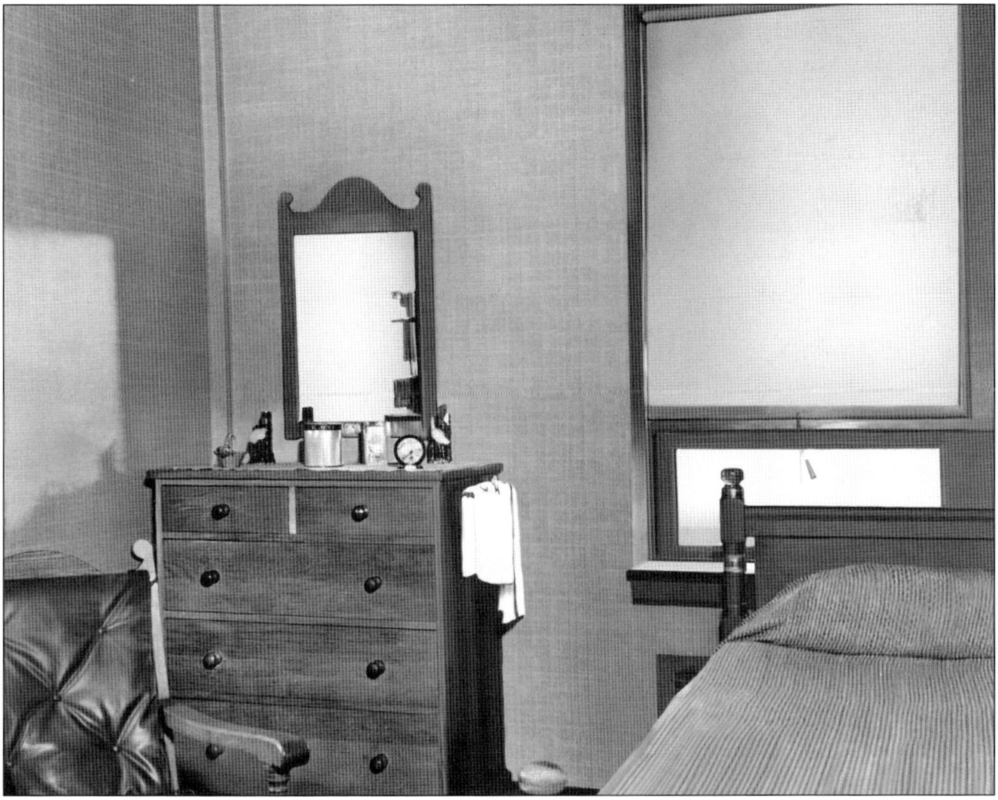

The Walnut Street YMCA offered housing for men. This is a photograph of a dormitory room. As the photograph illustrates, there was a bed, easy chair, and bureau. A desk and chair, which are not visible, were also part of the furnishings. When Dr. Eugene McGowan, the first African American school psychologist in Delaware came to Wilmington there were no integrated facilities for him to live so he stayed at the Walnut Street YMCA. It was suggested to him by Eldridge Waters, a school principal and member of the board of managers. Dr. McGowan said that the dorms were very nice. Dr. Byron K. Armstrong, one of the founders of Kappa Alpha Psi fraternity, lived at the Walnut Street YMCA for several years. These dormitory rooms also provided accommodations for visiting African American male dignitaries. The cost was $9.50 a week, which could be paid weekly or monthly. This included a weekly change of linen. (Courtesy of the Walnut Street YMCA.)

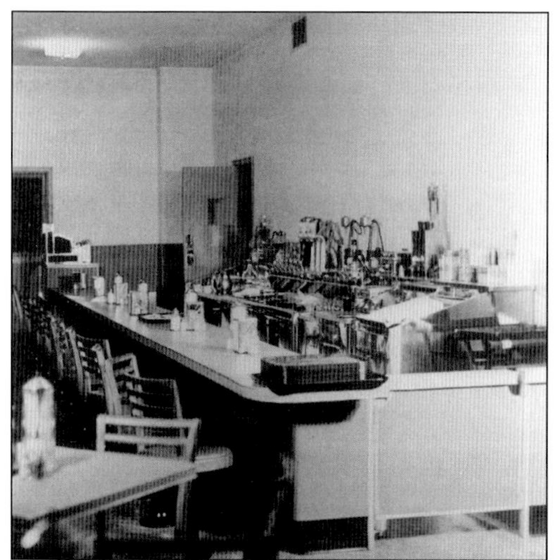

Since dining facilities in the city were segregated, the cafe served a broad population. In addition, it provided meals for the men who lived in the dormitories. The cafe could accommodate 50 people. For children, it was a place to buy an inexpensive treat. One of the favorite treats for children was buttered toast. Two slices could be purchased for 5¢. Later, the price increased to 10¢. The warm treat was wrapped in waxed paper with the butter melting on the insides of the paper. This was a favorite for tired and hungry young ballet and tap students after rigorous practice. It was also something most could afford. (Courtesy of the Delaware Historical Society.)

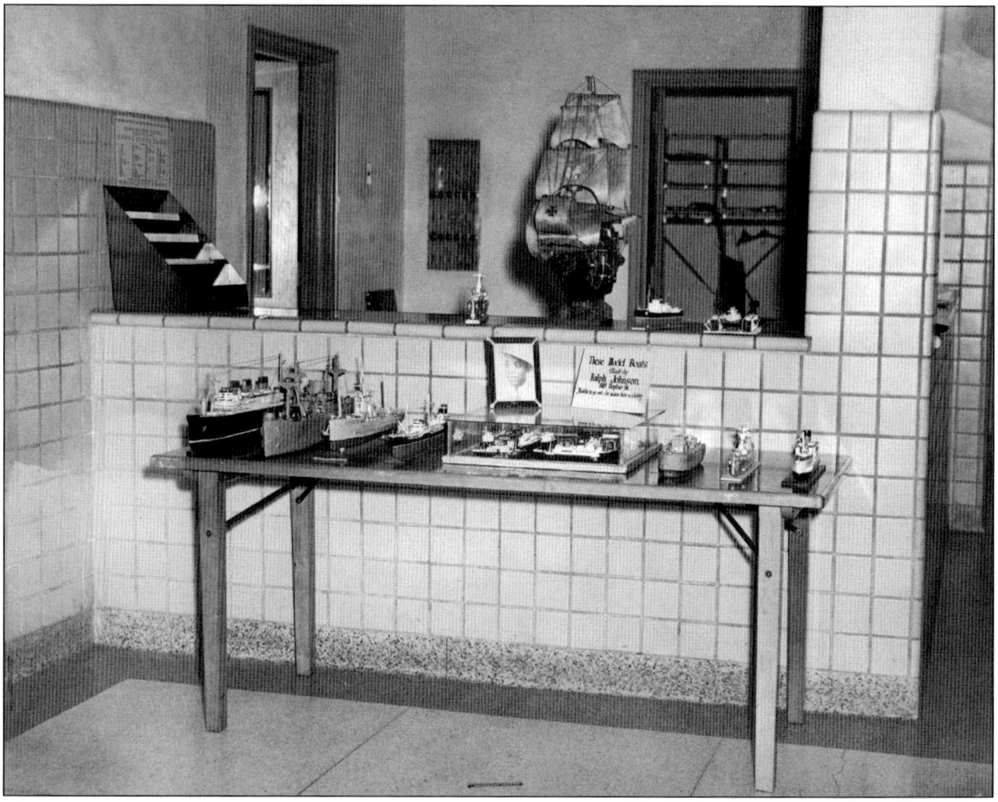

When one entered the building, they immediately saw the registration desk. This was managed by staff who welcomed visitors and monitored the activities of the young people. There was always a friendly face and the staff became favorites of both children and adults. In this photograph, the front desk also became a display area for the talents of a young man named Ralph Johnson. When Johnson became disabled, model-boat making became his signature. His art was displayed throughout the city and he taught the skill to others. This photograph was taken by Portfield Harris. Harris was a teacher but also had a photography business. (Courtesy of the Delaware Historical Society.)

Three

The Staff and Volunteer Leadership

WALNUT STREET CENTER COMMITTEE (Continued)

Mrs. Necola Andrews	Mrs. Theophilus Nix
Mrs. John Boston	Mrs. Harvey Peterson
Mrs. Richard Copper	Mrs. Winder L. Porter
Mrs. Samuel G. Elbert	Mrs. Phillip G. Sadler
Miss Martha Evans	Mrs. Harry Scott
Mrs. Robert Fleming	Mrs. Henry P. Street
Mrs. Samuel F. Holland	Mrs. George Sykes

STAFF - WALNUT STREET CENTER Y.W.C.A.

Center Director	Miss Elizabeth Jordan
Young Adult Program Director	Miss Marie K. Clarke
Y Teens Program Director	Miss June A. Gibosn
Health, Physical Education & Recreation	Miss Barbara Y. Washam
Clerical	Mrs. Carl Watts
Membership	Miss Carolyn Bailey
Membership Asst.	Mrs. Roland Ross

STAFF - WALNUT STREET BRANCH Y.M.C.A.

Executive	John B. Redmond
Youth and Adult Program	George H. Poe, Jr.
Industrial Services and Membership	Wesley J. Marshall
Physical Education	George H. Taylor
Building Superintendent	H. Sylvester Clark

CLERICAL AND DESK

Miss Doris Cannon	Edward Ingram
Mrs. William S. Young, Jr.	Francis G. Portlock

BUILDING MAINTENANCE

Annie Calloway	Joseph H. Gray
Rosa Lee Diggs	Alfred Lockett
Sara Fonville	Armstead H. Ransom
Heston Chandler	

This is a list of some of the employees at the YMCA and YWCA during the 1960s. These individuals were critical to the operation of the facility. The board of managers and other volunteers were equally important to the viability of the organization. A partial listing of the YMCA board is located at the top of the page. (Courtesy of the Delaware Historical Society.)

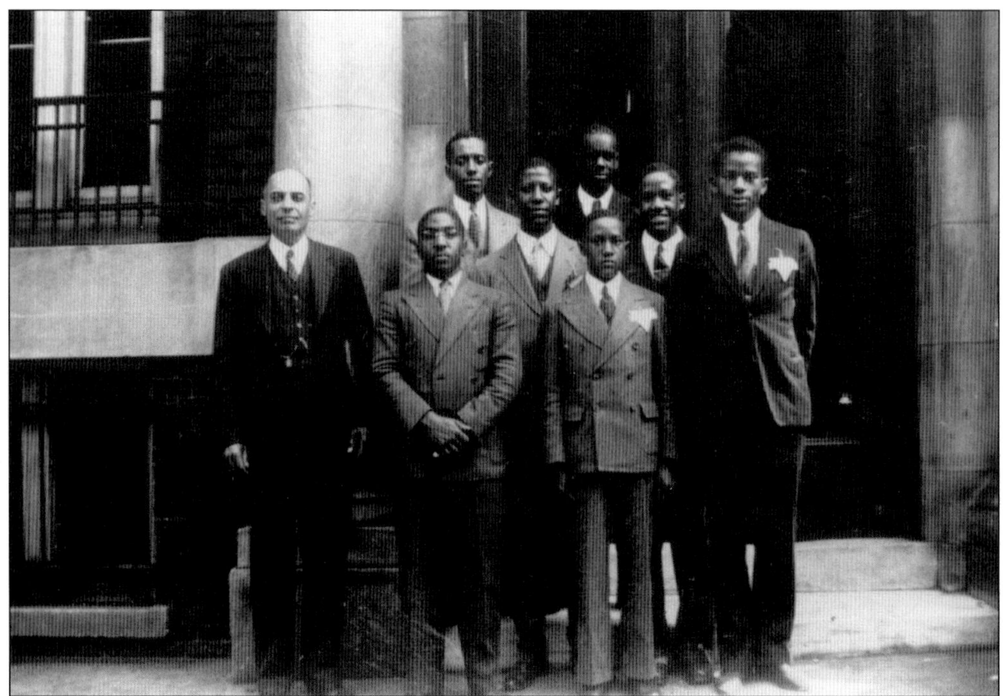

Boyd Overton, pictured on the left in the black three-piece suit, was the first executive secretary of the Walnut Street YMCA and was instrumental in opening the building and operating it in the first crucial years. He started in 1939 and left in 1943 to work in the Red Cross in India. Prior to coming to Wilmington, Overton was a YMCA executive in Cincinnati. In this photograph, he is with his first secretary William Young Sr. (first on the second row) and several other young adults. (Courtesy of the estate of William Young Sr.)

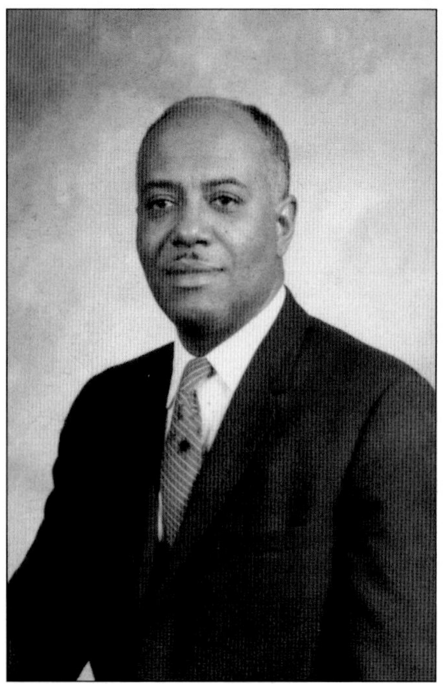

William Young Sr. was involved with the Walnut Street YMCA in its infancy. In 1939, after graduating from Howard University, he came to work as a clerical aide for Boyd Overton. He was able to participate firsthand before the structure was completed. Later, he was promoted to desk secretary with responsibility for youth clubs. After his work at the Y, he became a teacher and, later, a highly respected principal in the Wilmington Public School System. During his entire work career, he was actively involved with the Walnut Street YMCA as a volunteer eventually serving on the board. He is credited with writing the 50-year history of the organization. (Courtesy of William and Anita Young.)

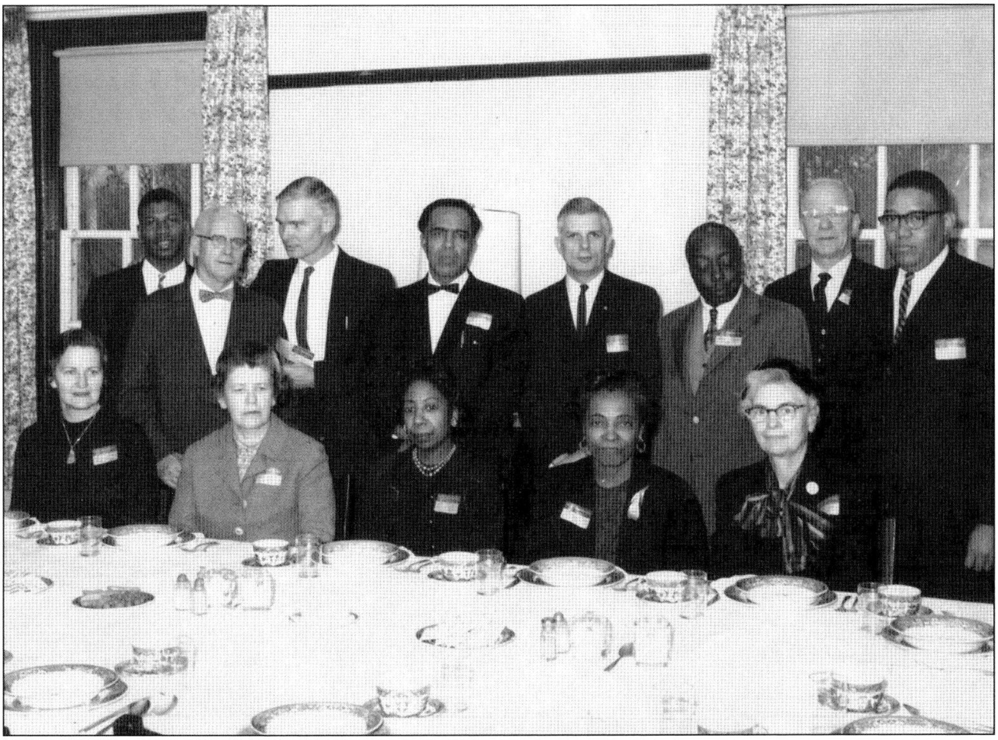

This is a joint meeting of the YMCA and YWCA representatives involving branch and general association entities. From left to right are (first row, seated) YWCA representatives two unidentified, Lennie Frisby Lewis, Elizabeth Jordan (Walnut Street YWCA executive director), and Barbara Miller; (second row, standing) Rev. Albert Rowe, J. Edgar Rhoads, unidentified, John B. Redmond, (Walnut Street executive director), two unidentified, Philip G. Rhoads, and Arthur Redding Jr. John Redmond was the second executive secretary serving first from 1943 to 1949 when he left to become the associate executive director of the Central Atlantic Area Council of the YMCA of Newark, New Jersey. He returned to Delaware serving from 1959 to 1972. During both of his terms, the programs grew and expanded. Redmond was also a minister and was highly respected in the community. In 1929, he graduated from Lincoln University and later graduated from Princeton Theological Seminary. (Courtesy of the Delaware Historical Society.)

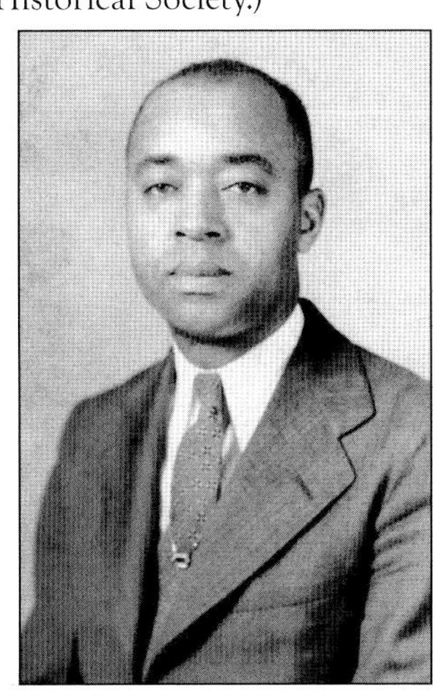

Roland J. Henry was another early member of the Walnut Street YMCA. He was part of the Industrial Club, which was the initial planning group for the organization. As a young man, Henry worked as a secretary for Eugene Redmond until he was drafted into the Army to serve in the Pacific. Redmond married Henry and his wife, Henrietta, in 1944. (Courtesy of the author.)

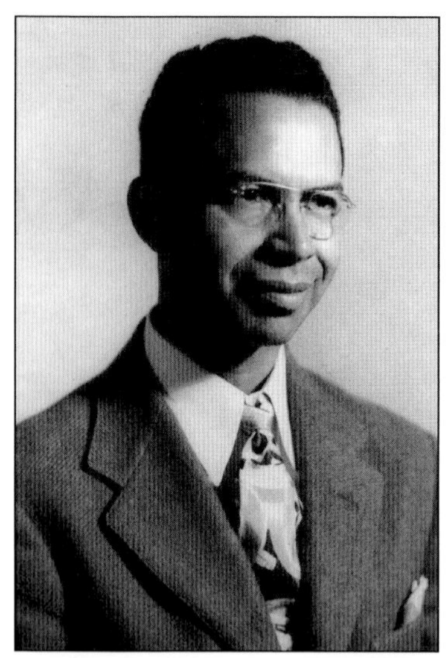

Hilmar Jensen, the third executive secretary of the organization, joined the organization in 1949. Prior to coming to Wilmington, he worked at the Trenton YMCA for 20 years. Jensen graduated from New Jersey State Teachers College and the City College of New York. He was also a World War I veteran. While in Wilmington, he was very active in the NAACP, the National Conference of Christians and Jews, and the Wilmington Board of Education. While serving as executive director of Walnut Street, Jensen died after an illness in 1954. (Courtesy of the Walnut Street YMCA.)

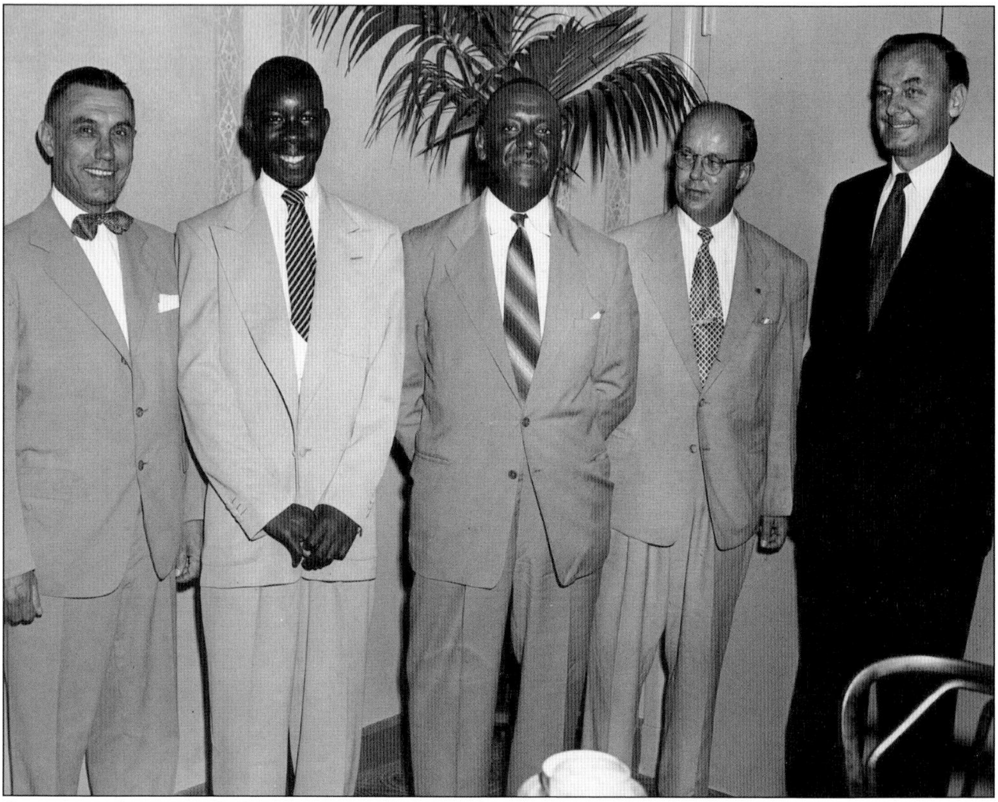

George Taylor joined the YMCA as the Boys' Work secretary. He is pictured here celebrating the win of Tilton Holt, the VFW marble champion. Holt played marbles at the Walnut Street YMCA and then earned fame as a national marble champion. He was featured in a 1950 issue of *Life* magazine. Taylor organized a celebration for Holt at Walnut Street on June 28, 1950. Pictured in the photograph from left to right are Democratic state senator J. Allen Freer Jr., Tilton Holt, George Taylor, Mike Frederick, and Republican senator John Williams. (Courtesy of the University of Delaware Library.)

Gilbert H. Jackson lived next door to the YMCA. Always athletic, he participated in numerous Walnut Street activities. Jackson was an outstanding football player at Howard High School and Delaware State College. He was also known for his aquatic abilities and was a lifeguard at the Kruse Pool. His first job was as the physical education director of the YMCA. He developed an extensive swimming program along with Barbara Washam, who was the physical education director of the YWCA. Together, they trained multitudes of young people how to swim and dive. Jackson and Washam also conducted Red Cross lifesaving activities. In addition to swimming, Jackson also coached the Big Five basketball team. Jackson left the Y in 1956 to begin his teaching and coaching career. He became the first African American basketball coach at Wilmington High School and one of the first African American basketball referees. (Courtesy of Gilbert Jackson III and Sheryll Jackson Slade.)

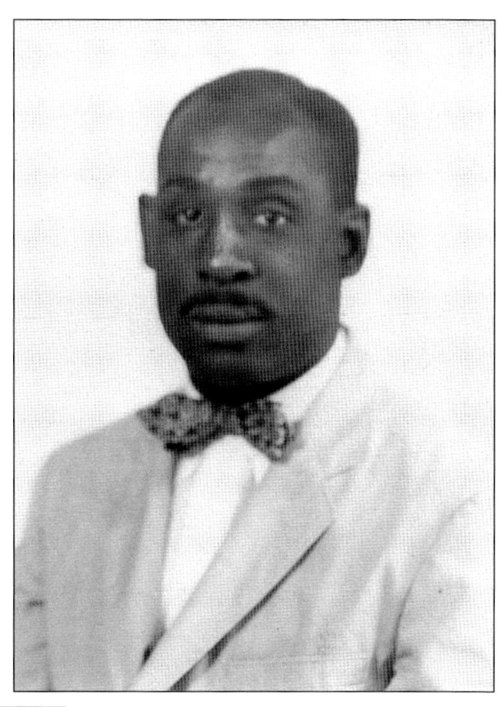

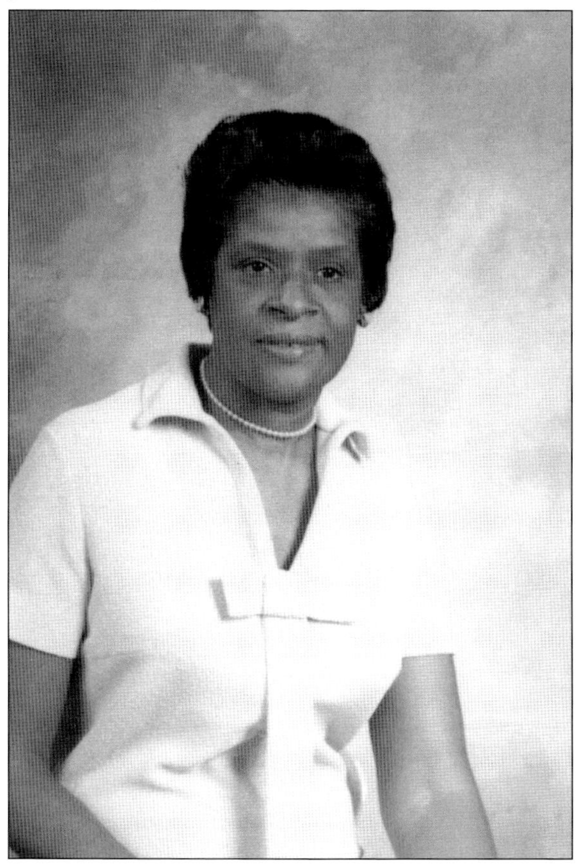

Cecile Young was a secretary to John Redmond from 1953 to 1970. Her husband, William Young, was one of the first employees of the Walnut Street YMCA. (Courtesy of William and Anita Young.)

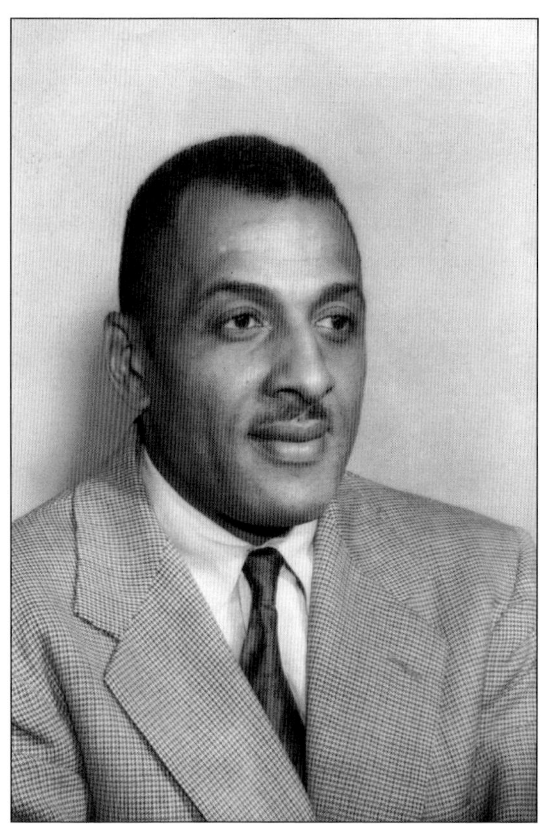

George Poe was secretary of Boys' Work. Poe came to Wilmington in 1955 after working in the Baltimore Druid Hill Branch YMCA as a physical director. He graduated with a degree in education from the University of Pittsburgh. Poe also held numerous jobs in recreation and physical education. (Courtesy of Evelyn Poe Jr.)

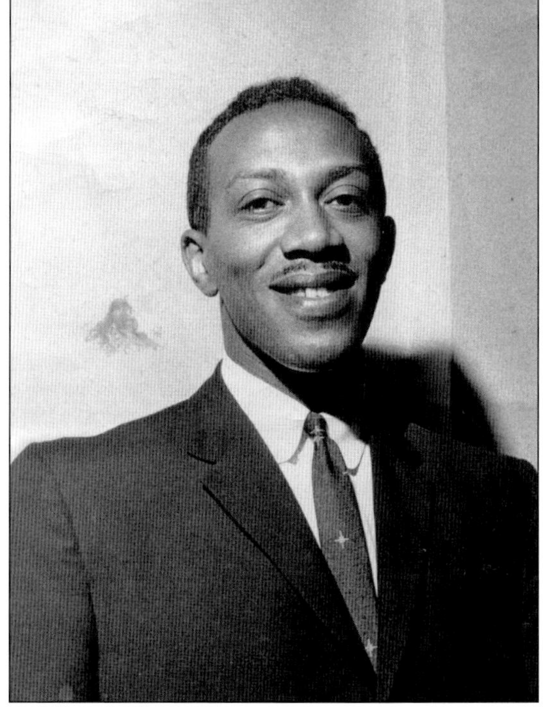

Eddie Ingram attended Howard High School and enrolled at Temple University. After serving in the Air Force, he worked as the night manager at the Walnut Street YMCA. At one point, he served as president of the board. (Courtesy of Niki Ingram, Esq.)

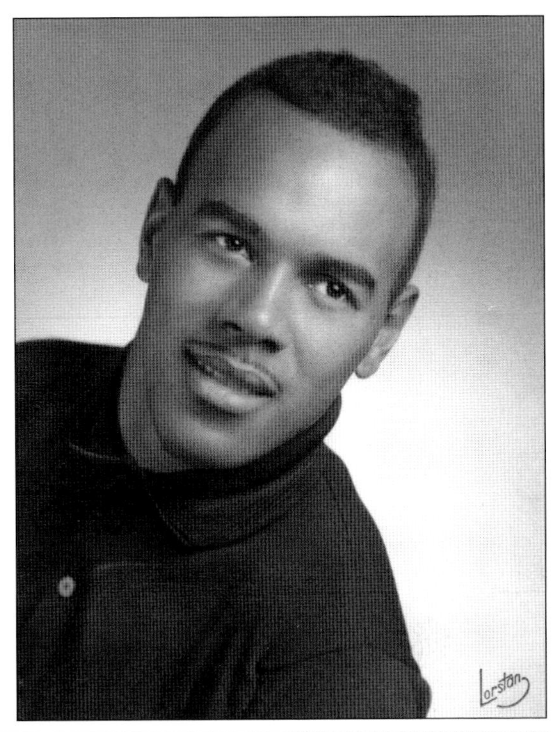

Ernest "Sammy" Congo worked at the YMCA from 1966 to 1975 as director of neighborhood groups and specialized services. This was nontraditional YMCA work, as he was employed to work with the Neighborhood Youth Corps and the Industrial Service Group. The Industrial Service Group was composed of the major businesses in the community. Following Dr. Martin Luther King's assassination, Congo worked with the outdoor gangs. As a student at Howard High School, Congo went to the Walnut Street YMCA for swimming and other physical activities. He eventually established a highly successful funeral business. (Courtesy of Ernest Congo.)

Herman McKinney is shown here registering young children at the desk. In order to participate in activities, children and adults had to have evidence of membership (Courtesy of the Walnut Street YMCA.)

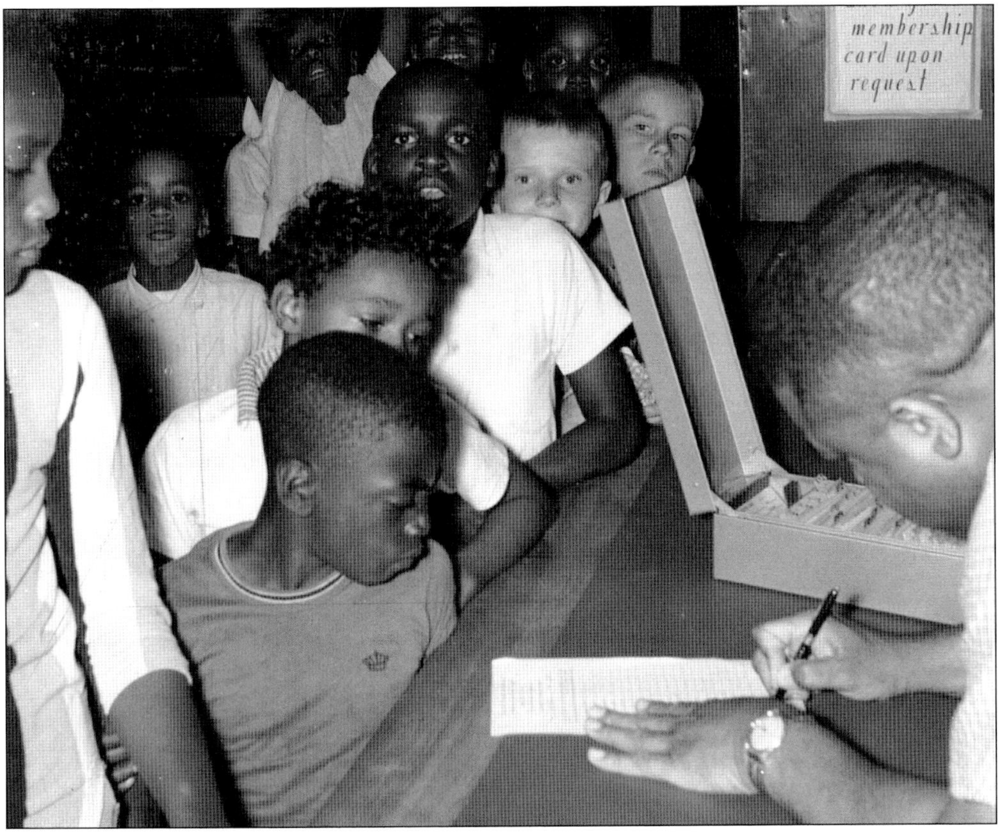

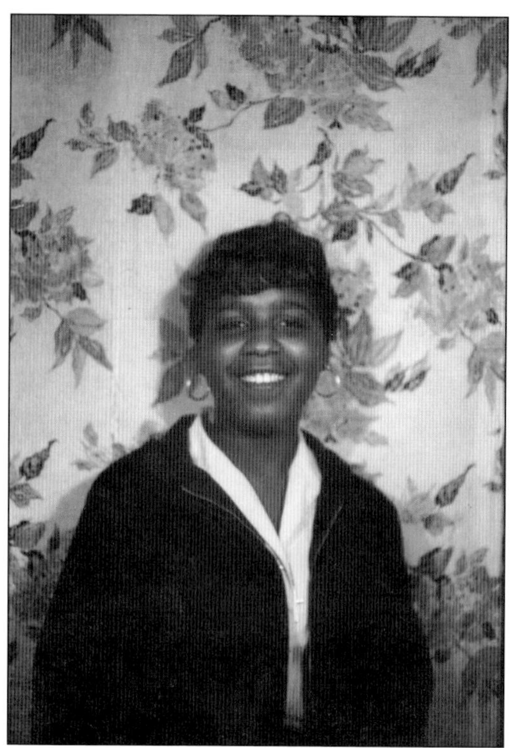

Doris Cannon participated in the co-op program at the YMCA while at Howard High School and was so impressive that George Taylor came to her home, personally, to ask her to work as a secretary when she graduated. In 1959, Cannon began her first job as secretary for youth membership at Walnut Street. She eventually worked for the YMCA for 30 years as a secretary for George Poe and George Taylor. (Courtesy of Doris Cannon.)

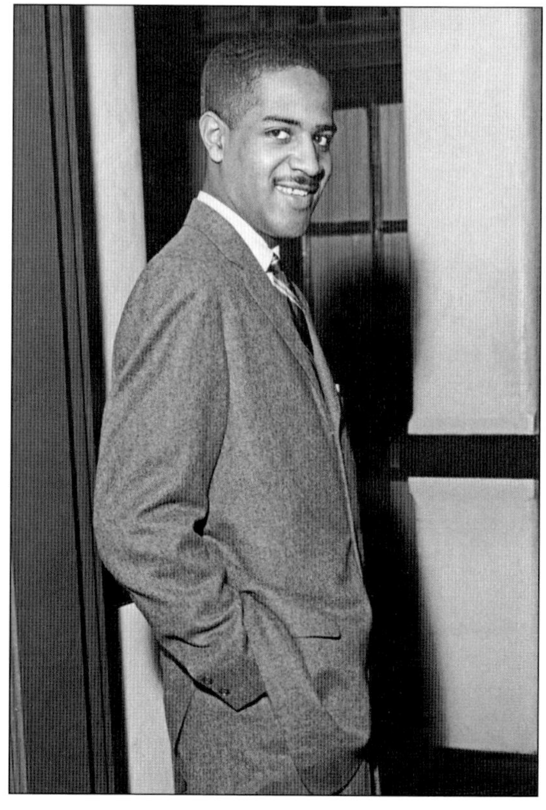

Harmon Carey participated in the YMCA as a child and later worked there in the 1960s as a teen director while attending graduate school at the University of Pennsylvania. In addition to working as a YMCA professional, Carey also volunteered. In 1970, he was credited with recruiting more members than anyone in the membership campaign of that year. Carey has had a lifelong commitment to preserving the history and culture of African Americans in Delaware. In 2023, he started WHGE 95.3 FM, the first African American–owned radio station in the State of Delaware. (Courtesy of Harmon R. Carey.)

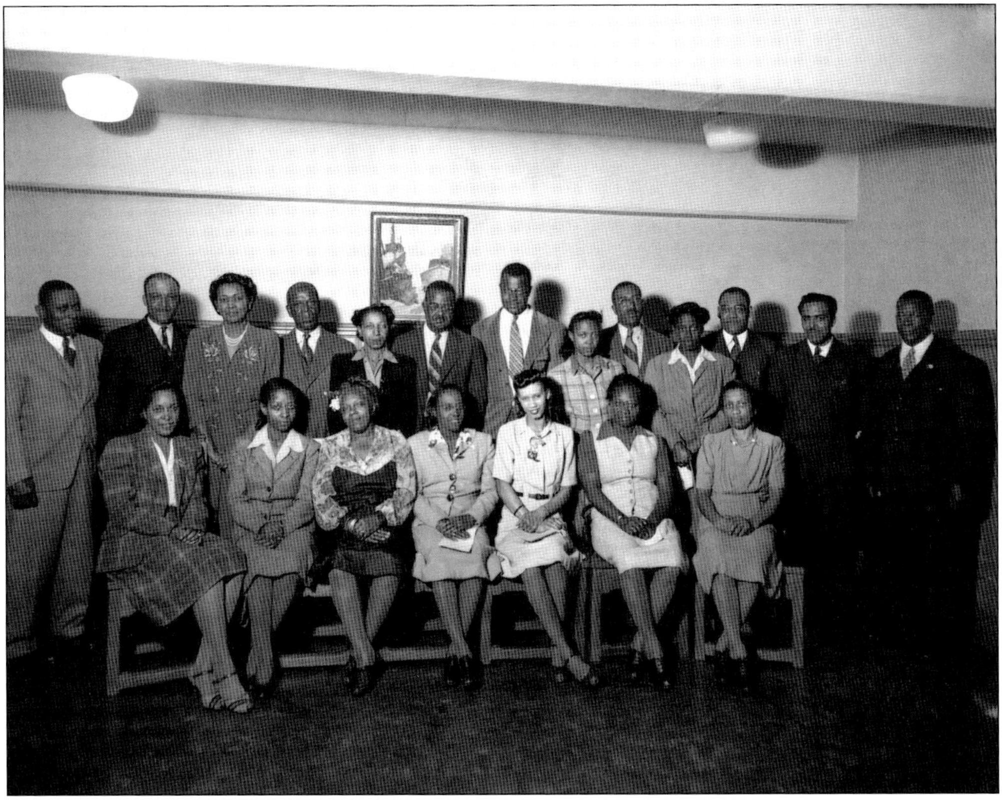

This is a 1940s group photograph of YMCA and YWCA staff and volunteer leadership. (Courtesy of the Walnut Street YMCA.)

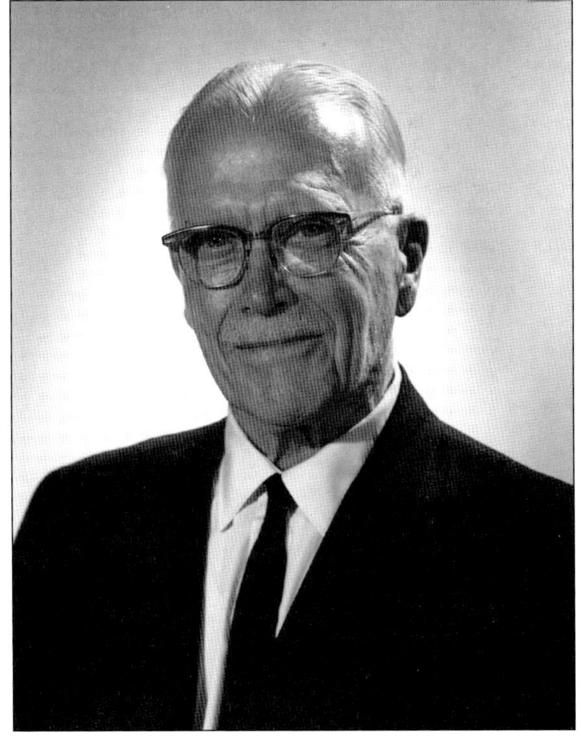

J. Edgar Rhodes was one of the most successful industrialists in Wilmington. He was also a Quaker. He served as vice president of the board of the Wilmington YMCA and as the first president of the board of managers at the Walnut Street YMCA. In addition to his YMCA activities, Rhodes was the 1946 chair of the United Negro College Fund Campaign, president of the National History Society, president of the Lincoln Club, and a member of the American Friends Service Committee, the Rotary, Boy Scouts, Wilmington Public Library the Delaware Camera Club, and the National Conference of Christians and Jews. (Courtesy of Hagley Museum and Library.)

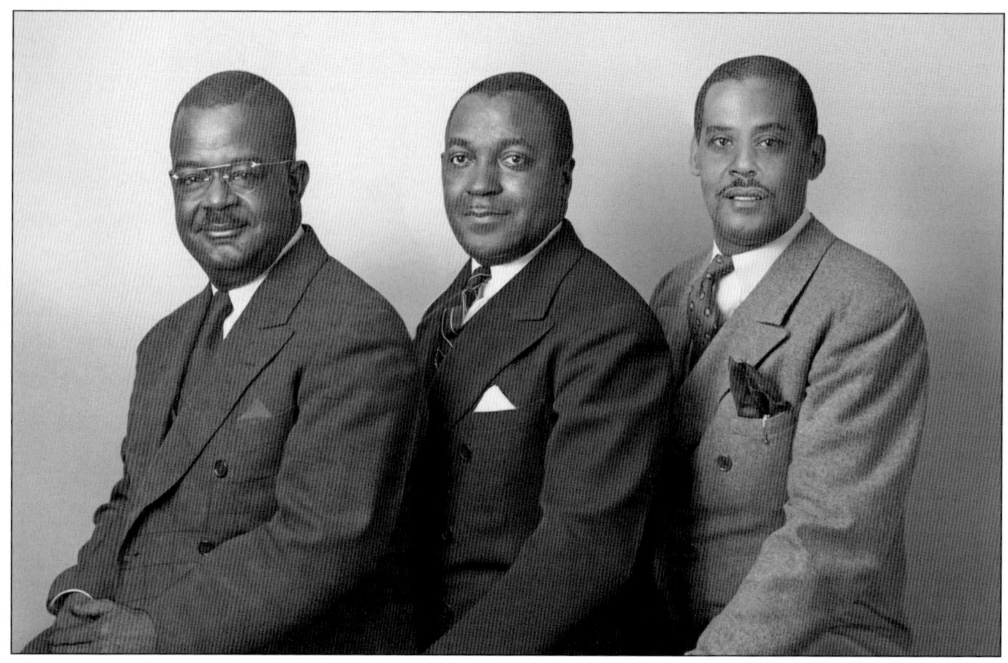

This 1940s photograph is of three prominent board of manager members of the Walnut Street YMCA. The first person on the left is William H. Emory who was a chauffeur for the wealthy Lakey family. Emory was the president of the Walnut Street YMCA board. In 1949, he was credited with bringing in the largest amount of money to the fundraising efforts. Sitting next to Emory is Edward R. Bell, owner of Bell's Funeral Home and member of the Wilmington City Council from 1948 to 1960. Bell served as deputy coroner of New Castle County in the 1950s and 1960s. Gomaster T. Gilbert is seated at the far right. Employed as a butler for the Paul DuPont family, Gilbert started volunteering with Walnut Street in 1941 as chair of the camping committee. All three men were members of the Monday Club, with Emory serving as president. (Courtesy of the Delaware Historical Society.)

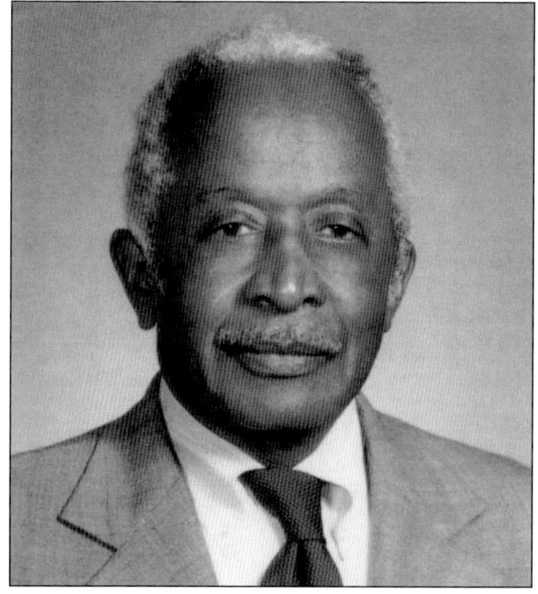

Louis L. Redding, the first African American attorney in the state of Delaware, was very active with the Walnut Street YMCA. Redding is most remembered for his role in *Brown v. Board of Education*. (Courtesy of the Delaware Historical Society.)

Portfield Harris was a teacher at Howard High School and a professional photographer but he was also very active with the Walnut Street YMCA and the Masons. (Courtesy of the Delaware Historical Society.)

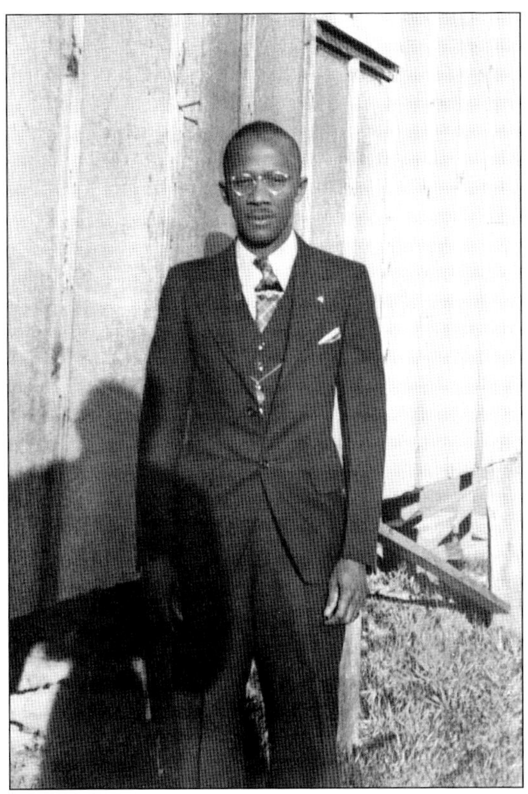

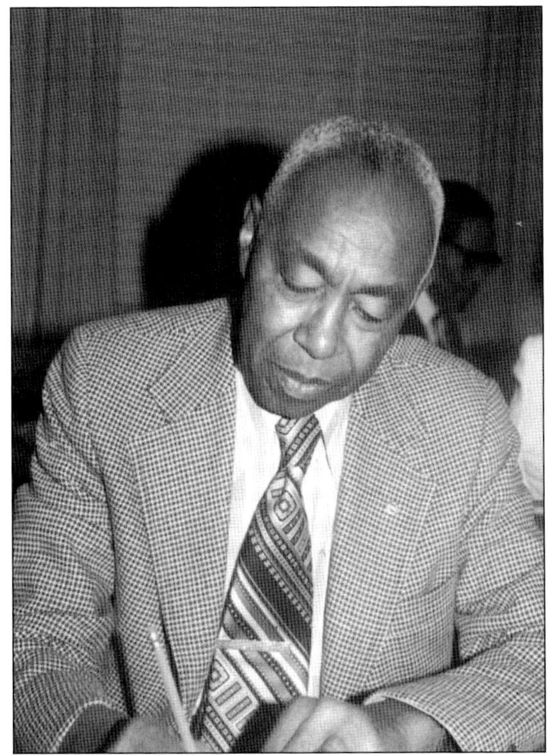

Eldridge Waters was a member of the board of managers and was active in the YMCA for most of his adult life. He was a teacher and, eventually, the principal of the Stubbs School. When Dr. Eugene McGowan came to Wilmington in the 1950s and could not find a place to live, Waters told McGowan about the dormitories at the Walnut Street YMCA. (Courtesy of the Delaware Historical Society.)

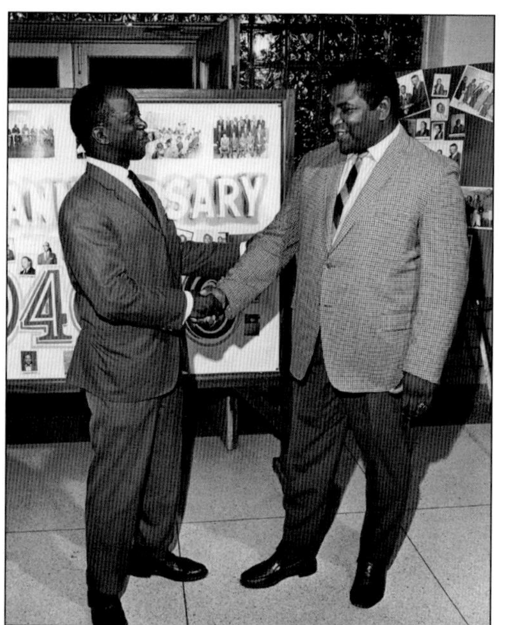

This photograph shows Calvin P. Hamilton shaking the hand of former boxer Maynard Jones. Jones, a light heavyweight, was known as the "Delaware Dynamiter." He also participated in many Walnut Street YMCA activities. Calvin P. Hamilton was a major contributor to the Walnut Street YMCA. He served as president of the board and chair of several committees. His father was an early member and volunteer of the Y. Hamilton served on the board for most of his adult life. He was also the first African American registered architect in the State of Delaware. Some of the projects he designed were Ezion-Mt. Carmel Methodist Church, William Anderson Community Center, Westown Square, buildings on the Delaware State University campus, Brandywine Village, and the Terry Building on the Delaware Technical and Community College campus. (Courtesy of the Walnut Street YMCA.)

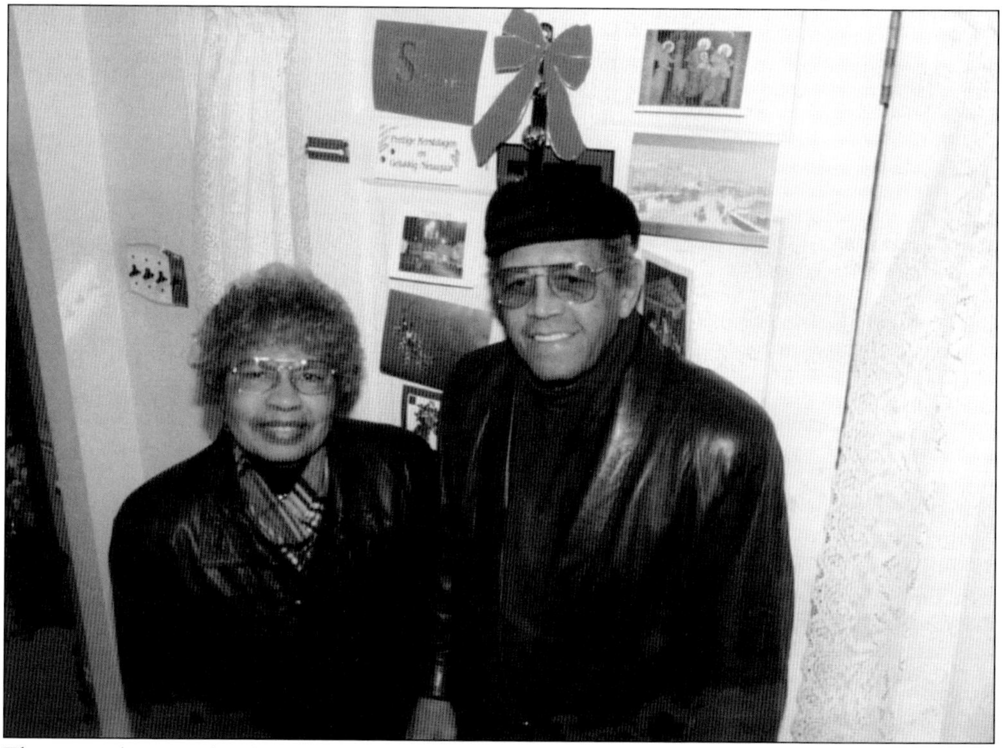

This is a photograph of Forrester Lee and his wife, Jeanne. Forrester came to Walnut Street YMCA in 1946 as the physical director, having served in the same role at the Spring Street Branch in Ohio. He stayed until 1948 when he left to become the executive secretary at the YMCA West Side Branch in Red Bank, New Jersey. Forrester returned to Walnut Street in 1964 to serve as the associate secretary for industrial services. During his early years at Walnut Street, he greatly expanded the swimming program. (Courtesy of Sheryll Jackson Slade and Gilbert H. Jackson III.)

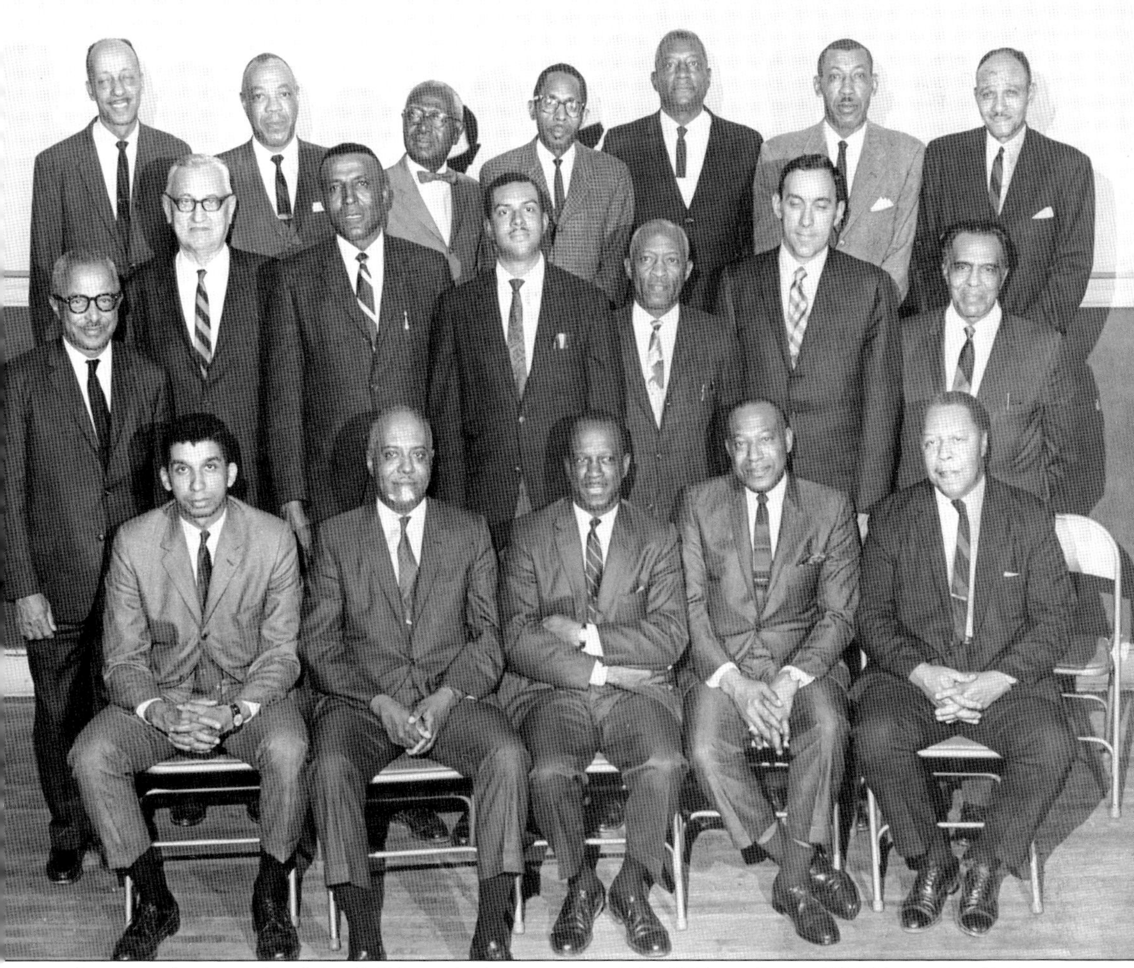

This is a photograph of the full board of managers of the Walnut Street YMCA in the 1960s. The members represented many different professions. Some were educators, religious leaders, and business leaders. In the photograph are Dr. Eugene McGowan, the first African American school psychologist in Wilmington; Dr. Joseph E. Johnson, the first African American principal of an integrated school in Delaware; and Calvin P. Hamilton, the first African American architect in the State of Delaware. The members from left to right are (first row) Dr. Joseph E. Johnson, William S. Young, Jr., Calvin P. Hamilton, Jr., the Reverend Maurice J. Moyer, and Dr. Eugene McGowan; (second row) James White, Clarence Fulmer, Theophilus Andrews, William S. Young III, Samuel L. Peterson, Fred Hickman and John B. Redmond, executive secretary; (third row) James T. Gardner, Charles L. Simms, Harvey King, Floyd Nutter, Franklin Butler, Charles Brown Sr., and S. Chester Deshields. (Courtesy of the Walnut Street YMCA.)

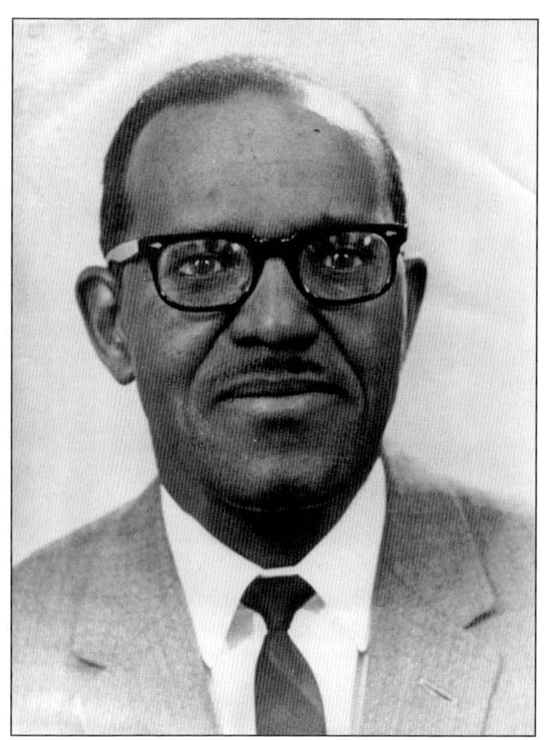

Ned Brown, a member of the board of managers, also served on the camp committee. Brown's participation on the board was significant because he represented the African American community of Belvedere. The Walnut Street YMCA had programs in the surrounding communities and Belvedere was one of them. Brown was president of the Belvedere Civic Association and an active member of the board of trustees of the Absalom Jones School. There were many Y programs at the school. (Courtesy of the Brown family.)

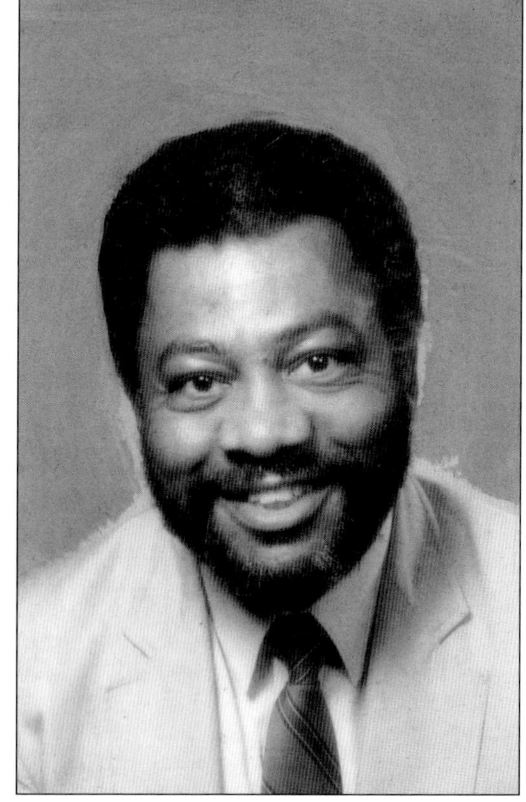

Dr. James Newton was the president of the board of managers in the early 1980s. He was a respected professor at the University of Delaware and was highly regarded as a scholar in Delaware African American history. Newton was also a well-known fine artist. (Courtesy of Lawanda Newton.)

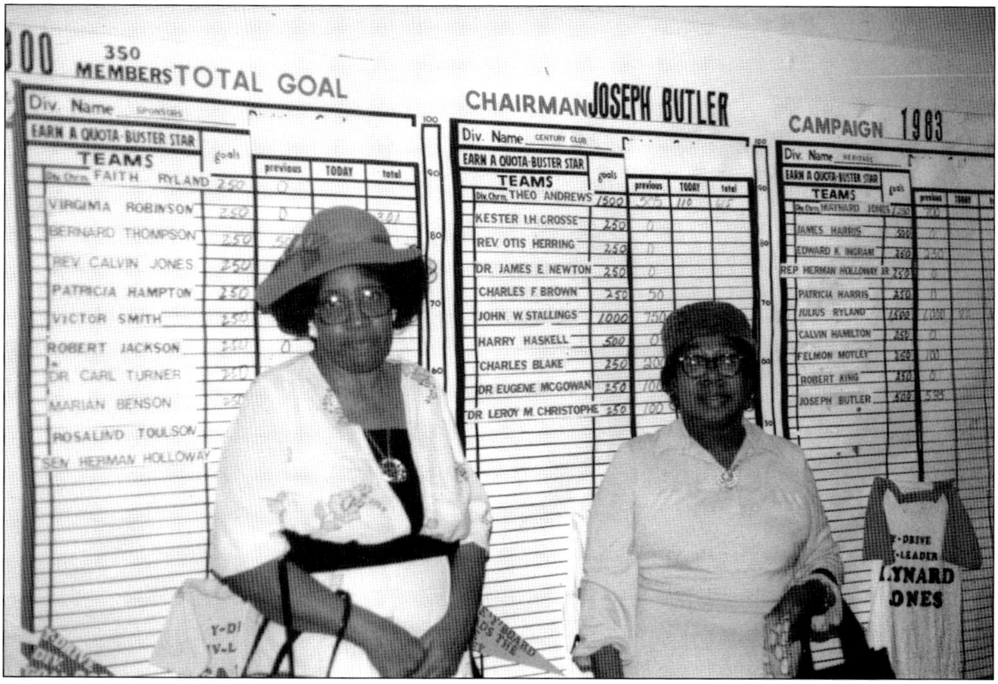

This 1983 membership drive is being highlighted because the individuals involved represent diverse leaders in the community. They were Faith Hyland, Virginia Robinson, Bernard Thompson, Rev. Calvin Jones, Patricia Hampton, Victor Smith, Robert Jackson, Dr. Carl Turner, Marian Benson, Rosalind Toulson, Sen. Herman Holloway, Theophilus Andrews, Kester I.H. Crosse, Dr. James Newton, Charles F. Brown, John Stallings, Harry Haskell, Charles Blake, Dr. Eugene McGowan, Dr. Leroy M. Christophe, Maynard Jones, James Harris, Edward Ingram, Rep. Herman Holloway, Jr., Patricia Harris, Julius Ryland, Felmon Motley, Robert King, and Joseph Butler. The two volunteers pictured are Elizabeth Bankley (left) and Kathryn Brady. (Courtesy of the Walnut Street YMCA.)

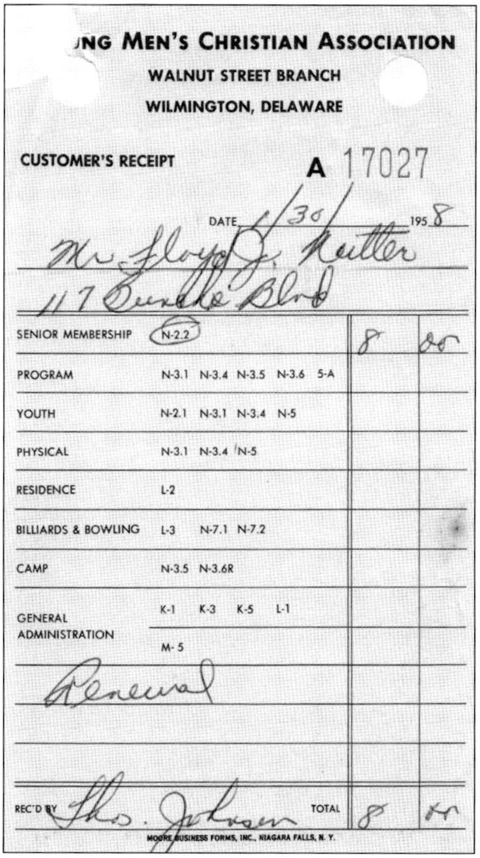

This membership dues receipt belonged to Floyd Nutter, who was a member of the board. The receipt also highlights the many different areas of the organization. There were fees for senior membership, youth, physical activities, dormitory residence, billiards, bowling, camp, and general administration. (Author's collection.)

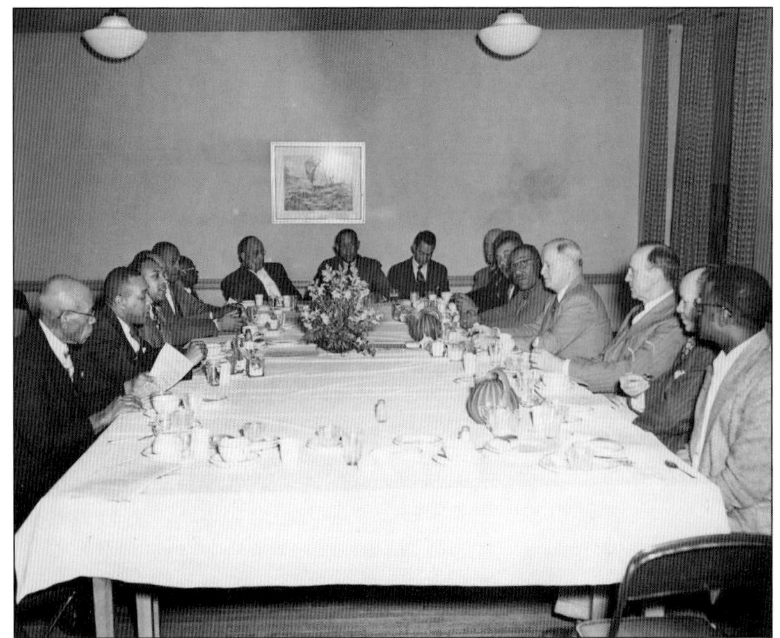

This photograph shows a 1950s board of managers meeting. It should be noted that the board was racially diverse. (Courtesy of the Walnut Street YMCA.)

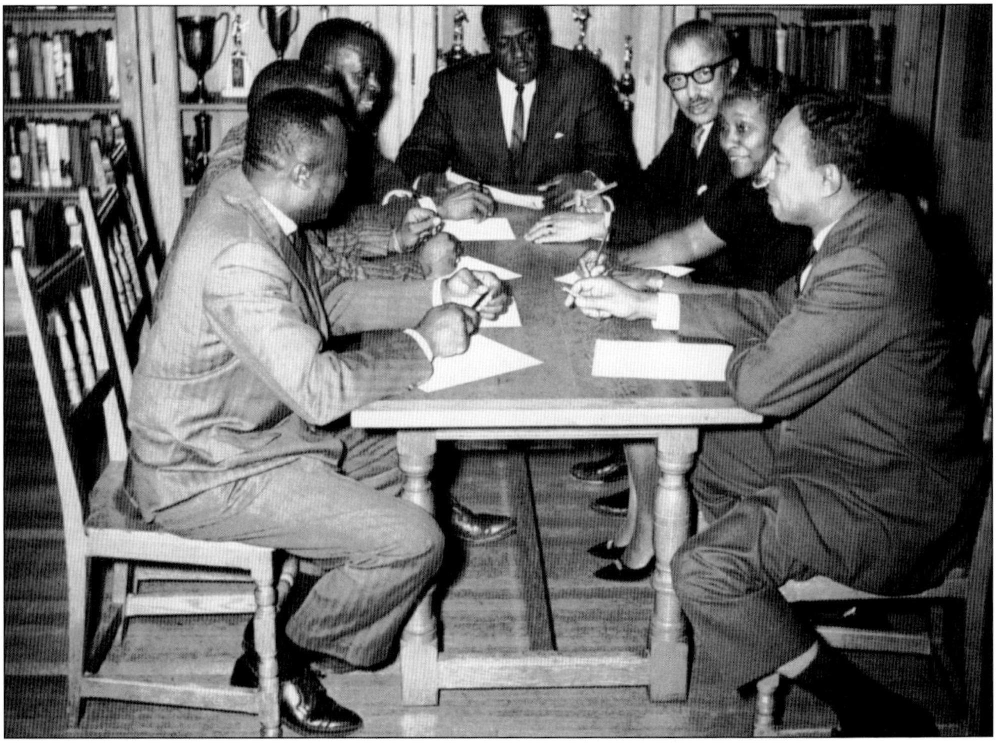

This is a meeting of the 1966 campaign leadership. Walter L. Purnell was campaign chair. Henrietta Henry was co-chair, and Joseph Johnson was membership chair. (Courtesy of the author.)

Four

THE SWIMMING PROGRAM

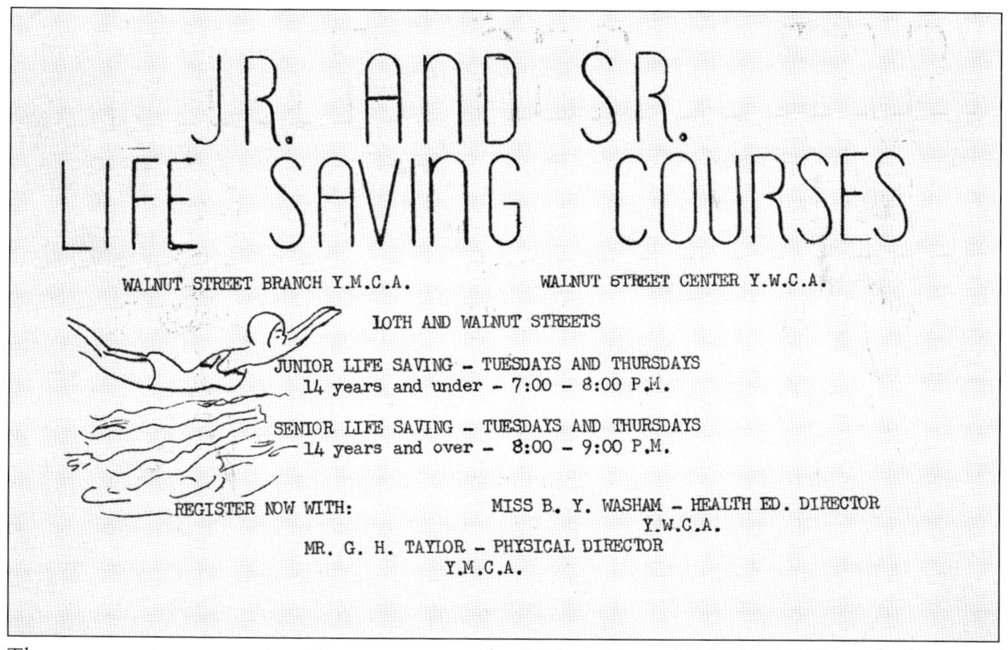

JR. AND SR.
LIFE SAVING COURSES

WALNUT STREET BRANCH Y.M.C.A. WALNUT STREET CENTER Y.W.C.A.

10TH AND WALNUT STREETS

JUNIOR LIFE SAVING - TUESDAYS AND THURSDAYS
14 years and under - 7:00 - 8:00 P.M.

SENIOR LIFE SAVING - TUESDAYS AND THURSDAYS
14 years and over - 8:00 - 9:00 P.M.

REGISTER NOW WITH: MISS B. Y. WASHAM - HEALTH ED. DIRECTOR
Y.W.C.A.
MR. G. H. TAYLOR - PHYSICAL DIRECTOR
Y.M.C.A.

There was a rigorous swimming program at the Walnut Street YMCA/YWCA, which started immediately after the building opened. The swimming pool was the only indoor pool for African Americans in Wilmington and the surrounding area. Lessons were provided for both children and adults. In addition to basic swimming and diving, there were lifesaving programs. Many of the young people who learned to swim at the Y went on to become award-winning swimmers and divers. This flyer highlights the lifesaving classes. (Courtesy of Dolores Washam and Lynn Clayton Jones.)

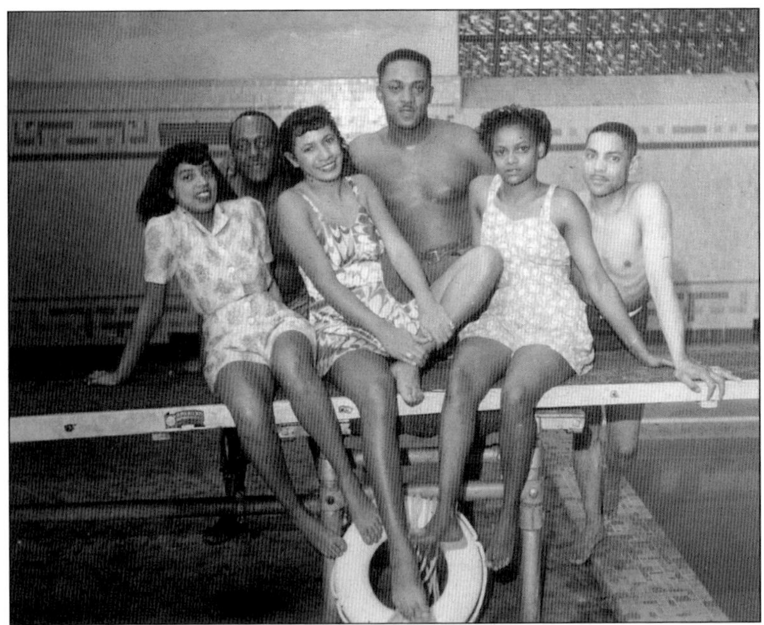

This photograph from the 1940s was taken by Portfield Harris. The pool was such a novelty that staff and members posed in the facility. In this photograph, the only identifiable individuals are George Taylor, second from left, who was the Boys' Work secretary, and Francis Portlock, on the far right, who was a desk clerk. (Courtesy of the Delaware Historical Society.)

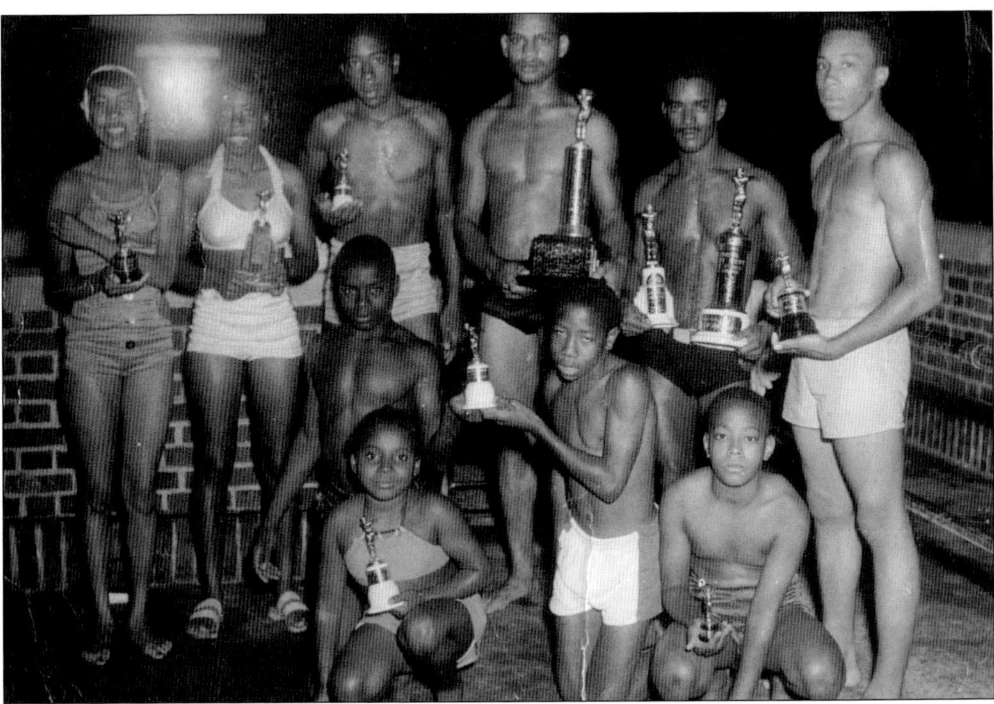

This is a 1940s photograph of award-winning swimmers. From left to right are (first row, crouching) Donald Comegys, Betty Ann Naylor and two unidentified; (second row, standing) Yvonne Bratcher, Barbara Washam, unidentified, Francis James, Maurice Wilson, and Lawrence Taylor. Wilson was known throughout the community as an outstanding diver. He is holding two trophies. (Courtesy of Dolores Washam and Lynn Clayton Jones.)

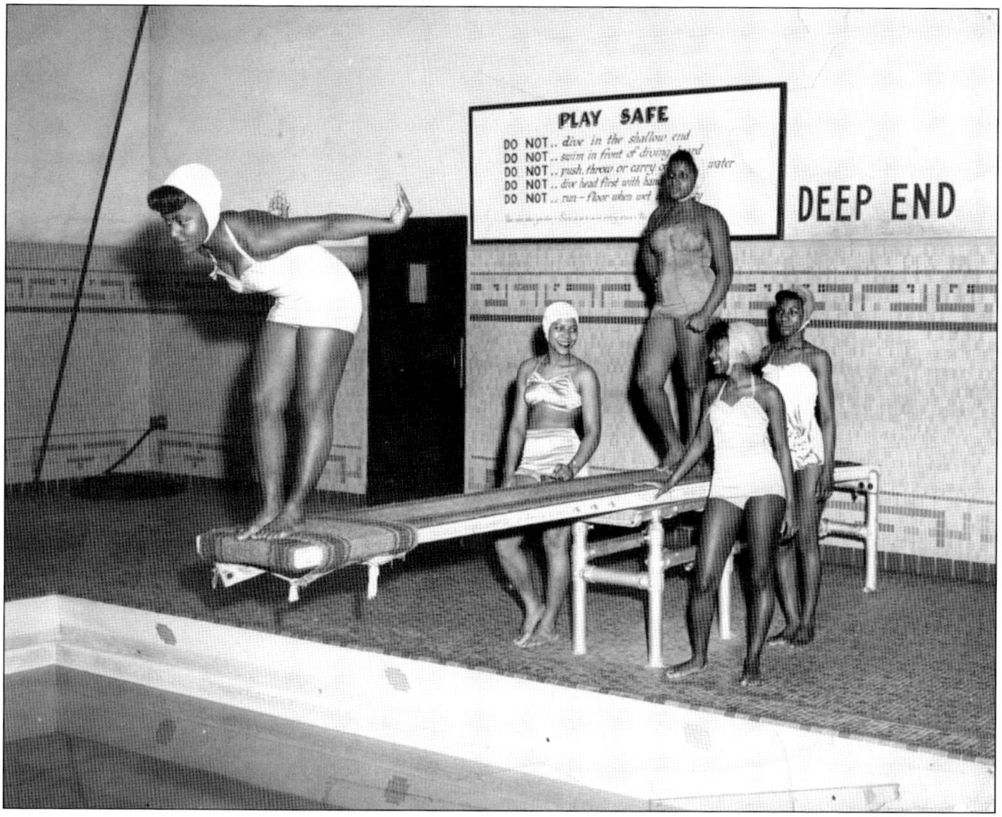

This photograph shows women during a diving lesson being conducted by Barbara Washam, physical education director for the YWCA (she is not seen in the photograph). The woman on the diving board is her sister Dolores Washam. The women waiting their turn are, from left to right, Phyliss Allen, Betty Ann Naylor, Kay Rideout, and unidentified. (Courtesy of Dolores Washam and Lynn Clayton Jones.)

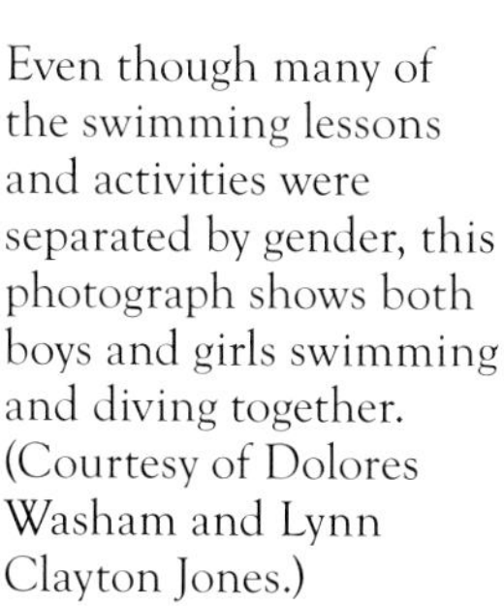

Even though many of the swimming lessons and activities were separated by gender, this photograph shows both boys and girls swimming and diving together. (Courtesy of Dolores Washam and Lynn Clayton Jones.)

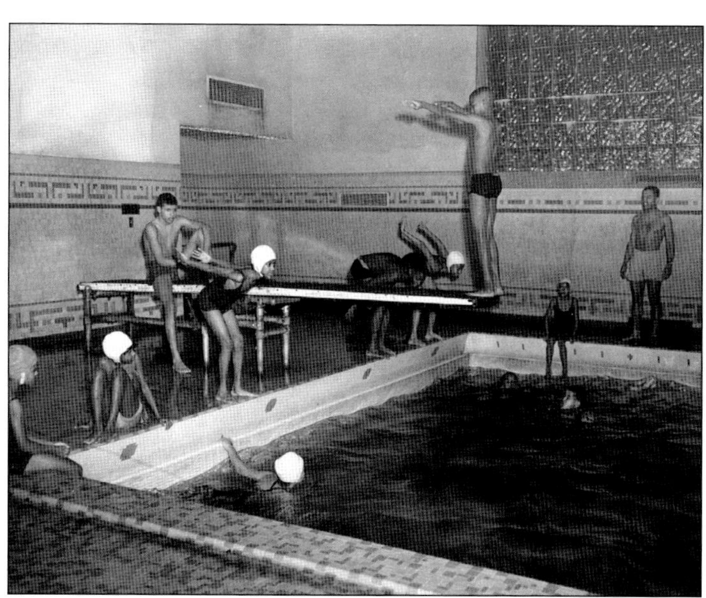

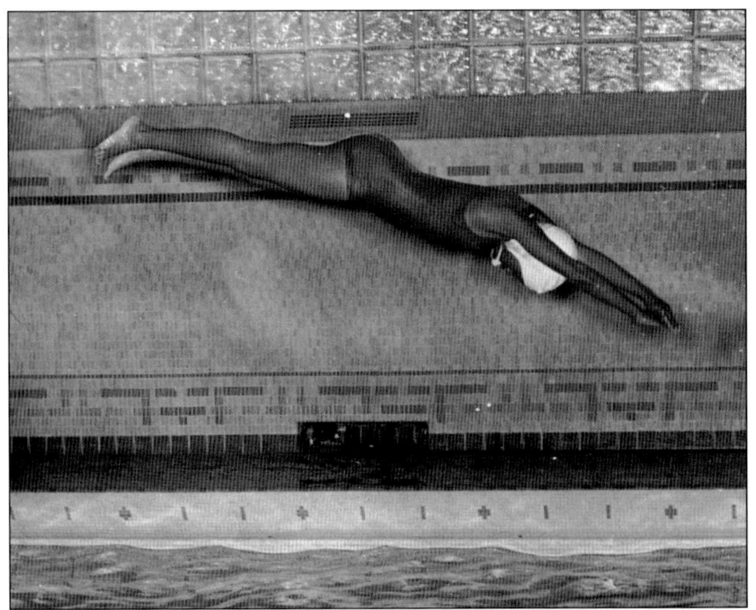

This young woman is practicing her diving technique. She appears to be between 10 and 12 years old. (Courtesy of Dolores Washam and Lynn Clayton Jones.)

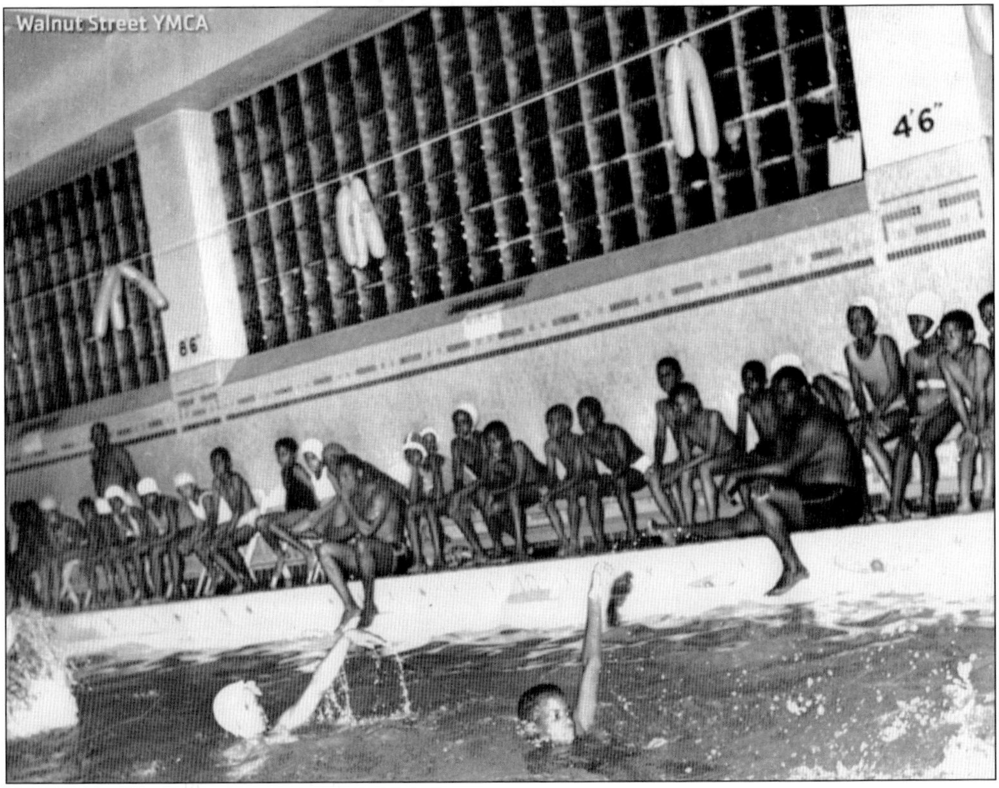

This photograph shows how many children might be swimming at one time. At least 26 children are pictured and others seem to be hidden. There are two male adults supervising the activity. This image is also important because it shows an architectural feature of the swimming pool area. The architect built a wall of glass blocks to ensure there would be plenty of light in the facility. (Courtesy of the Walnut Street YMCA.)

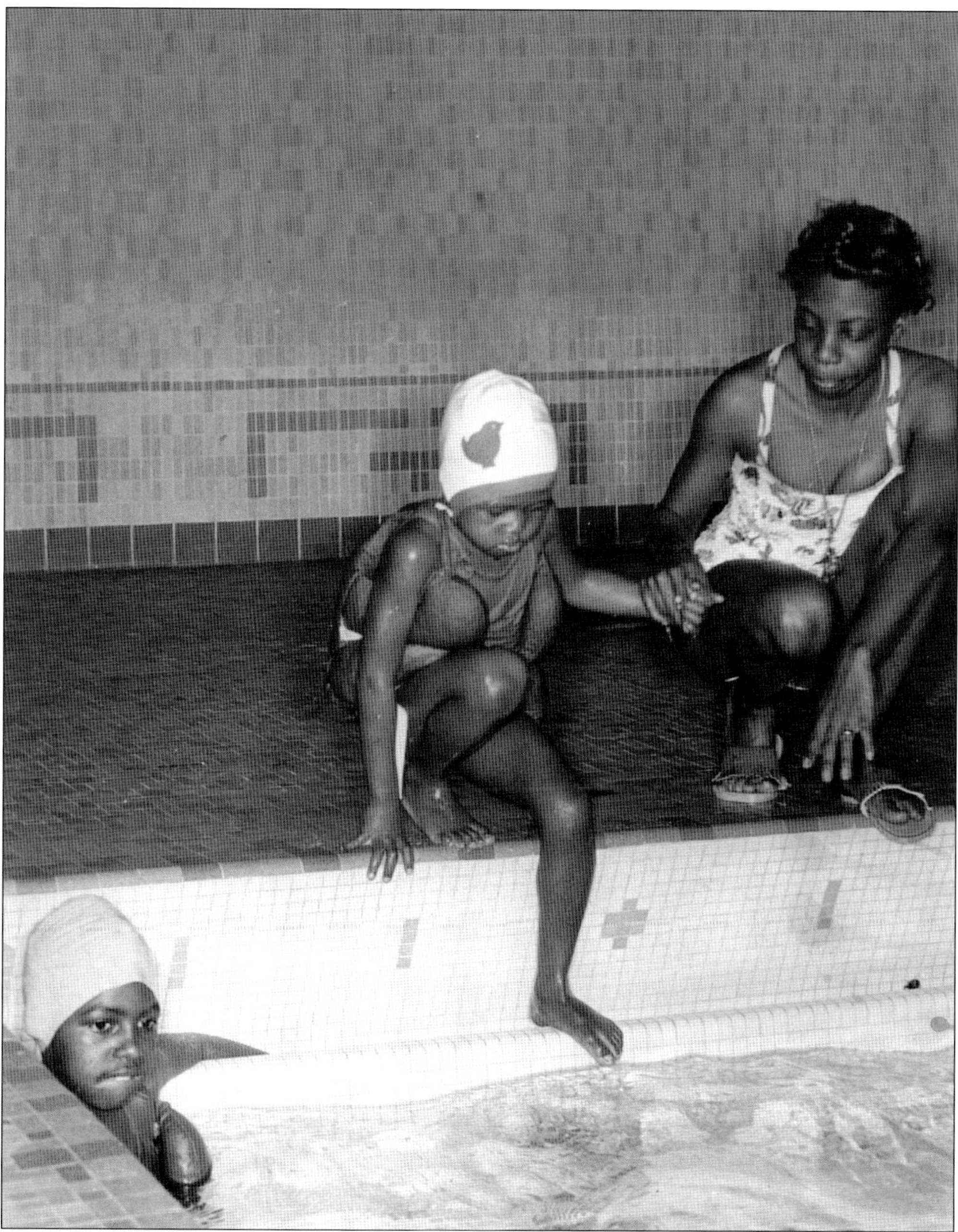

Barbara Washam, the physical education director of the YWCA, taught numerous children how to swim. She is pictured here teaching what appears to be a preschool child. Washam was of the opinion that children should be taught to swim when they are very young. She was an excellent swimmer as a child while attending the Walnut Street Y. Washam also taught swimming at Kruse Pool, an outdoor facility for African Americans. (Courtesy of Dolores Washam and Lynn Clayton Jones.)

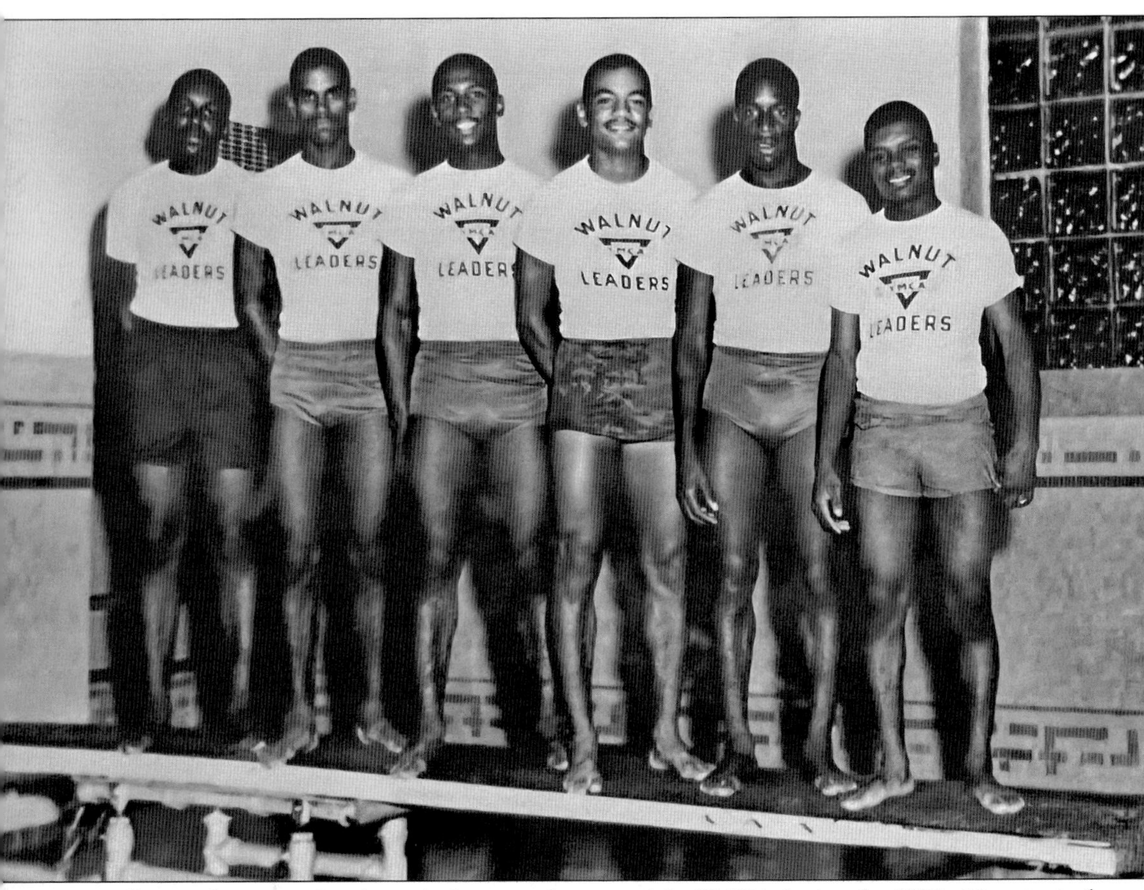

Gilbert Jackson was the physical education director of the YMCA during the 1950s. He recruited Barbara Washam to become the physical education director of the YWCA. Jackson also taught swimming and lifesaving. He and Washam became well-known for their emphasis on the sport. Jackson recognized talent and formed the elite group called the Walnut Street Team Leaders. They were the best swimmers and divers. Many of them were recognized for their athletic abilities. Pictured from left to right are Ellsworth Wilson, Richard Cephas, Arthur Redding Quentin Sterling, Willard Cephas, and Donald Comegys. Richard Cephas accepted a scholarship to Michigan State University for track even though he received offers from Dartmouth, William & Mary, and Indiana University. He was the NCAA record holder for the high hurdles, qualified for the 1960 Olympic trials, and was inducted into the University of Michigan Hall of Fame. Sterling was a football star and winning track coach. Willard Cephas was a swimming and diving champion, winning a state diving championship on the 30-foot platform. He was so motivated that he woke up at 4:00 a.m., got to the Y at 5:00 a.m., and swam for two hours before going to school. At one point, he lived two miles from the Y and walked through the rain and snow. (Courtesy of the estate of Gilbert H. Jackson Sr.)

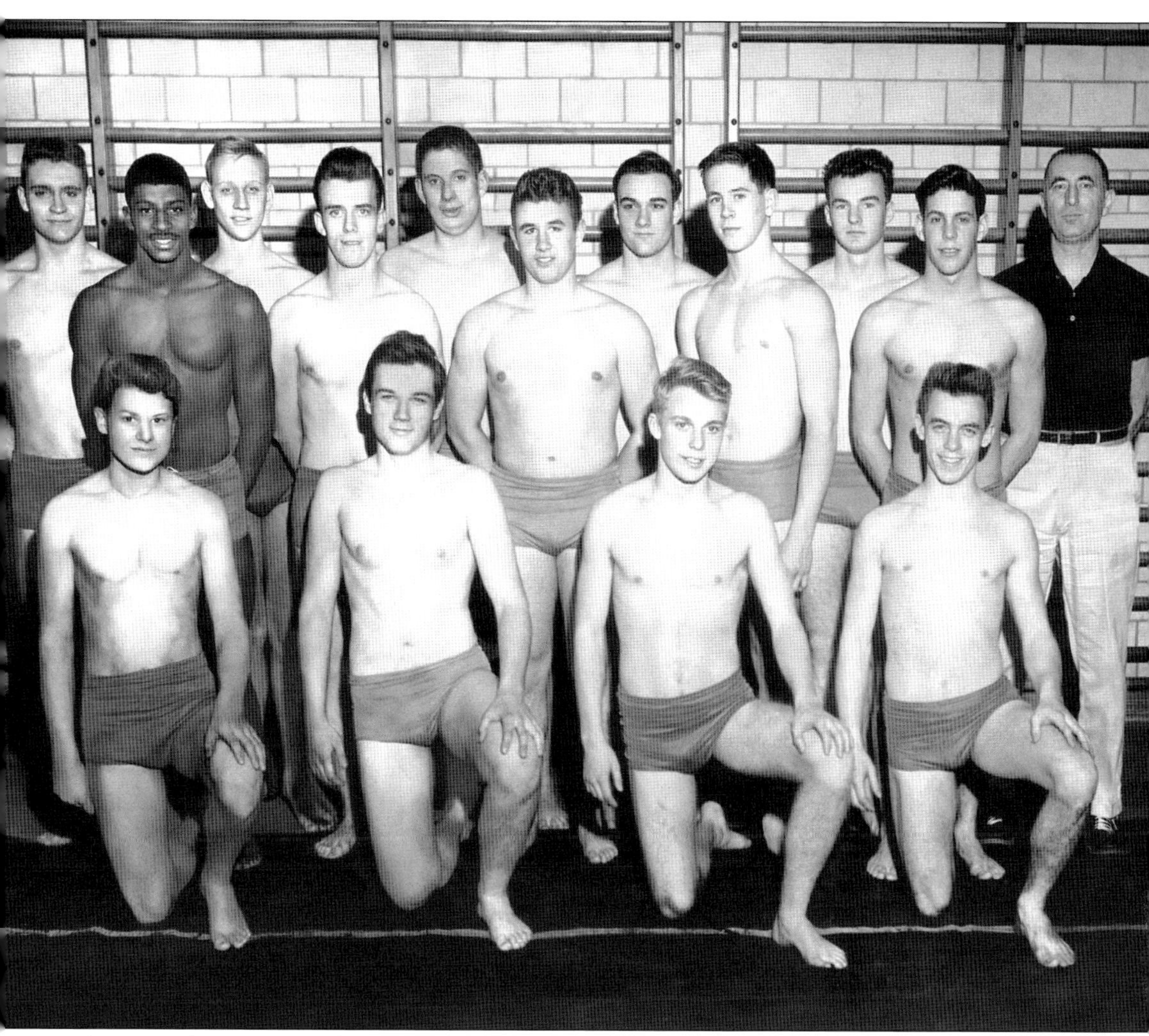

Lafayette Jackson was a scholar athlete setting records early in his career. During his time at Bancroft Jr. High School, he won awards in the 25-yard backstroke and 100-yard freestyle. In 1958, 1959, and 1960, at P.S. DuPont High School, he was the undefeated Delaware Interscholastic diving champ. In 1961, at Syracuse University Jackson was a freshman diving champ. From 1962 to 1964, at Howard University, he was the undefeated CIAA one and three-meter diving champion. In addition to swimming, he was also an outstanding gymnast. Jackson credits Gilbert Jackson for teaching him how to swim and dive. He also notes that his friend Willard Cephas helped him perfect his dive. When Gilbert Jackson realized Lafayette and Willard needed more expert training, he elicited the help of Charles Banks of the Wilmington YMCA to perfect their diving skills. (Courtesy of Lafayette Jackson.)

PHYSICAL COMMITTEE

John L. Simms - Chairman
Miss Jeannette Dixon - Secretary
Stewart J. A. Rivers
Maynard Jones
William A. Oliver
Charles B. Hayes
Daniel Hicks
Willard Cephas
Andrew McFarley
Harry Scott
David Gray
Clifton Crawford

JUNIOR LEADERS

Lafayette Jackson	Claven Jones
Marion Wright	Wilbert Waters
Llewellyn Bell	William Smither
Otho Stewart	Ronnie Jackson

This list of individuals is from the summer 1958 swimming schedule. The young men in the junior leaders were the top swimmers. Note that Lafayette Jackson and Llewellyn Bell are on that list. The list also included the adult members of the physical education committee. (Author's collection.)

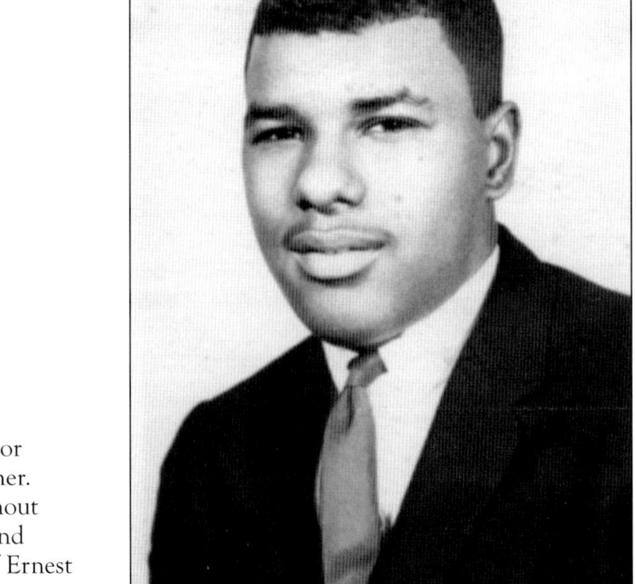

Ronnie Jackson was one of the junior leaders and was an excellent swimmer. Jackson continued to swim throughout his adult years at the P.S. DuPont and Central YMCA pools. (Courtesy of Ernest "Ronnie" Jackson.)

Maurice Pritchett was very active in the Walnut Street YMCA as a child. Among other activities, he participated in the camp program. Pritchett credited Gilbert Jackson for developing his basketball skills when he played itty-bitty basketball. Pritchett later became a basketball champion at Howard High School and Delaware State College. After graduating from college, he played semipro basketball for a short period of time. Pritchett returned to Wilmington to become an outstanding principal at Bancroft School. The Maurice Pritchett Academy has been named in his honor. (Courtesy of Juanita Pritchett.)

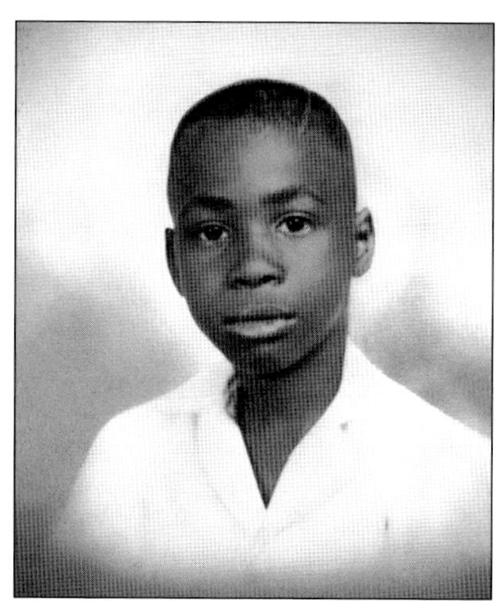

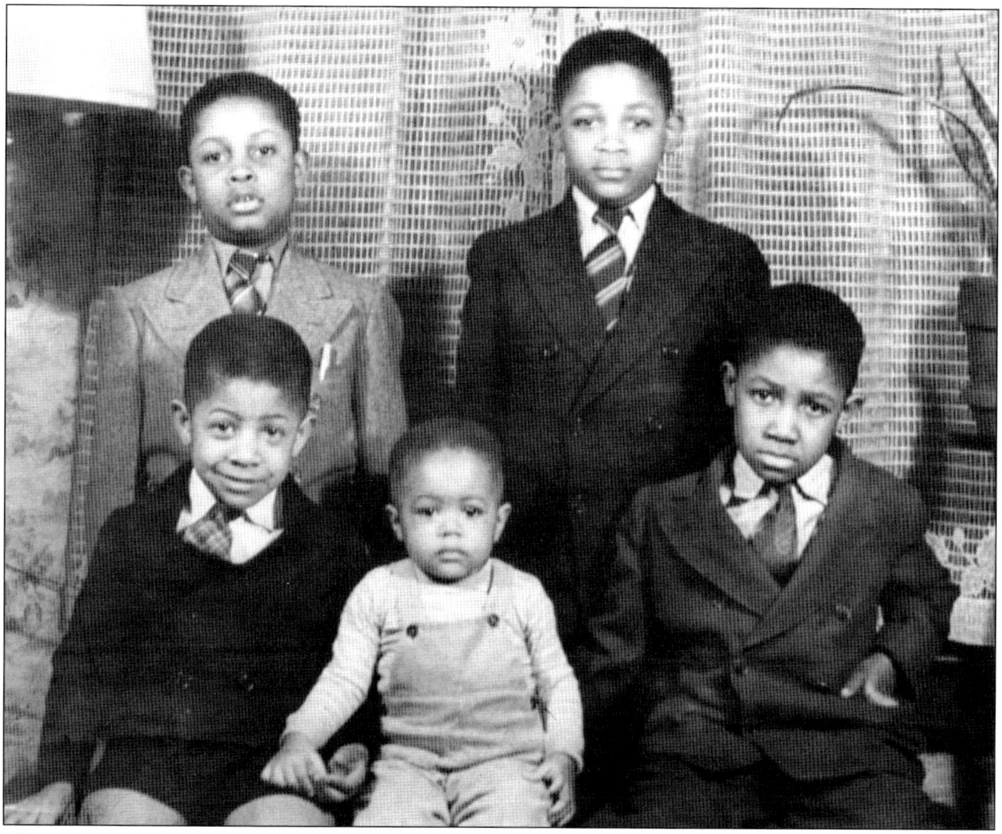

This is a picture of the boys in the Roberts family. They moved to Wilmington in the 1940s from Indianapolis, Indiana. As they traveled by train, the children became very excited when they saw the ocean. Their father, Chester Roberts, soon realized he needed to enroll his sons in swimming classes at the Walnut Street YMCA to prevent them from drowning. The children participated in other activities at the Y. Their mother, Alma Thomas, became very active in the Walnut Street YWCA. Pictured from left to right are (first row) Lesley Roberts, cousin John Fredrick Leeke, and Thomas Roberts; (second row) Chester Roberts and David Roberts. (Courtesy of Thomas Roberts.)

PHYSICAL DEPARTMENT SUMMER S

JUNE JULY AUGUST

MONDAY	TUESDAY	WEDNESDAY	THURSI
9:00-10:00 Low Beginners	9:00-10:00 Low Beg. Swim Instructions	9:00-10:00 Low Beginners	
10:00-10:30 Minnow Club	10:00-11:00 Low Beginners Instructions	10:00-10:30 Minnow Club	
10:30-11:00 Fish Club	11:00-12:00 Rec. Swim	10:30-11:00 Fish Club	
11:00-11:30 Flying Fish		11:00-11:30 Flying Fish	
11:30-12:15 Shark Club		11:30-12:15 Shark Club	
		1:00-3:00 Co-ed Rec. Swim	
4:00-5:00 Jr. Swim Team	4:00-5:00 Jr. Swim Team	4:00-5:00 Jr. Swim Team	4:00-5: Jr. Sw
5:30 - 7:00		C O M M U N I T Y	U S E O F
7:00-7:45 Teenage Co-ed Rec		7:00-8:00 Club Period	7:00-8: Club Pe
8:00-8:30 Adult Beg. Swim Lessons	8:00-9:45 Life Saving	8:00-8:30 Adult Co-ed Swim Lessons	8:00-9: Life Sa
8:30-9:15 Rec. Swim Adults		8:30-9:15 Rec Swim	

SWIMMING POOL RULES:
1. A YMCA rule prohibits anyone
2. A warm soap and water bath i
3. Two or more experienced swim

GYMNASIUM: After May 31, gymnasium facilities availab
Pollywogs instructions for boys ages 6-8 a

E

FRIDAY	SATURDAY
9:00-10:00 Low Beginners	8:30-9:15 Pollywogs
10:00-10:30 Minnow Club	9:30-10:30 Beginners
10:30-11:00 Fish Club	10:30-11:30 Swimmers
11:00-11:30 Flying Fish	
11:30-12:15 Shark Club	
L	
7:30-8:45 Family Night Swim	

swimming alone
ired before entering the water.
ay enter pool anytime.

n request. (Membership required)
tall must be enrolled.

This is the 1958 summer swimming schedule at the Walnut Street Y. The classes and activities ran from 9:00 a.m. in the morning until 9:15 p.m. at night. There was instruction for both children and adults. The classes were programmed based on ability and went from "pollywogs" to "sharks." There was a junior swim team that practiced four days a week. Lifesaving lessons were held twice a week. (Author's collection.)

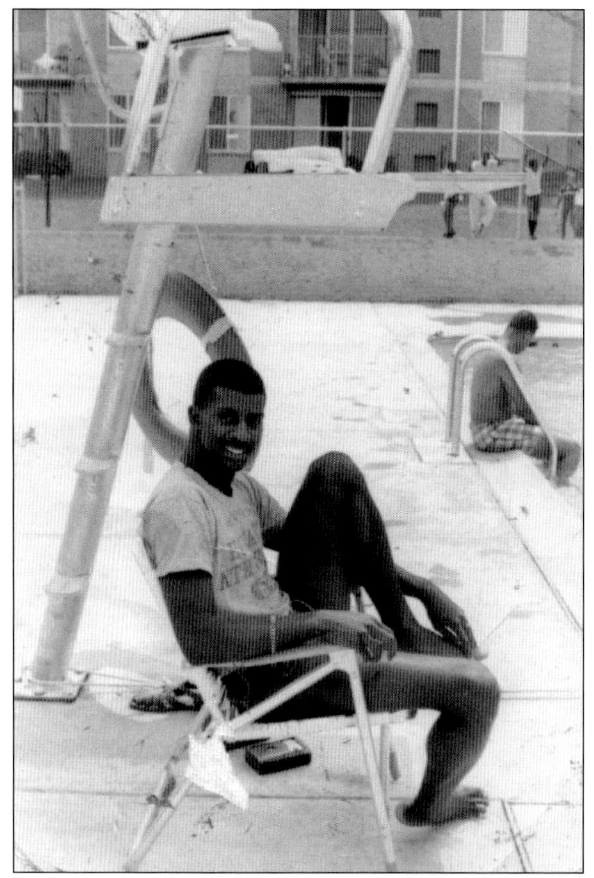

Lafayette Jackson, in addition to being an outstanding swimmer and diver, was also a lifeguard. Here we see him sitting at his lifeguard post on a summer's day. The training at the Walnut Street YMCA and YWCA provided many opportunities for young people. When Gilbert Jackson, the physical education director, became the first manager of Eden Park Pool, he decided to hire as many African American lifeguards as he could. He had trained young people in lifesaving skills and had many swimmers to choose from. Two of his outstanding swimmers, James Llewellyn Bell and Lafayette Jackson, were only 15 years old and did not meet the age requirement of 16 to become lifeguards. Gilbert Jackson knew they had the skills and petitioned for them to become lifeguards at 15 years old. (Courtesy of Lafayette Jackson.)

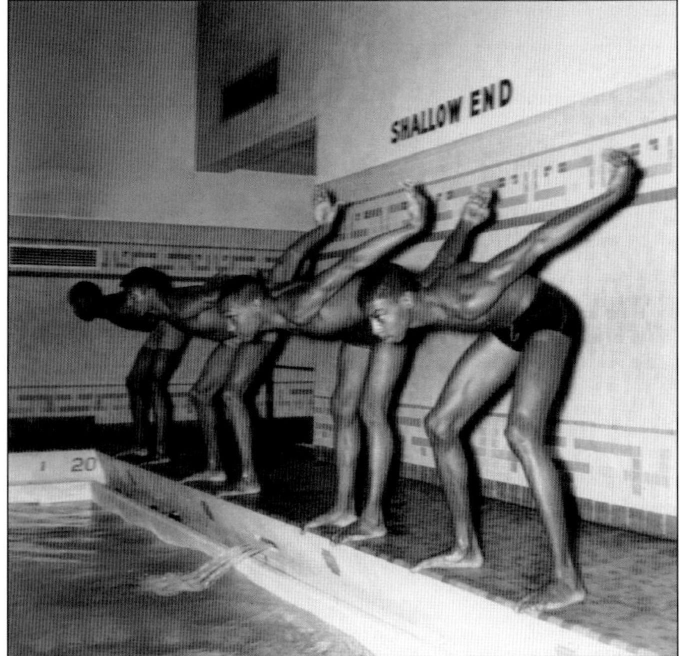

These swimmers are ready to dive in the pool. Notice their form—it is apparent they have received excellent training. (Courtesy of the Walnut Street YMCA.)

Five

The Camp Program

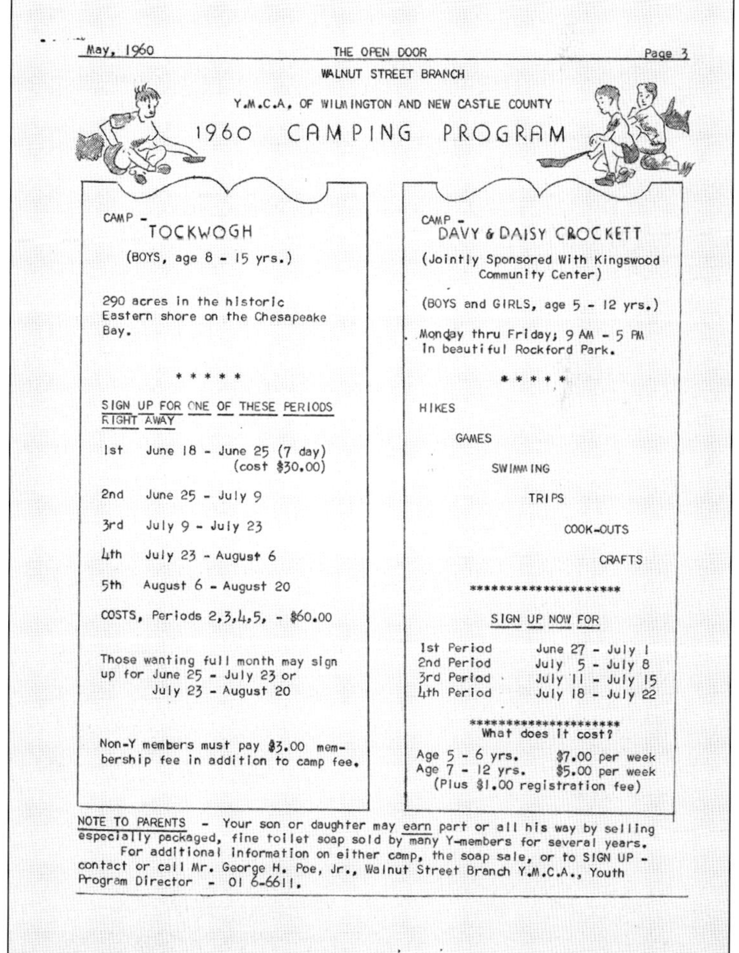

May, 1960 THE OPEN DOOR Page 3

WALNUT STREET BRANCH

Y.M.C.A. OF WILMINGTON AND NEW CASTLE COUNTY

1960 CAMPING PROGRAM

CAMP - TOCKWOGH

(BOYS, age 8 - 15 yrs.)

290 acres in the historic Eastern shore on the Chesapeake Bay.

* * * * *

SIGN UP FOR ONE OF THESE PERIODS RIGHT AWAY

1st June 18 - June 25 (7 day) (cost $30.00)

2nd June 25 - July 9

3rd July 9 - July 23

4th July 23 - August 6

5th August 6 - August 20

COSTS, Periods 2,3,4,5, - $60.00

Those wanting full month may sign up for June 25 - July 23 or July 23 - August 20

Non-Y members must pay $3.00 membership fee in addition to camp fee.

CAMP - DAVY & DAISY CROCKETT

(Jointly Sponsored With Kingswood Community Center)

(BOYS and GIRLS, age 5 - 12 yrs.)

Monday thru Friday; 9 AM - 5 PM In beautiful Rockford Park.

* * * * *

HIKES

GAMES

SWIMMING

TRIPS

COOK-OUTS

CRAFTS

****

SIGN UP NOW FOR

1st Period	June 27 - July 1
2nd Period	July 5 - July 8
3rd Period	July 11 - July 15
4th Period	July 18 - July 22

****

What does it cost?

Age 5 - 6 yrs. $7.00 per week
Age 7 - 12 yrs. $5.00 per week
(Plus $1.00 registration fee)

NOTE TO PARENTS - Your son or daughter may earn part or all his way by selling especially packaged, fine toilet soap sold by many Y-members for several years.
For additional information on either camp, the soap sale, or to SIGN UP - contact or call Mr. George H. Poe, Jr., Walnut Street Branch Y.M.C.A., Youth Program Director - OL 6-6611.

This copy of the camp brochure details the specifics of the camp programs. Camp Tockwogh was the overnight program for boys aged 8–15 years old. Each session ran for a week. Children were able to earn the camp tuition by selling toilet soap. The Davey & Daisy Crockett Camp was for both boys and girls aged 5–12. This day camp was in collaboration with Kingswood Community Center. It was held at Rockford Park. (Courtesy of the Delaware Historical Society.)

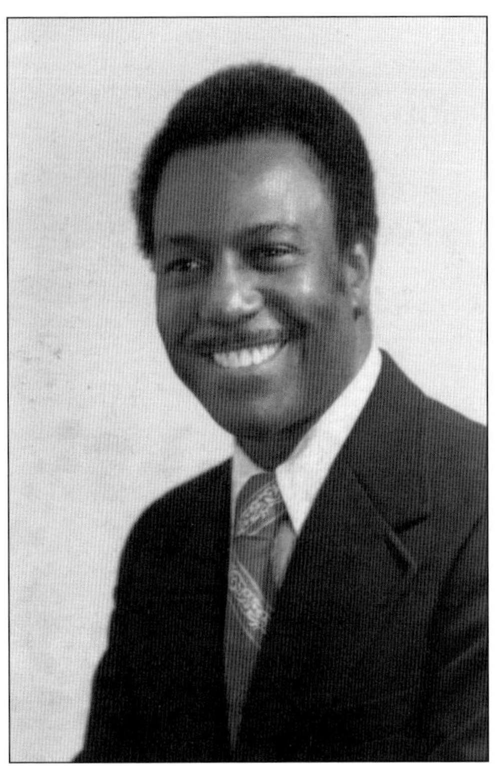

Raymond Woodard was the director of the Davey and Daisy Crockett Camp. He was a teacher at the Dunleith School. Previously, he served as a counselor at Camp Barnes. Woodard hired college students as camp counselors. A bus would come to the Dunleith community to pick up children who lived there. (Courtesy of Linda Woodard.)

All YMCA camp directors were required to complete specialized training. This is a photograph of Raymond Woodard at one of the trainings. He is the only African American participating in this event. (Courtesy of Linda Woodard.)

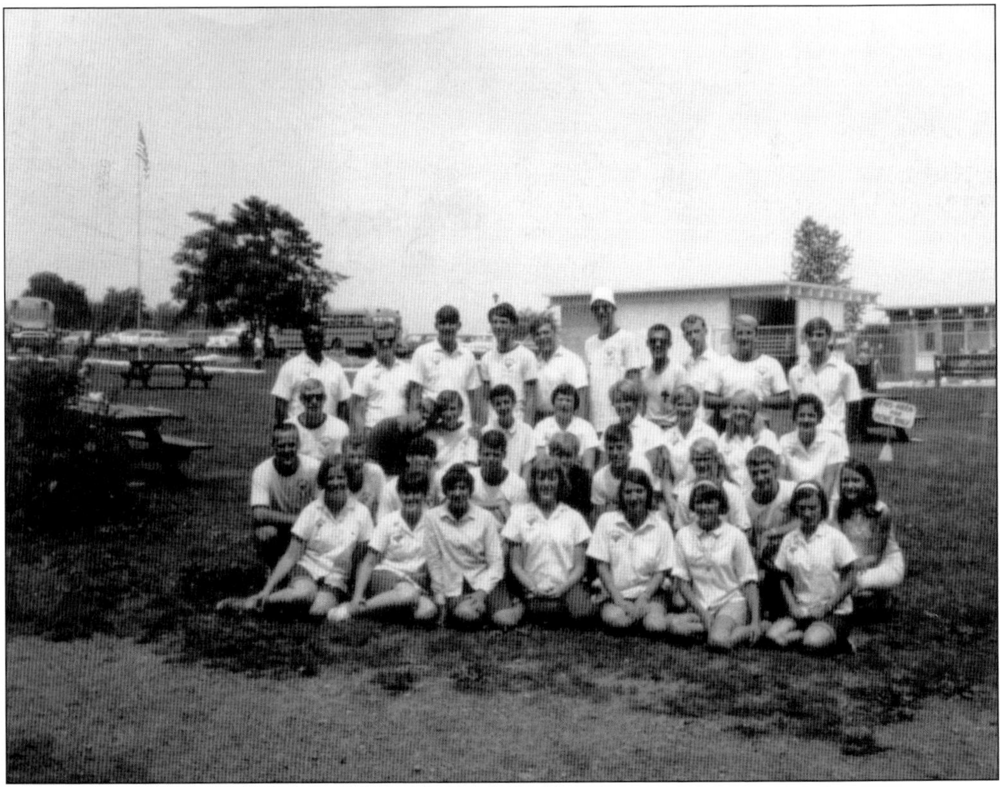

These children are getting on the bus to go to Rockford Park for the Davey & Daisy Crockett Day Camp. (Courtesy of the Walnut Street YMCA.)

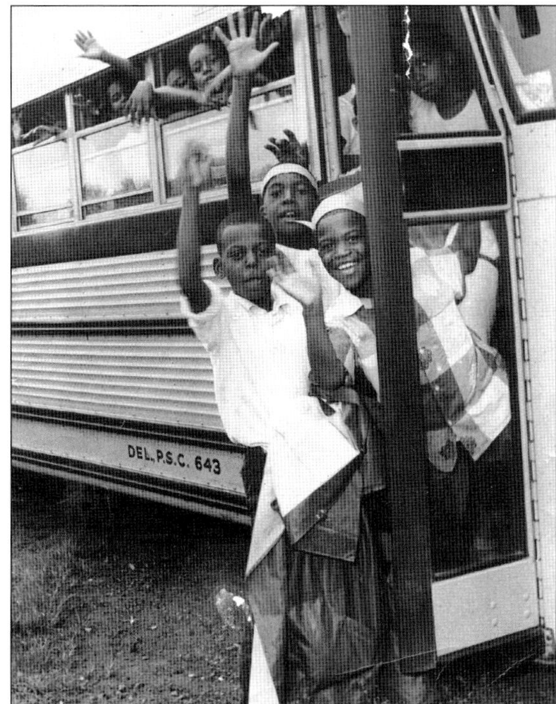

These young children are enjoying the fresh air and wide open spaces at Rockford Park. The large expanse of grass provided opportunities for many diverse outdoor activities. (Courtesy of the Walnut Street YMCA.)

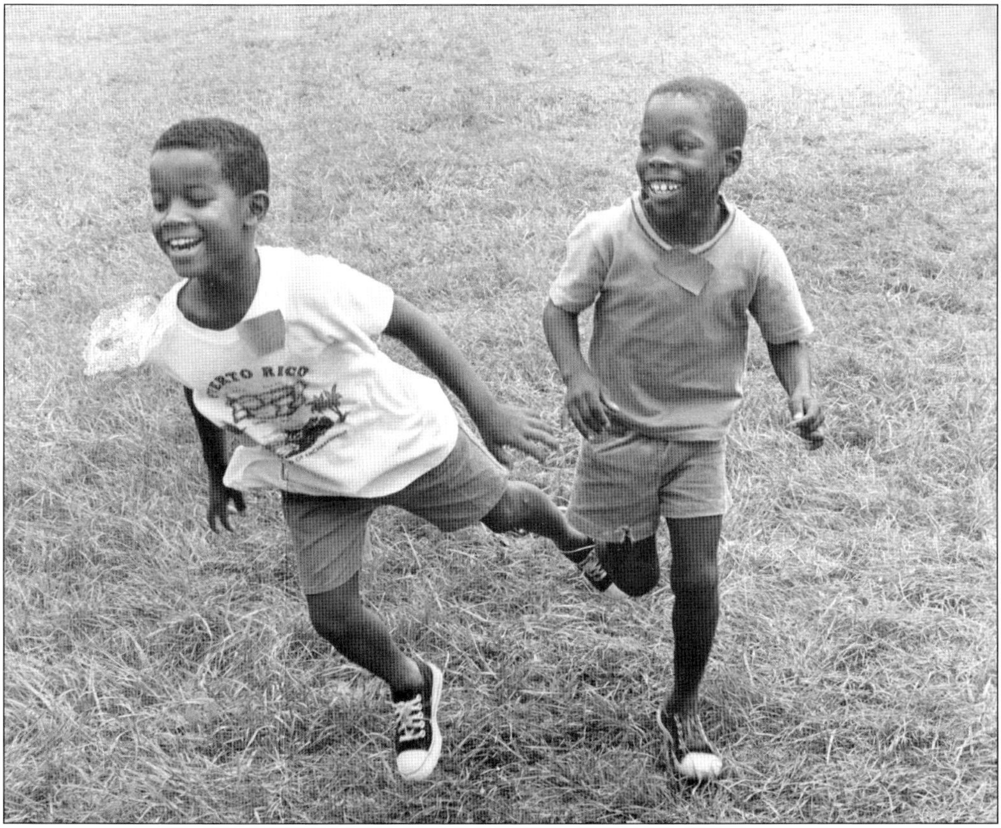

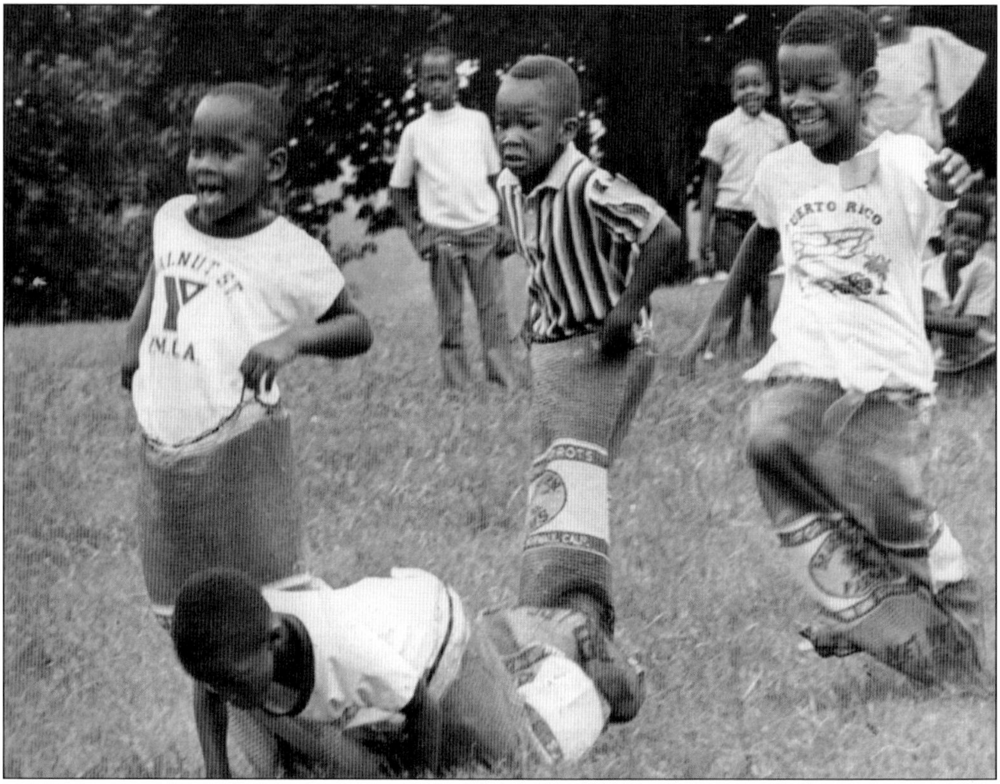

There were many outdoor activities at Rockford Park. Here, children participate in a sack race. (Courtesy of the Walnut Street YMCA.)

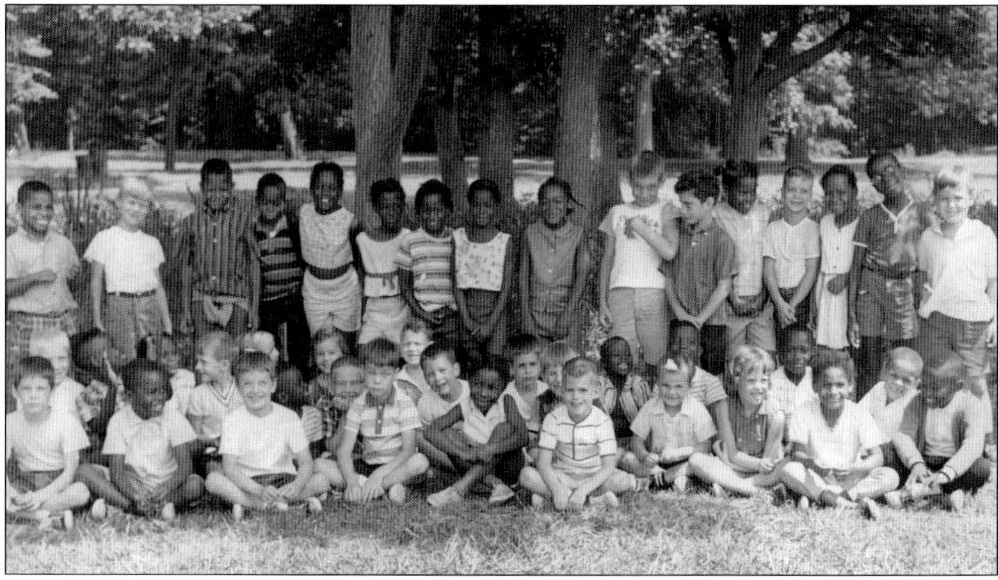

This group of day campers is an example of the integrated activities at Rockford Park. Even though the Walnut Street YMCA and YWCA were primarily African American in membership, during day camp activities the children often engaged with children from the white YMCA and YWCA. (Courtesy of the Walnut Street YMCA.)

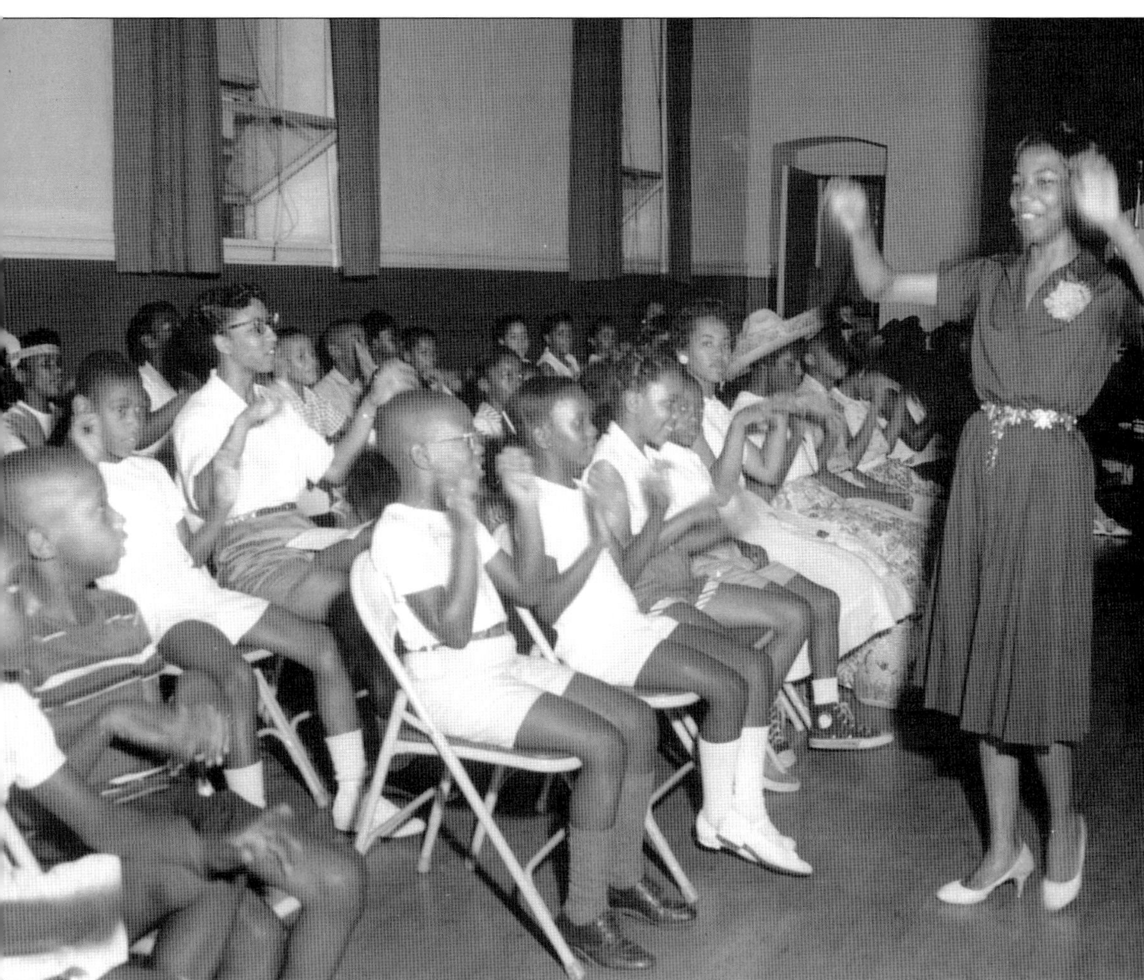

When there was inclement weather, the children met at the Walnut Street YMCA instead of Rockford Park. On this day, camp counselor Madeline Bolden Johnson is leading the children in a camp song. They are probably preparing for the closing activities. Other counselors are also present in this photograph. The woman with the glasses on the second row is Cynthia Elliott Oates. On the first row, the woman looking at the camera next to the girl in the hat is Sylvia Henry Cain, who later worked as a secretary at the Walnut Street YMCA. All of these young women were college students. (Courtesy of Dolores Washam and Lynn Clayton Jones.)

"DAVY & DAISY CROCKETT DAY CAMP CAMPOREE"

Mistress of Ceremonies - Marlene Hazzard

Opening Song "Do Lord". . . . . Campers

Biblical Recitation . . . . . . Crystal Burris

Greeting. . . . . Mr. Raymond Woodard, Director

Drilling & Acrobatics. . .. .Miss Henry's Group

Acrobatics . . . . Miss Elliott's Group

Song "Ten Green Bottles" . . . . Campers

Song " One Finger, One Thumb" . . . . . Campers

Square Dance. . . . . Mrs. Jenkins' Group

"The Doll Playlet" . . . . Miss Anderson's Group

Indian Dance - NAVAJO TRIBE (Mrs. Harris' Group

"Puppet Show". . . . . Miss Bolden's Group

Singing "DAVY & DAISY CROCKETT SONG"
Miss Johnson's Group

"Bear Hunt" . . . . Campers

EXHIBITION . . . . Arts & Crafts
James Johnson

Song "Jacob's Ladder". . . . . Campers

Song "Tell Me Why" . . . . Campers

TAPS . . . . Campers

Remarks . . . Mr. Charles Simms, Board Sponsor

Remarks - Mr. George H. Taylor, Youth Secretary

This is the closing activity for the Davey & Daisy Crockett Day Camp program. Each of the camp counselors led an activity. (Courtesy of the Delaware Historical Society.)

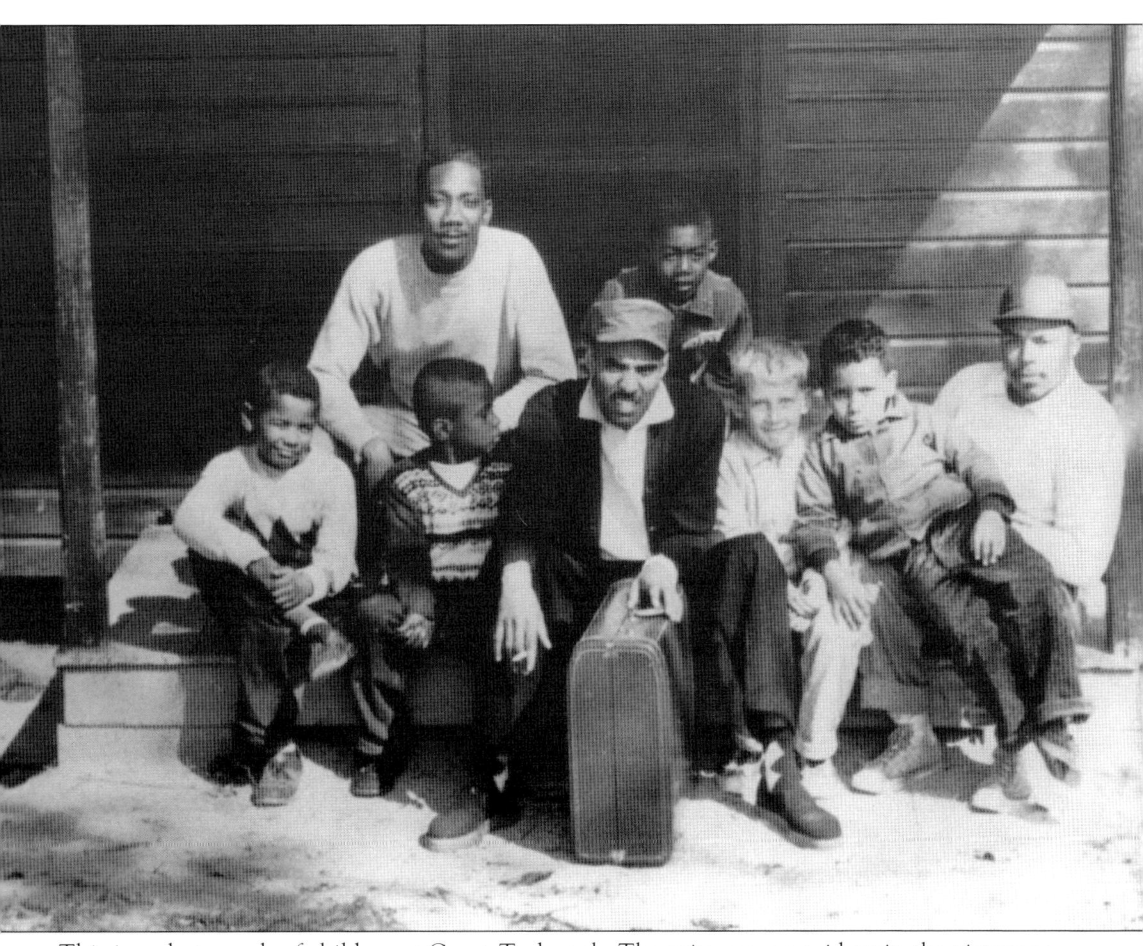

This is a photograph of children at Camp Tockwogh. The suitcases are evident in the picture as the children and their counselors sit outside of one of the cabins. The man on the second row is David Gray, who was very active in the Y. He and his wife headed the Theater Guild. Gray was an outstanding actor as well as a respected photographer, and he documented many of the activities in the African American community in the 1950s and 1950s. His family was best known, however, for the successful funeral business they operated on the East Side of Wilmington. (Courtesy of the Delaware Historical Society.)

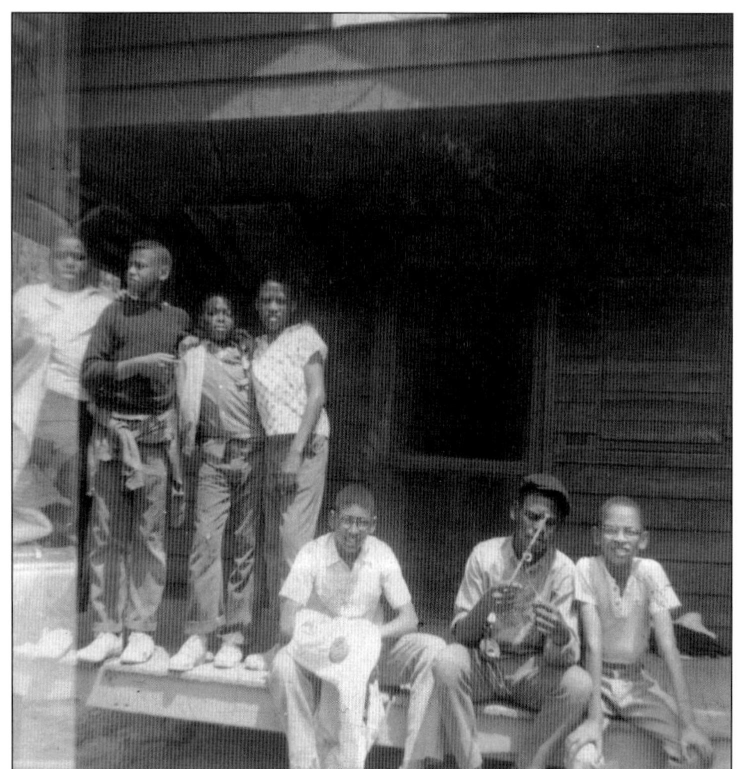

These are children outside of a cabin at Camp Tockwogh. It was one of the most frequented overnight camp for boys. They usually spent one week there engaging in such pursuits as swimming, sports activities, and arts and crafts. (Courtesy of the Walnut Street YMCA.)

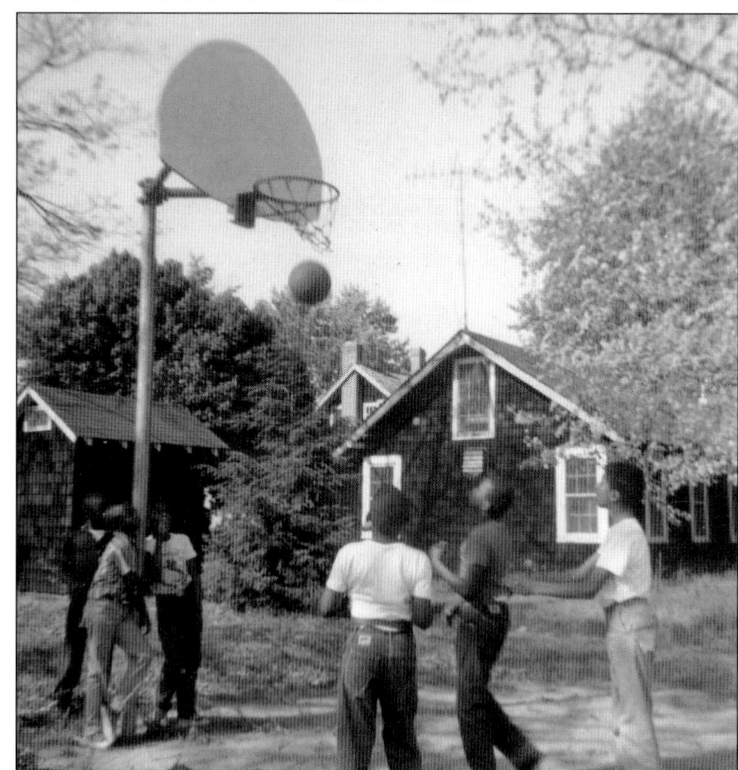

There were many activities at Camp Tockwogh. Children would swim, fish, and play outdoor games. Here they are playing basketball. (Courtesy of the Walnut Street YMCA.)

Six

The Dance Program

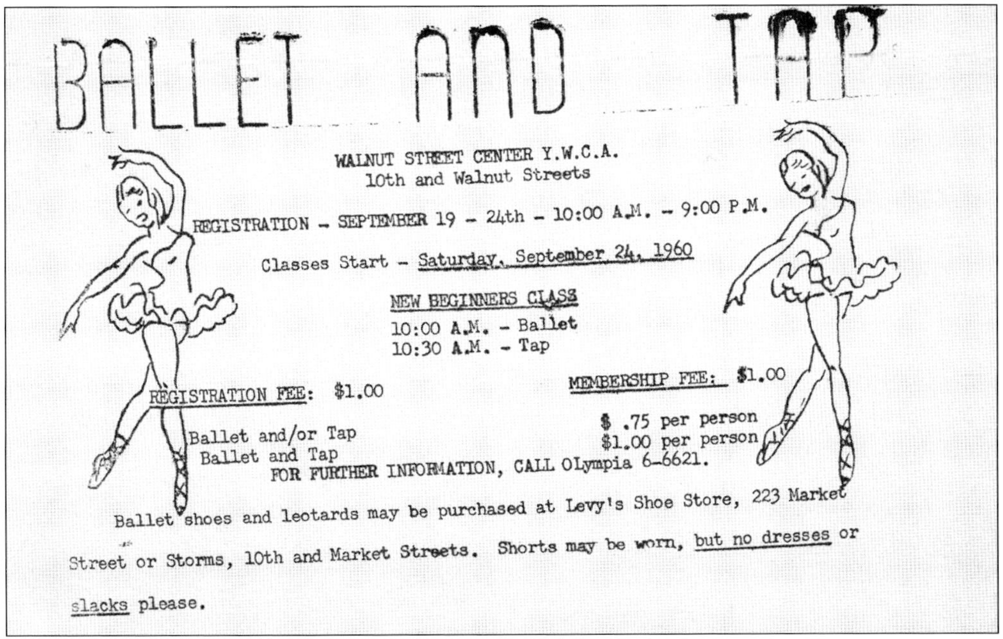

BALLET AND TAP

WALNUT STREET CENTER Y.W.C.A.
10th and Walnut Streets

REGISTRATION - SEPTEMBER 19 - 24th - 10:00 A.M. - 9:00 P.M.

Classes Start - Saturday, September 24, 1960

NEW BEGINNERS CLASS
10:00 A.M. - Ballet
10:30 A.M. - Tap

REGISTRATION FEE: $1.00 MEMBERSHIP FEE: $1.00

Ballet and/or Tap $ .75 per person
Ballet and Tap $1.00 per person

FOR FURTHER INFORMATION, CALL OLympia 6-6621.

Ballet shoes and leotards may be purchased at Levy's Shoe Store, 223 Market Street or Storms, 10th and Market Streets. Shorts may be worn, but no dresses or slacks please.

The dance program was initiated as soon as the building opened in 1940. It was operated by the YWCA. Taking dance lessons at the Walnut Street YWCA was almost a rite of passage for many African American young people in Wilmington and the surrounding area. Every year in June, there was a dance recital called the *Musical Hit*. This is a flyer for the dance program in the 1950s. (Courtesy of Dolores Washam and Lynn Clayton Jones.)

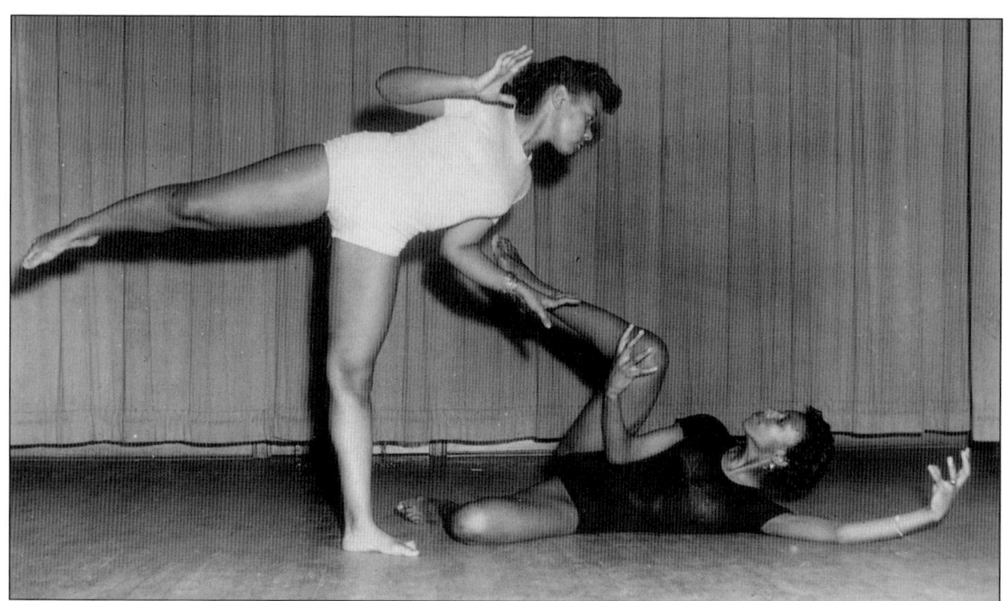

This 1947 photograph is a selection from the *Musical Hit.* The young woman on the floor is Gertrude Redding. The woman standing is Dolores ?. (Courtesy of Dolores Washam and Lynn Clayton Jones.)

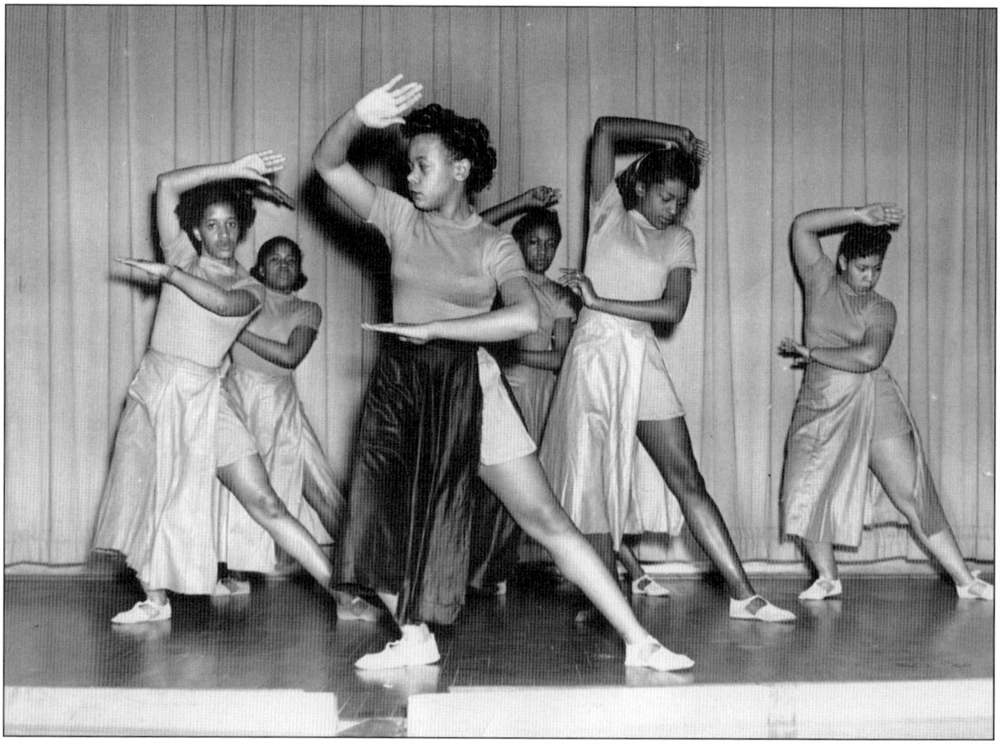

This is another selection from the 1947 *Musical Hit*. These young women were probably influenced by Katherine Dunham, who was the foremost African American modern dancer during the 1940s. She started the Katherine Dunham Dance Company, the only independent African American dance company during that time period. (Courtesy of Dolores Washam and Lynn Clayton Jones.)

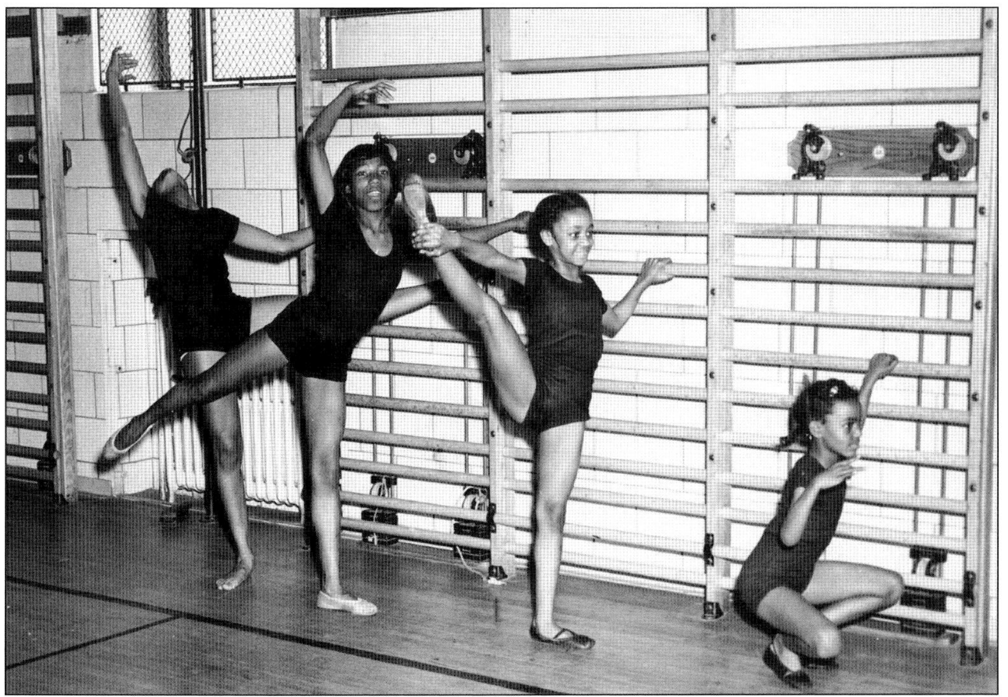

Dance classes at the YWCA always started with warm-up exercises at the barre. Here, students are doing those exercises. They are, from left to right, unidentified, Madeline Bolden Johnson, and two unidentified. (Courtesy of Dolores Washam and Lynn Clayton Jones.)

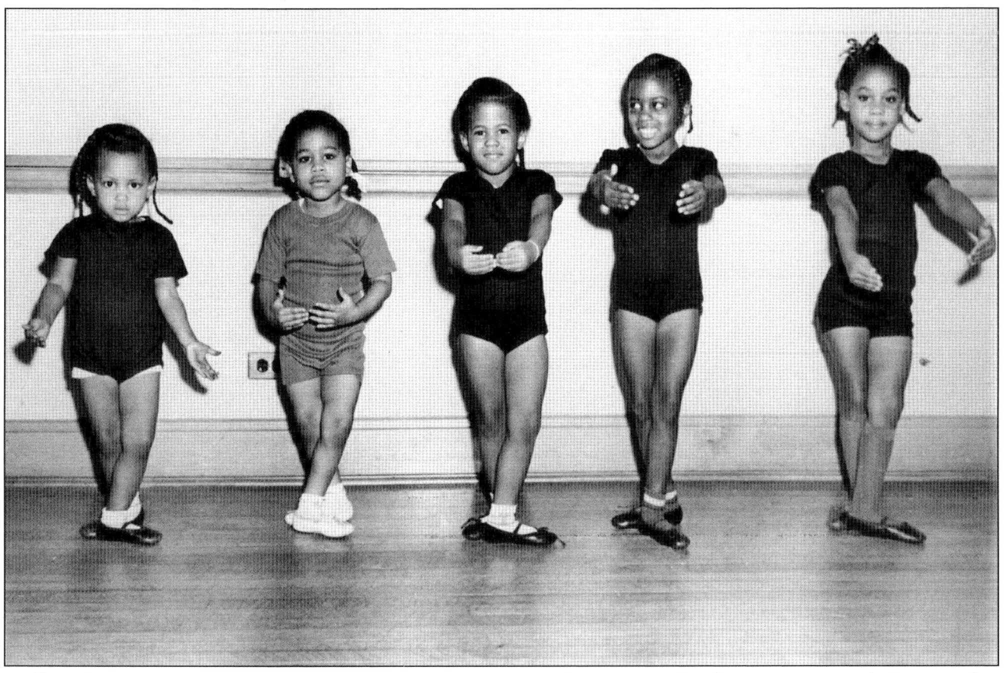

Ballet classes were offered to very young children. These preschoolers are, from left to right, unidentified, Beiley Byrd, Debbie Jackson, Francine Hammond, and Brenda Andrews. (Courtesy of Dolores Washam and Lynn Clayton Jones.)

PROGRAMME

BY THE SEA

Sharon Kirk	Debra Jackson
Cynthia Clark	Priscilla Brunswick
Charlotte Paine	Cheryl Howell
Francine Hammond	Brenda Love
Sydella Davis	Cortez Baylock
Sandra Debrick	Jean Warlaw
Loretta Monroe	Barbara Brown

Beily Byrd

STRUTTERS ON THE BOARDWALK

"Stepping out with my Baby"

Rosalyn Harris	Sandra Nelson
Carolyn Thomas	Lenora Petty

ACROBATS

Sharon Kirk	Debra Jackson
Cynthia Clark	Priscilla Brunswick
Charlotte Paine	Cheryl Howell
Francine Hammond	Brenda Love
Sydella Davis	Cortez Baylock
Sandra Debrick	Jean Warlaw
Loretta Monroe	Barbara Brown

Beilv Byrd

LITTLE PEASANTS

Ann Waters	Joyce Holden
Shelia Boyer	Marguerite Quinn
Martina Gardner	Kathryn Quinn

Rosalyn Harris

THE FORTUNE TELLER

Sandra Johnson

During the *Musical Hit*, there was always a physical program brochure. This is a brochure from the 1950s with some of the participants listed. (Courtesy of the Delaware Historical Society.)

This section of the program lists some of the adult staff. Bessie Morgan was the director of programs for the YWCA. David Gray was the director of the Theater Guild. They both were highly artistic and created much of the scenery for the dance productions. Ilona Ivinski was the dance teacher. She traveled from her home in Smyrna Delaware every Saturday to begin classes at 9:00 a.m. and taught until 4:00 p.m. Ivinski was one of the most sought-after dance teachers in the state; she taught in Smyrna and at Ursuline Academy in Wilmington. Helen Griffin was the pianist and played during the dance classes on Saturdays and for the *Musical Hit*. She was a professional piano teacher in Wilmington. Lillian Stafford was the costume designer and seamstress. She created elaborate costumes. Some of her creations still survive in the possession of some of the dance students. (Courtesy of the Delaware Historical Society.)

ACKNOWLEGEMENTS

SCENERY	Mrs. Bessie Morgan Mr. David Gray
PROGRAMS	Mrs. Rudolph Johnson
BALLET AND TAP Choreographer	Mrs. Ilona Ivinsci
PIANIST	Miss Helen Griffin
GUEST	Warren Guy Madeline Bolden Charlestine Lewis
COSTUMES	Mrs. Lillian Stanford

HEALTH EDUCATION COMMITTEE

Mrs. Eva W. Sydney, Chairman

Mrs. Marion Donnell	Mrs. Virginia Outlaw
Mrs. Hattie Brooks	Mrs. Gertrude Young
Mrs. Emma Edwards	Mrs. Ruth Winchester
Mrs. Blanche Fleming	Mrs. Lula Stinson

Miss Barbara Y. Washam, Director

Parents were active participants in the *Musical Hits.* They dyed and embellished leotards and ballet shoes. Most were on hand, backstage, to apply makeup on their child and to help them change. One of the parents, Elizabeth Hunt, is pictured here with some of the young dancers. From left to right are Carolyn Thomas, Stephanie Hunt Evans, and Jeanne Nutter. (Author's collection.)

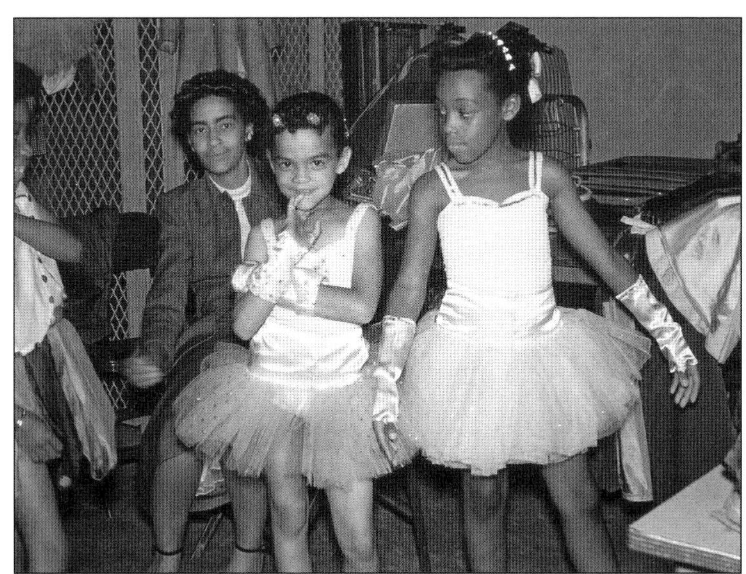

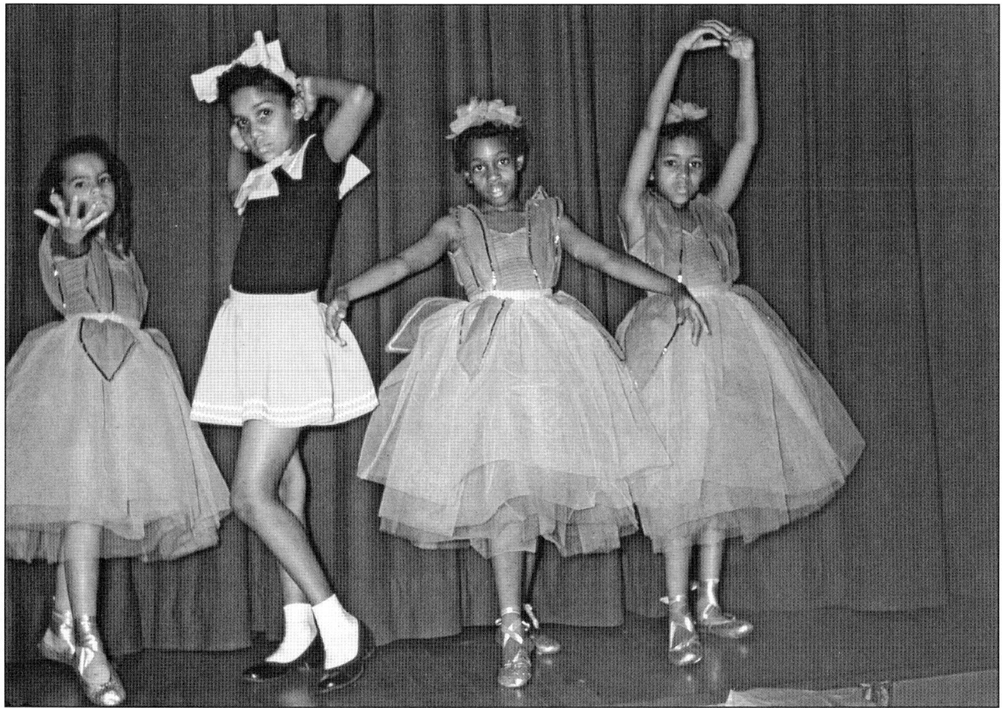

The *Musical Hit* featured numerous acts. In this picture are Stephanie Hunt Evans, Sydella Davis Boone, Jeanne Nutter, and Judith Gupton Wiley. Evans, Nutter, and Wiley were in a selection called "April Showers." They wore pink plastic raincoats, carried umbrellas, and sang the song "April Showers." At a certain point, they took off the raincoats and threw away the umbrellas to reveal the costumes they were wearing, which represented the May flowers created by the April showers. Sydella was in a dance called "By the Sea." The children in that selection portrayed bathing beauties from the 1920s. (Author's collection.)

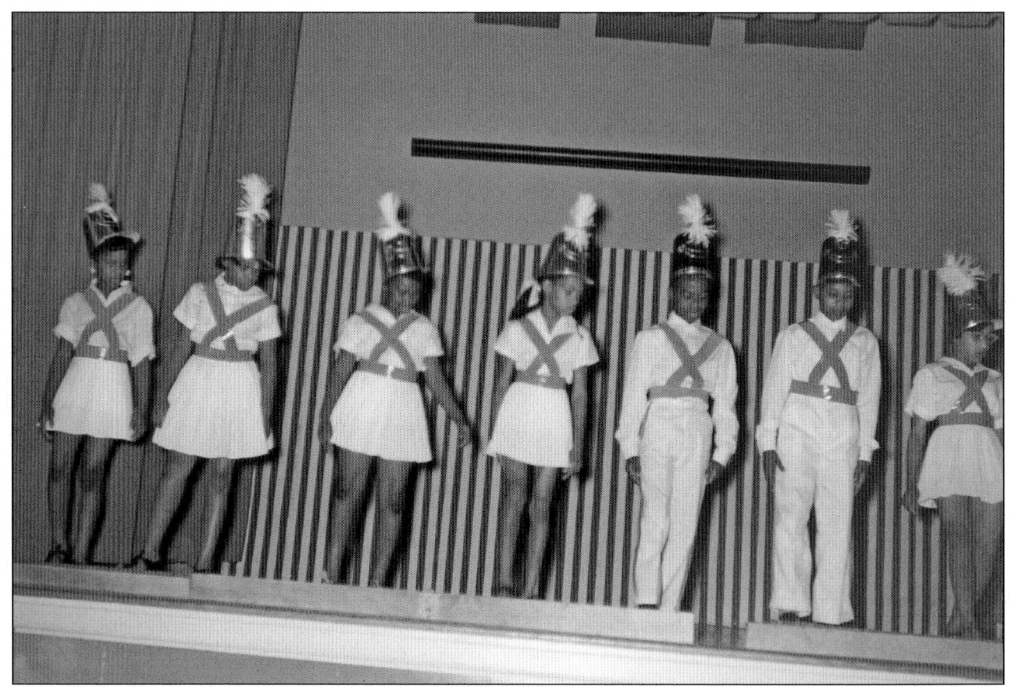

These young tap dancers were portraying tin soldiers. Pictured from left to right are three unidentified, Sheryll Jackson Slade, Douglas Lee, Herbert Gardner, and Sandra Jackson Mullens. (Author's collection.)

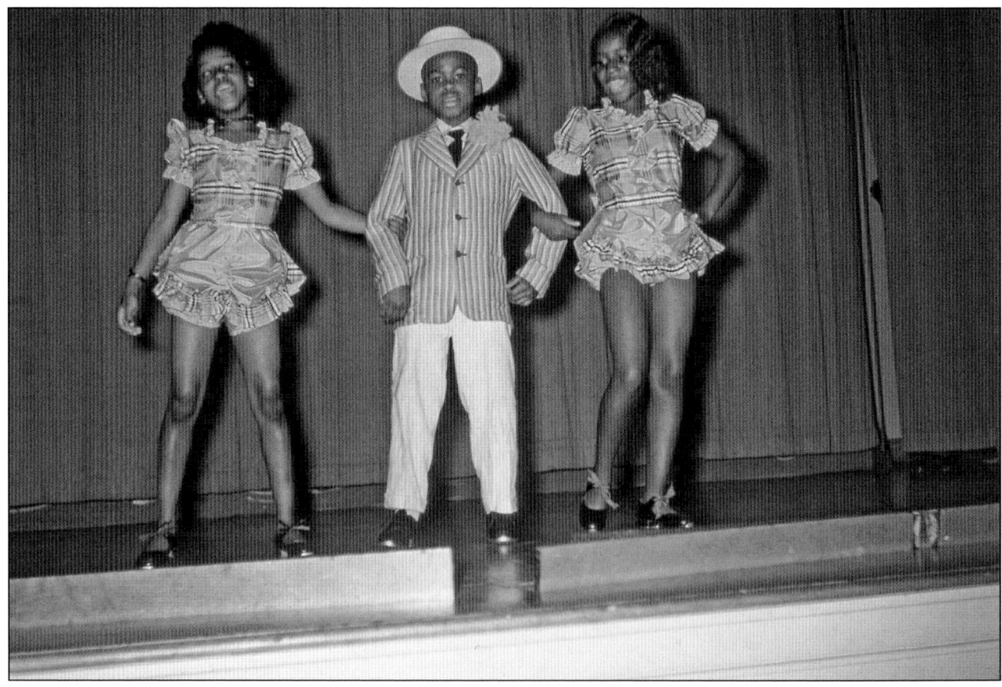

The tap dancers are, from left to right, Marita Harding, Douglass Lee, and Brenda Thomas. Brenda, the niece of costume designer Lillian Stafford, was one of the best all-around dancers. She was excellent in ballet, tap, and toe. (Author's collection.)

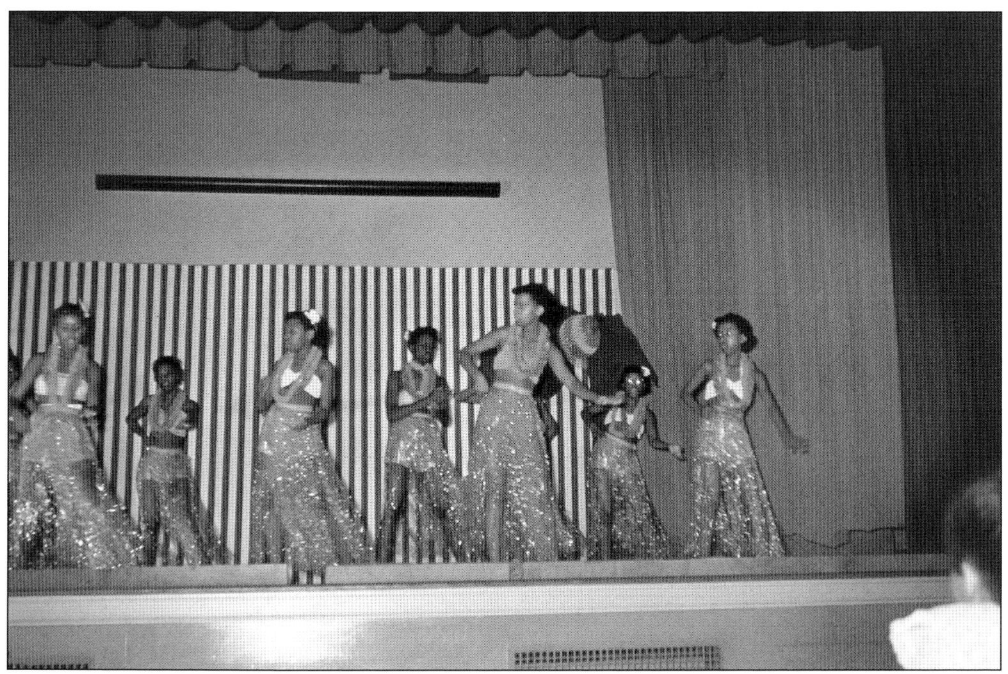

This Hawaiian Dance was in tribute to Hawaii becoming the 50th state in 1959. The dancers are wearing bright pink grass skirts. They are, from left to right, Brenda Thomas, unidentified, Jeanne Nutter, Elizabeth White, Martina Garner Woods, unidentified, and Peggy Corbin. (Author's collection.)

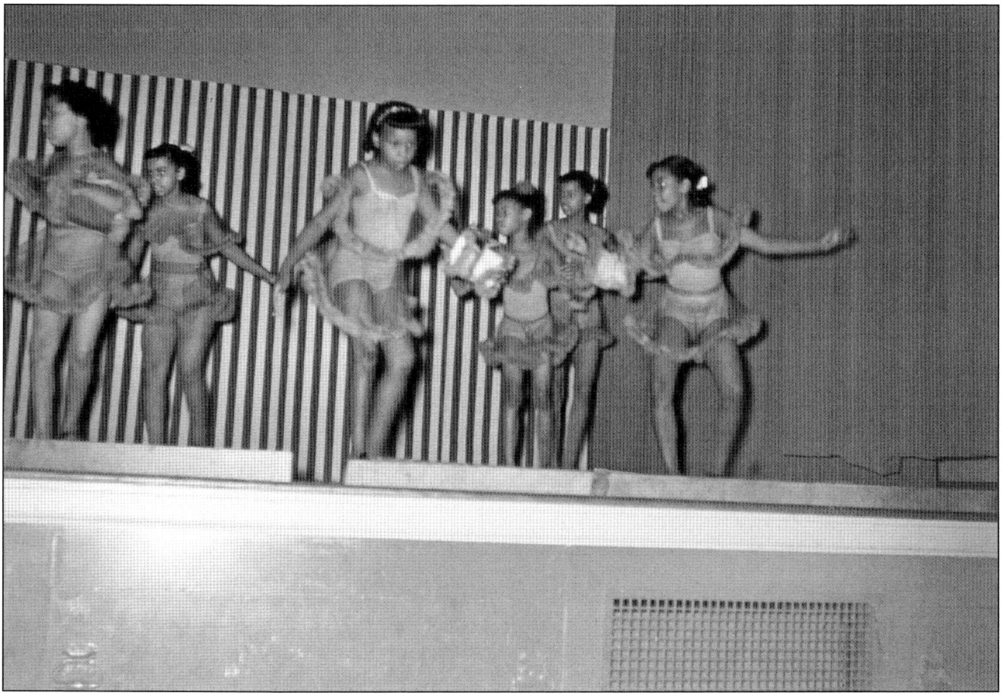

These dancers are also part of the recital. From left to right are unidentified, Loretta Roy, unidentified, Sheryll Jackson Slade, Martina Gardner Woods, and unidentified. (Author's collection.)

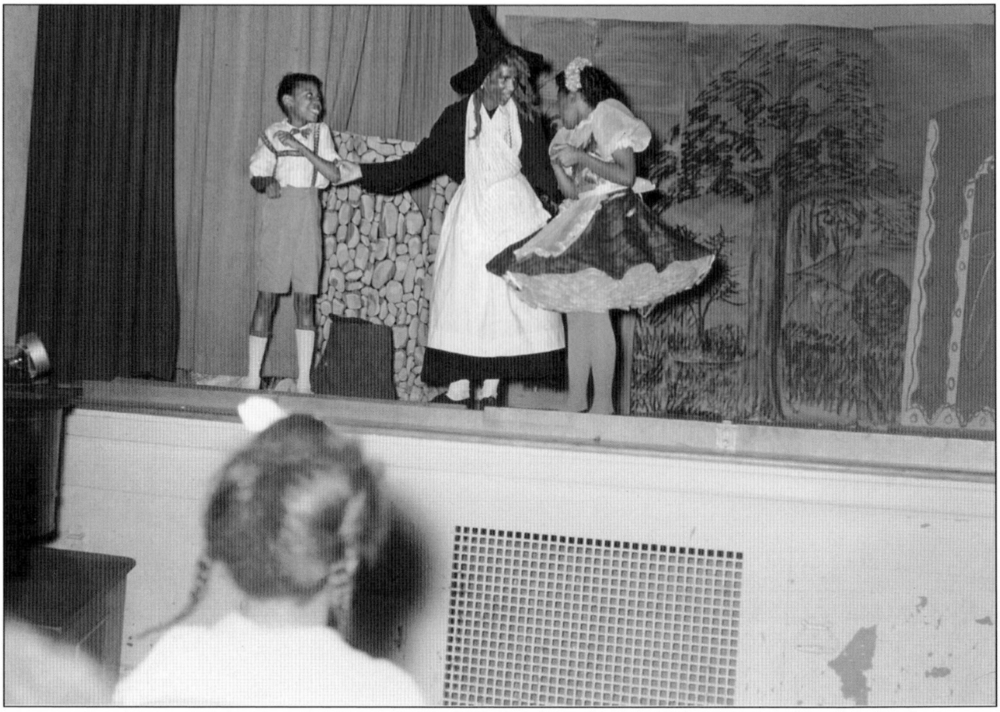

Sometimes, the recital included stories, and one year, the story was *Hansel and Gretel*. From left to right are Carolyn Thomas (Hansel), Florence Morris Collins Hardy (the witch), and Jeanne Nutter (Gretel). The ballet teacher, Ilona Ivinski, had her mother make delicious gingerbread cookies which were attached to the house. One of the best parts of playing Hansel or Gretel was that they ate those wonderful delicacies. At the end of the show, many of the other little ballet dancers scrambled to get some of the remaining cookies. (Author's collection.)

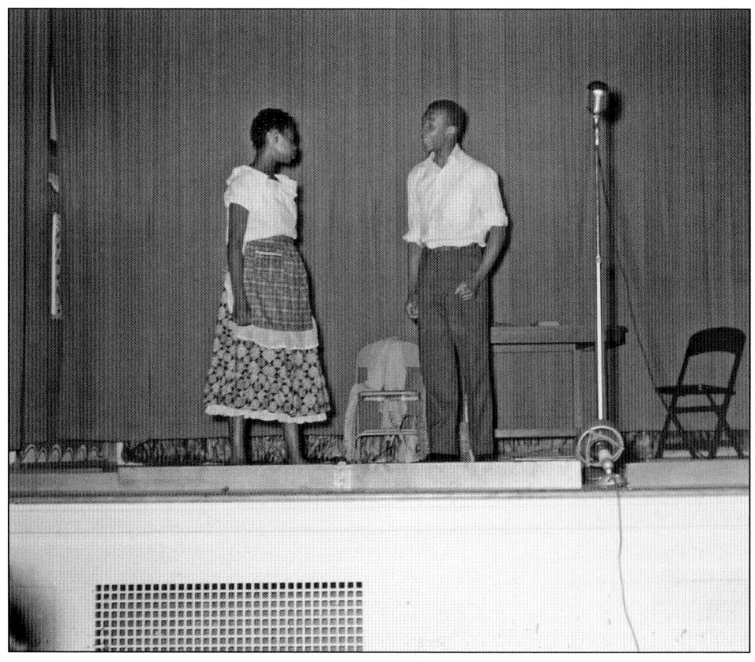

The story of *Hansel and Gretel* included a mother and father, played by Elizabeth White and unidentified. (Author's collection.)

During the 1940s, in addition to modern dance, there was also ballet. Evonne Ross Ingram took classes as a young woman. She is seen here performing in one of the *Musical Hits*. From left to right are unidentified, Evonne Ross Ingram, unidentified. (Courtesy of Niki Ingram, Esq.)

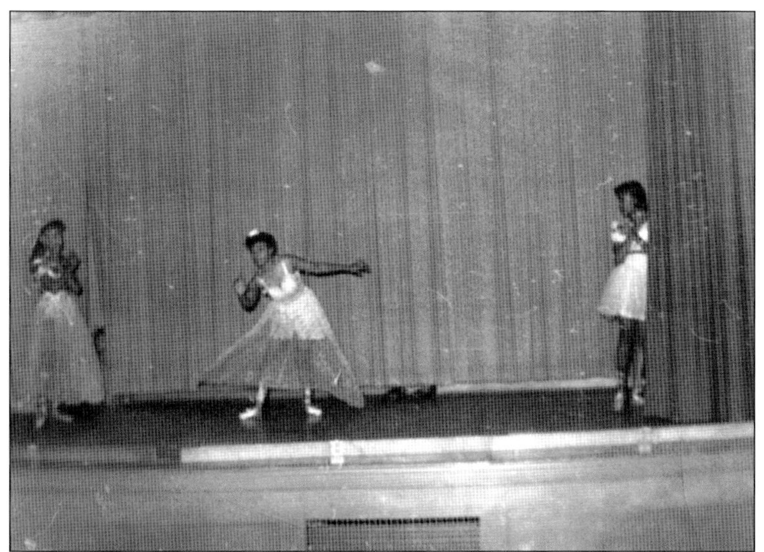

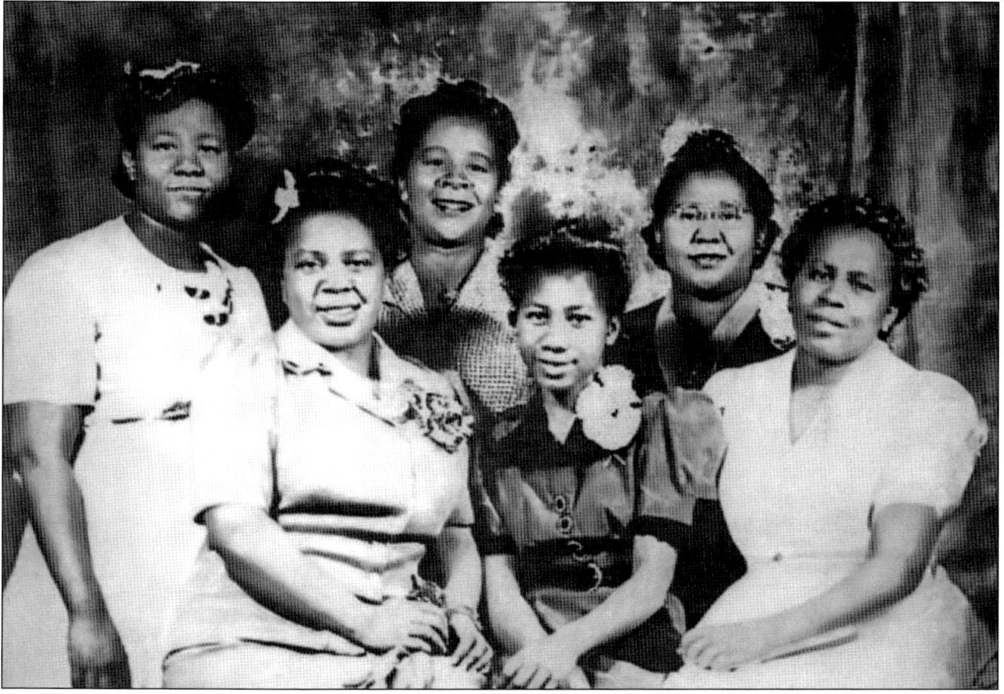

The stunning costumes were created mostly by Lillian Stafford and her team. She was a talented designer and dressmaker. Her regular job was as a domestic with the McGuire family in Wilmington, Delaware. She was born in Ridgely, Maryland, where her family owned a farm where they grew and raised all of their food. The family was self-sufficient, and this is probably where Lillian acquired her sewing skills. In the 1950s, she moved to Wilmington and raised her late sister's children Marvin Thomas and Brenda Thomas Boyd. Brenda took ballet lessons at the Y and was a very accomplished dancer. This was also the time when Lillian became the costume designer for the ballet productions at the Walnut Street YWCA. The photograph shows the women of the Thomas family. From left to right are Clara, Lillian, Estelle, Beatrice, Martha, and Adelaine the mother of the family. (Courtesy of Marvin Thomas.)

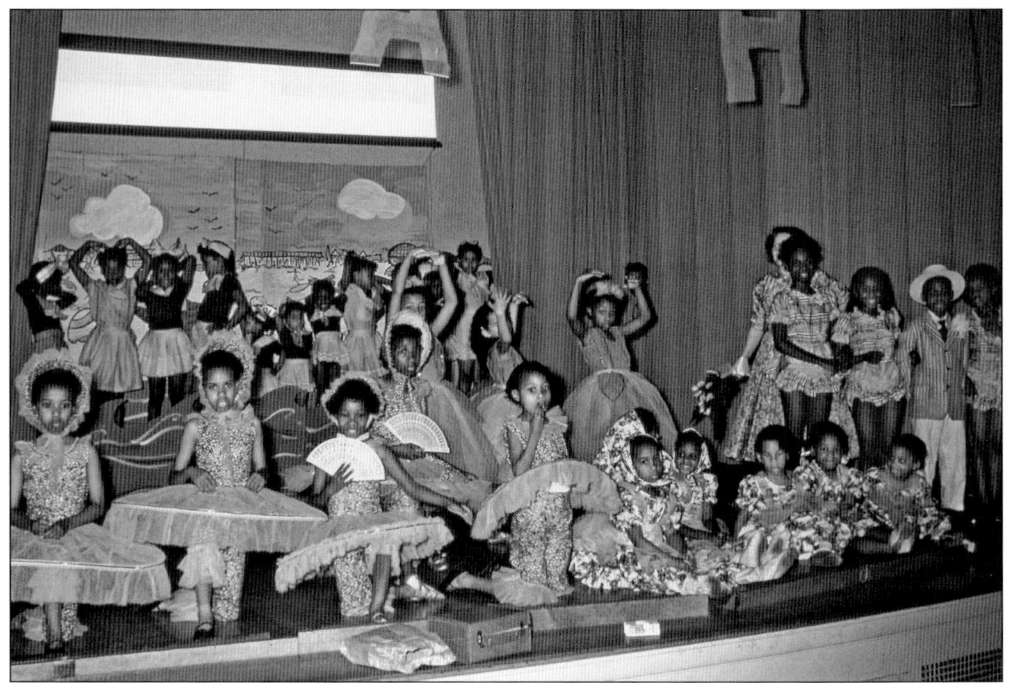

At the end of the *Musical* Hit, the students always took a final bow and posed for a group photograph. Ilona Ivinksi, the ballet teacher, can be seen on the far right holding a bouquet of flowers. She is partially hidden by a dancer. This is from one of the 1950s productions. (Author's collection.)

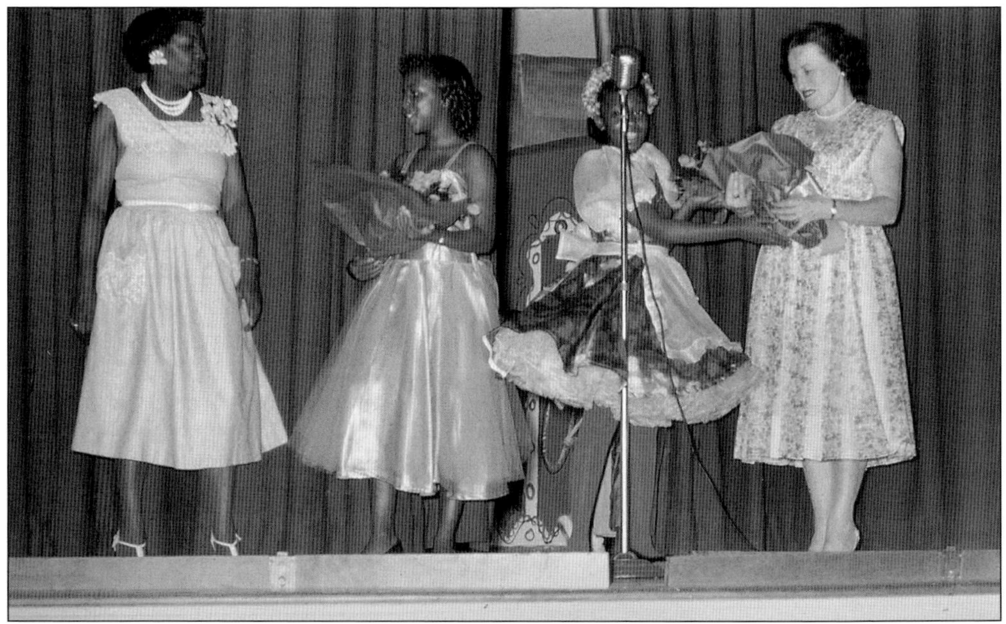

At the end of the every ballet recital, the dance teacher and the pianist were presented with a bouquet of flowers. Here, from left to right, are Helen Griffin, the pianist, being handed flowers by dancer Brenda Thomas. Next to Brenda, Jeanne Nutter is presenting flowers to Ilona Ivinski, the dance teacher. Each year, different dancers were chosen to make the presentations. (Author's collection.)

Seven

SPORTS AND ATHLETICS

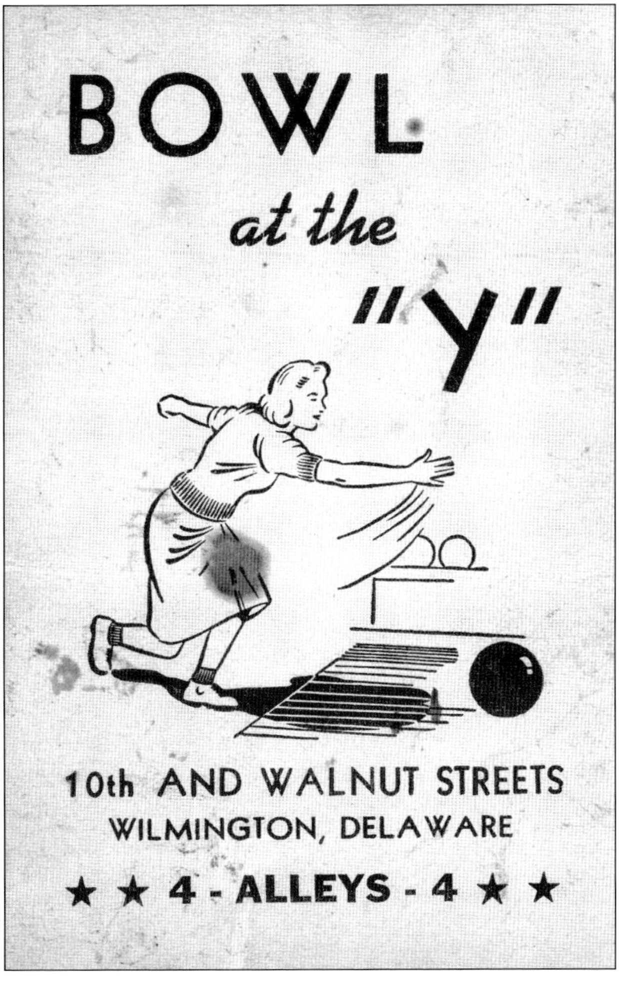

Athletic activities were a major component of the programming for both the Walnut Street YMCA and the YWCA. Full-time physical education directors were always part of the staff, and they operated very comprehensive programs. Bowling, basketball, gymnastics, and other sports were offered to children and adults. There were also organized competitive teams. This is a brochure advertising bowling. (Courtesy of the Delaware Historical Society.)

BOWL
at the
"Y"
10th AND WALNUT STREETS
WILMINGTON, DELAWARE
★ ★ 4 - ALLEYS - 4 ★ ★

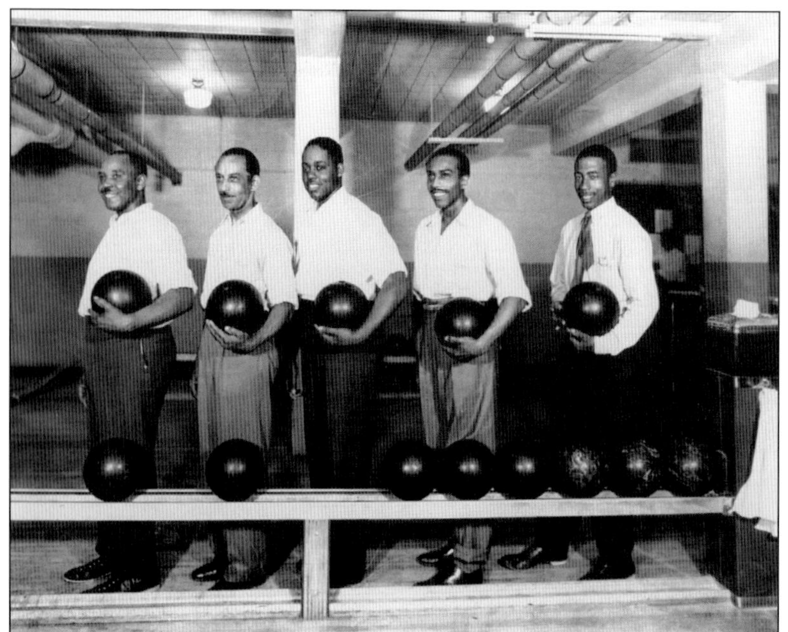

This is a 1940s photograph of the men's bowling team. Bowling was a very popular sport, and the league continued well into the 1970s or 1980s. (Courtesy of the Delaware Historical Society.)

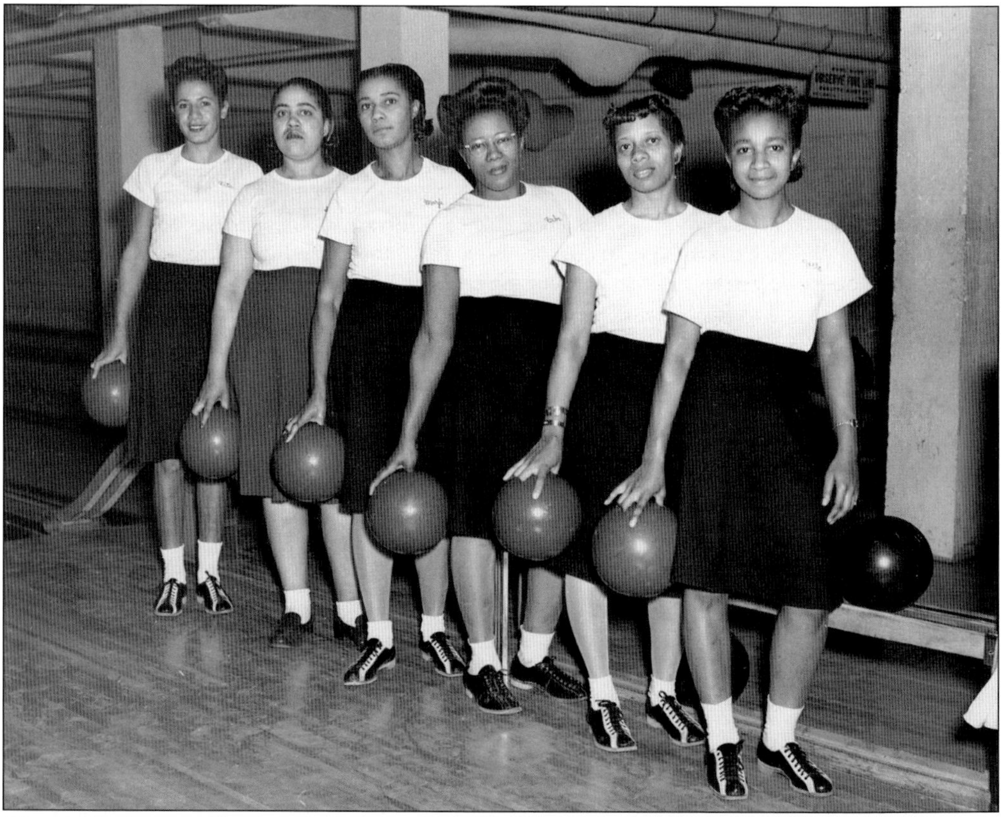

This 1946 photograph is of the Hornets, which was the women's bowling team at that time. It is not known how many years this particular team existed, but women bowled at the Y until the 1980s. (Courtesy of Dolores Washam and Lynn Clayton Jones.)

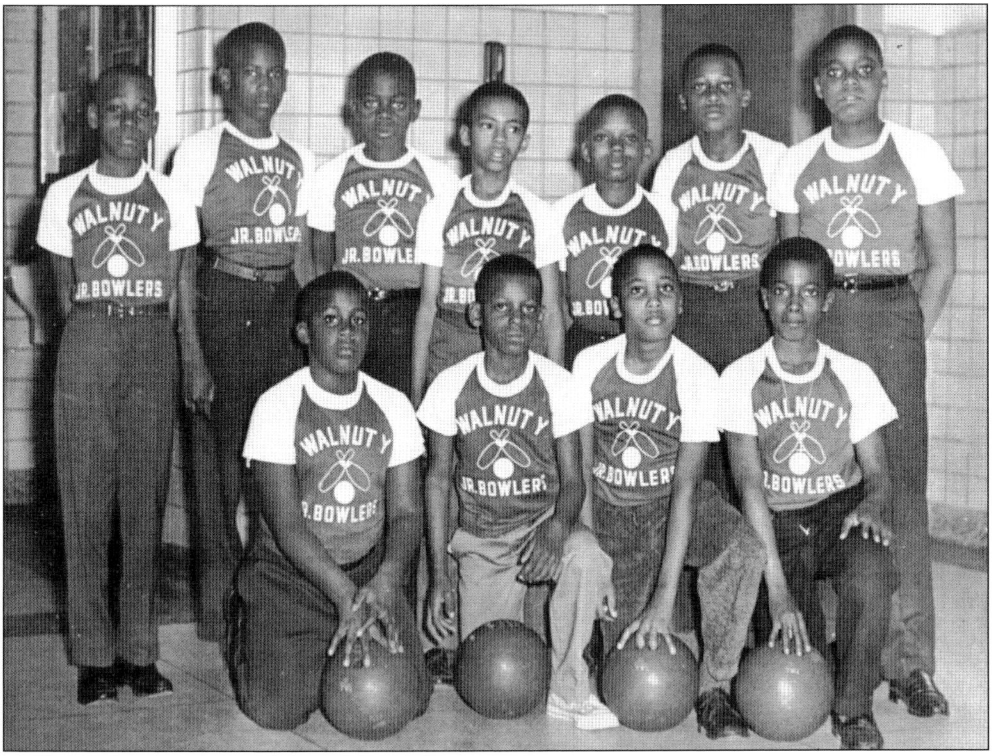

This is a 1960s photograph of the Walnut Y junior bowlers. The volunteer leaders were Barbara Huff, William Holmes, and Robert McGhee. Some of the group members were in the 126 Points Club. Those were youth who bowled at least 126 points. The members of the elite group were Robert McGhee, Charles Brown, David Huff, Enman Terrance, William Alston, Paul Dryden, William Benyard, Don Brown, Stephen Dryden, Terrance Holmes, Julius Jackson, John Woolford, and Darryl Cooper. (Courtesy of the Walnut Street YMCA.)

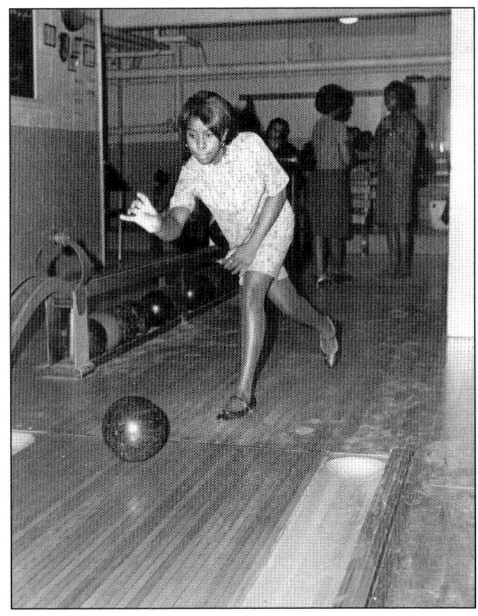

This photograph was taken on January 11, 1967, at the junior state bowling tournament in Dover, Delaware. Pictured here is Lisa Johnson, captain of the Y Swannettes bowling team. They were the first-place winners in the senior division. A very important female bowler who learned to bowl at the Walnut Street YMCA is Jill Nelson. She was the first African American female in Delaware to bowl a perfect score of 300 points. Nelson made history in the sport of bowling. (Courtesy of the Walnut Street YMCA.)

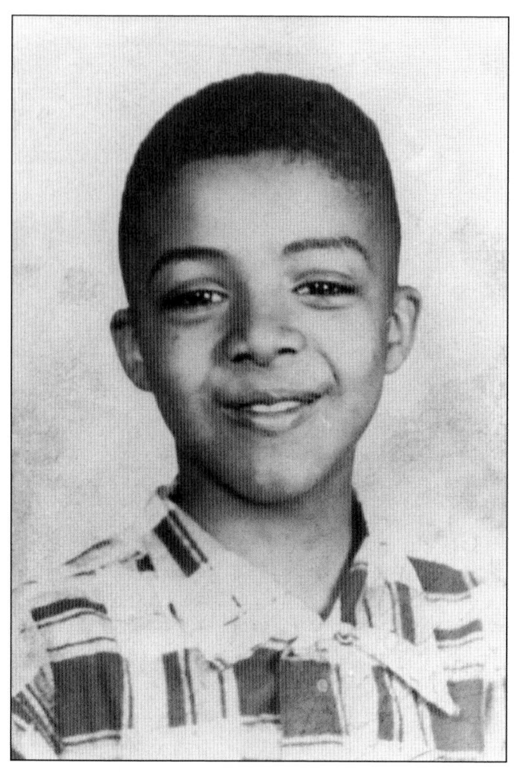

The bowling alley was a source of income for many young men who were employed as pin boys. This was the era before automatic pin-setting machines. The pins had to be picked up and set by individuals, and the Y hired young boys for the task. Alphonso Brock, pictured here, was one of those young men. He earned 25¢ a game, which was a nice income for a young teenager in the 1950s. This was quite a bit more than Lloyd Casson made in the 1940s as a pin boy. At that time, the going rate was 10¢ a game. (Courtesy of Alphonso Brock.)

Marion Brister was quite an active bowler with the Walnut Street Y. She participated in one of the bowling teams from the 1950s to the 1980s. It was one of the most meaningful activities of her life. (Courtesy of Marion Brister.)

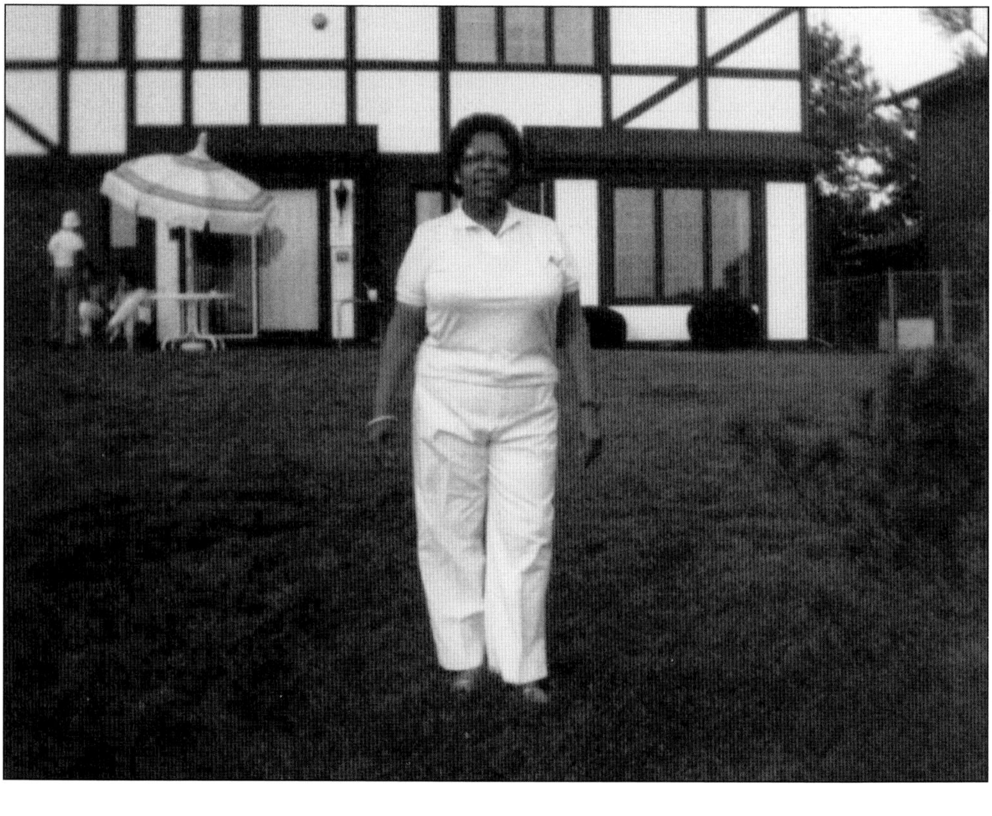

Page 2 THE OPEN DOOR May, 1960

MONDAY CLUB TAKES BOWLING HONORS

The Monday Club entry finished as champions of this year's YMCA Bowling League, defeating the Hawks, led by captain Bernard Sewell and 2nd half winners. The Monday Club then went to Brooklyn, N.Y., to win the team championship in the National N.B.A. Tournament. Captain Clarence I. Carter and the other Monday Club team members are to be congratulated. Individual champ performers in the season just closed were: Chris Smith, high 3 game series - 646; high single fame score - 267; and highest average score for season - Bernard Sewell.

Champions of the YMCA mixed league, winning 61½ games and losing 30½, was the team of Noah Daniels, capt., Chris Smith, Mrs. Frances Daniels and Mrs. Salena Benjamin.

KEEP COOL
IN THE 'Y' POOL
THIS SUMMER

URGE YOUR FRIENDS
TO JOIN TOO
BE A 'Y - BOOSTER'

SUMMER PROGRAM FOR BELVEDERE & ABSALOM JONES

Anticipation is great as to the activities for the swiftly coming summer season. Walnut Street Center YW is ready! There will be daily "camp outs" at Belvedere, as usual. Absalom Jones School will hum with crafts and games. Indoors: puzzles, guessing games and brain twisters. Outdoors: ball games, tennis, baseball, directed by our Miss Barbara Washam. Crafts, sewing and homemaking will be inside and the entire day from 9:00 to 4:00 P.M. will be under the supervision of the YWCA staff.

YW REGIONAL CONFERENCE HELD IN PITTSBURGH

The Eastern Regional YWCA Conference met in Pittsburgh, Pennsylvania, April 22 - 24. It is notable that 26 delegates from Wilmington attended. Of this number, 10 were members at Walnut Street Center: Mrs. Eldridge Shelton, Vice-Chairman, Center Committee; Mrs. Phillip G. Sadler, Religious Emphasis Committee; Miss Patricia Wilson, a Y-teen; Miss Helen Wiggins, of the Y-teen Committee; Miss Doris Thomas, a young adult (Club Clique); and from the staff, Mrs. J. L. Morgan and Misses Marie Clark and Elizabeth Jordan. The conference listened to the key-note speech of the President of the National YWCA, Miss Lilace Barnes, the Mayor of Pittsburgh, and other officials of the conference. Many matters vital to the program of the YWCA came before the meeting: the meaning and privileges of membership, the Christian directives of the association; the needs for good housing, better educational opportunities for all people; intergroup and interracial living.

Workshops on these topics were carried out in the actual area of the problems posed, with large groups visiting places and situations that had to do with many phases of YWCA program. The entire number of Associations are now looking forward to the National Convention, to be held in Denver, Colorado, May, 1961. At this convention, new rulings will be voted for the advancement of the work of the YWCA, based upon the studies made at the four Regional Conferences this Spring.

SUMMER CLASSES
CAN BE OFFERED

LATIN DANCE & SEWING - $10.00 per class
10 Lessons
PARTY FOODS & CHARM - $ 6.00 per class
10 Lessons

Air Conditioned rooms will be provided for these classes. Dates to be announced

If interested, call Mrs. Bessie Morgan at OI 6-6621 before June 15th.

The Monday Club was part of the YMCA Bowling League. In 1960, they were champions of the league. Later that year, they competed in Brooklyn, New York, and won the National NBA championship. The article in the *Open Door* chronicles those accomplishments. The captain of the Monday Club team was Clarence Carter. The high scorers were Chris Smith and Bernard Sewell. (Courtesy of the Delaware Historical Society.)

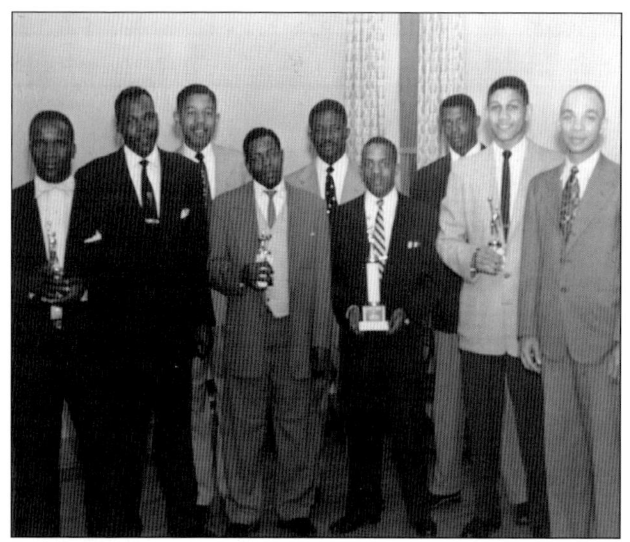

The Big Five was the men's basketball team. They were excellent players and won numerous championships. They are pictured here holding the trophies won in 1953 as the Penn-DE basketball champs. They are, from left to right, Nathan "Doc" Hill, Irvin Gordy, Elbert Stubblefield, James " Scrappy" Robinson, Mitch Thomas, Eggie Harris, Rodney Collins, William Wailes, and Harry Scott, coach. Harry Scott had been an outstanding basketball player and had earned an excellent reputation. (Courtesy of the Walnut Street YMCA.)

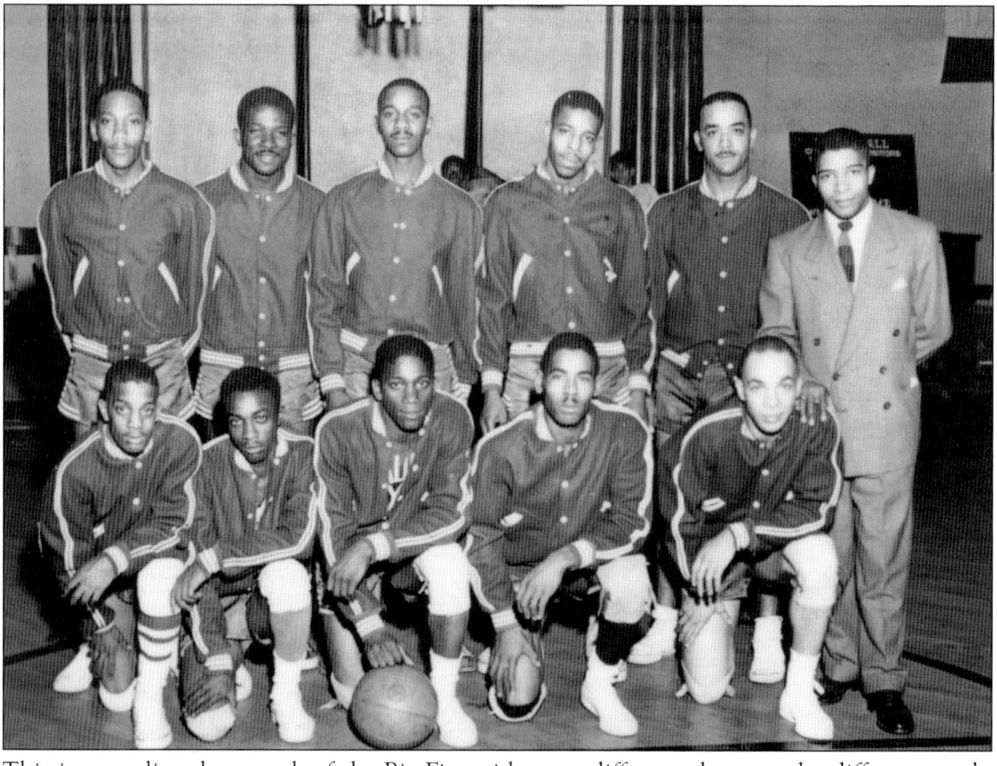

This is an earlier photograph of the Big Five with some different players and a different coach. Pictured from left to right are (first row) Eggie Harris, Charles Brown, unidentified, Newell Ruffin, and Harry Scott; (second row) David Gray, Mitch Thomas, three unidentified, and Paul Haughton (coach). Paul Haughton was the physical education director at that time. He had been a star athlete in his earlier years. He then joined the Walnut Street YMCA and coached the Big Five in addition to managing the other activities of the physical department. He left Walnut Street to assume duties at another YMCA in Annapolis, Maryland. His hand is placed on the shoulder of Harry Scott, who became the next coach of the team. (Courtesy of the Walnut Street YMCA.)

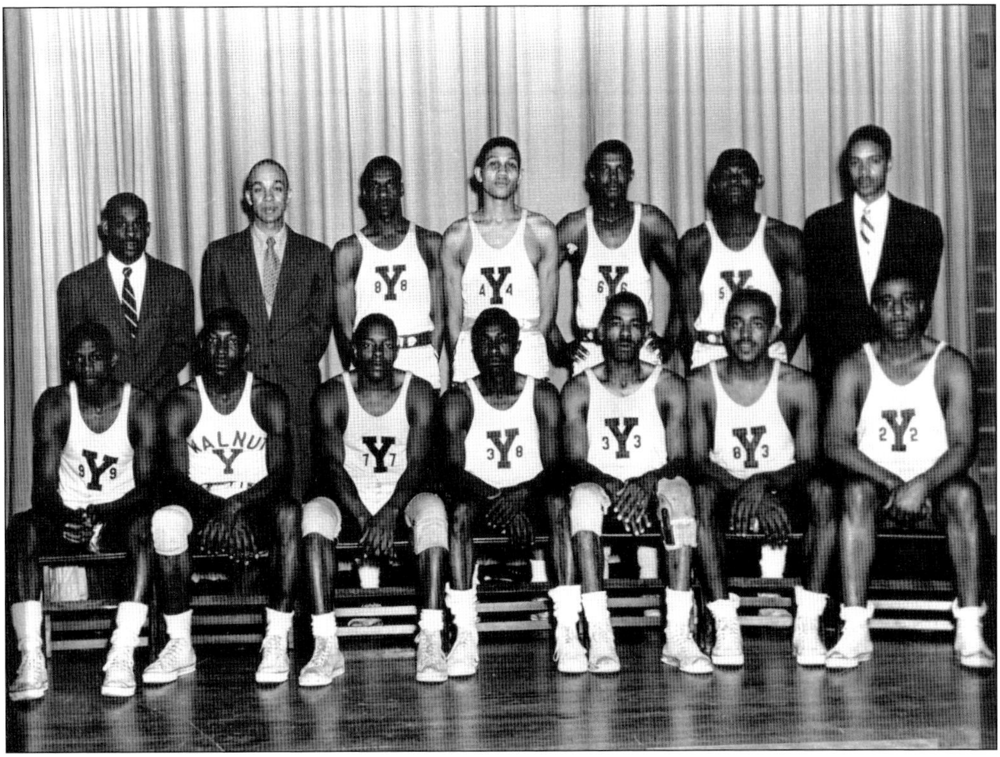

This is a later photograph of the Big Five. This team won the state Amateur League Basketball Tournament. From left to right are (seated, first row) Ivory Collins, "Money" Southerland, "Scrappy" Robinson, Charlie Brown, Newell Ruffin, Johnny Sims, and Pete Butler; (second row, standing) Gilbert Jackson (coach), Harry Scott (coach) Walter Russell, William Wales, Rodney Collins, Bob Perry, and Bob Brown (manager). (Courtesy of the estate of Gilbert Jackson.)

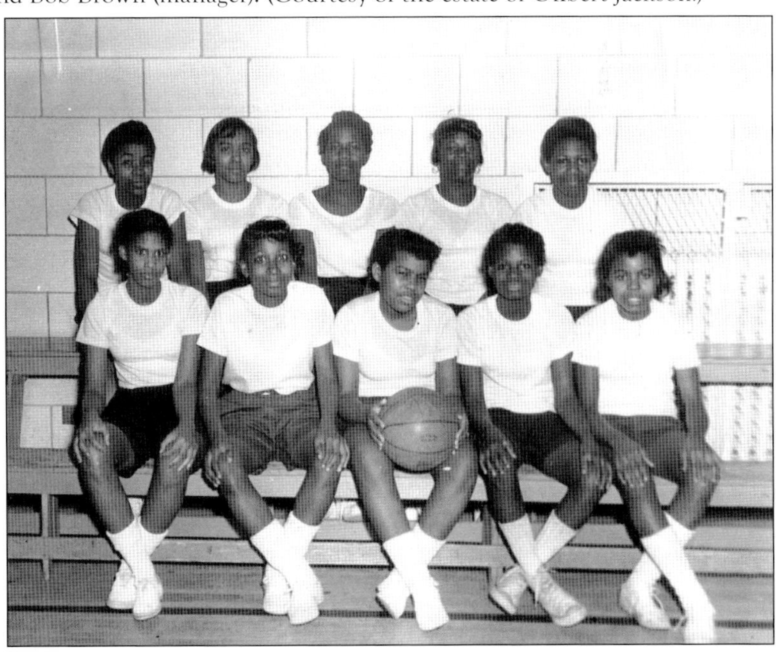

This is a 1960s photograph of the girls' basketball team. The only identified player is Florence Morris Collins Hardy, who is the first person on the left of the first row. (Courtesy of Dolores Washam and Lynn Clayton Jones.)

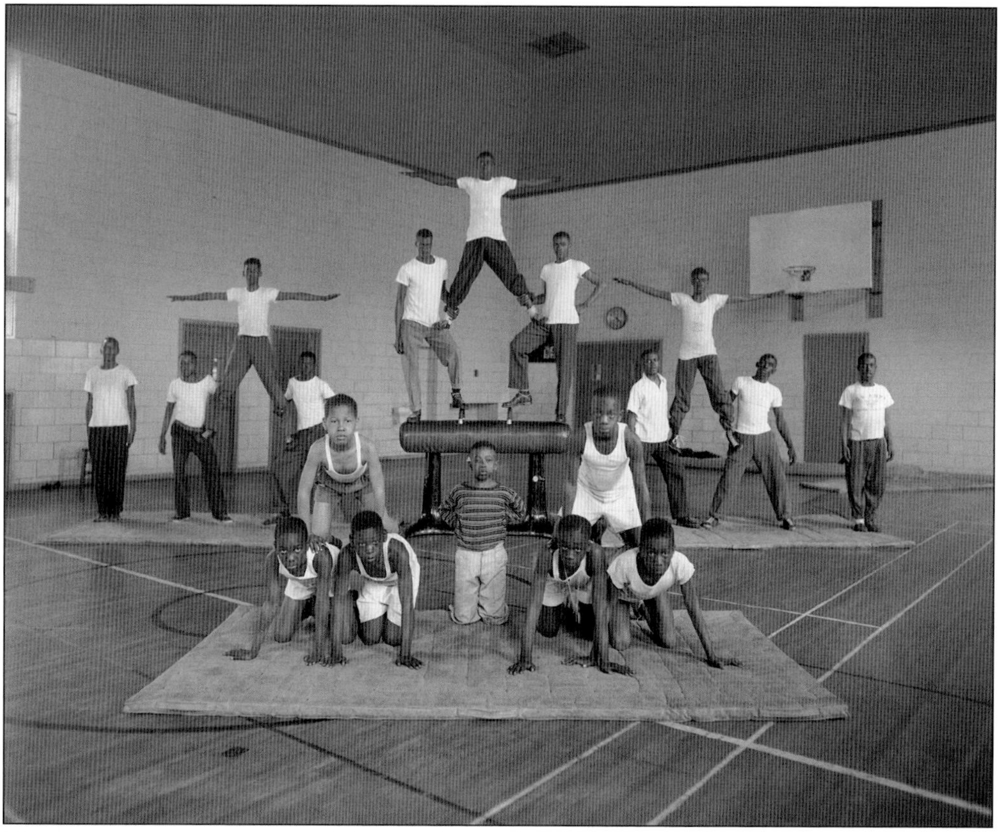

The gymnastics program started shortly after the building opened. It trained young boys as well as teenagers. This 1940s photograph shows both groups displaying their skills. (Courtesy of the Delaware Historical Society.)

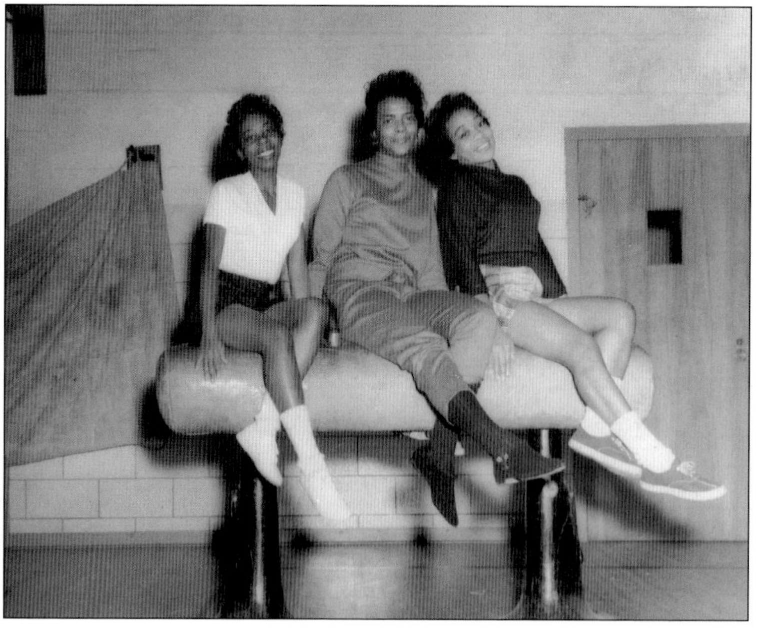

Women also participated in the gymnastics program. Pictured from left to right are Barbara Washam (the physical education director) and two unidentified women. This photograph was taken in the 1950s. (Courtesy of Dolores Washam and Lynn Clayton Jones.)

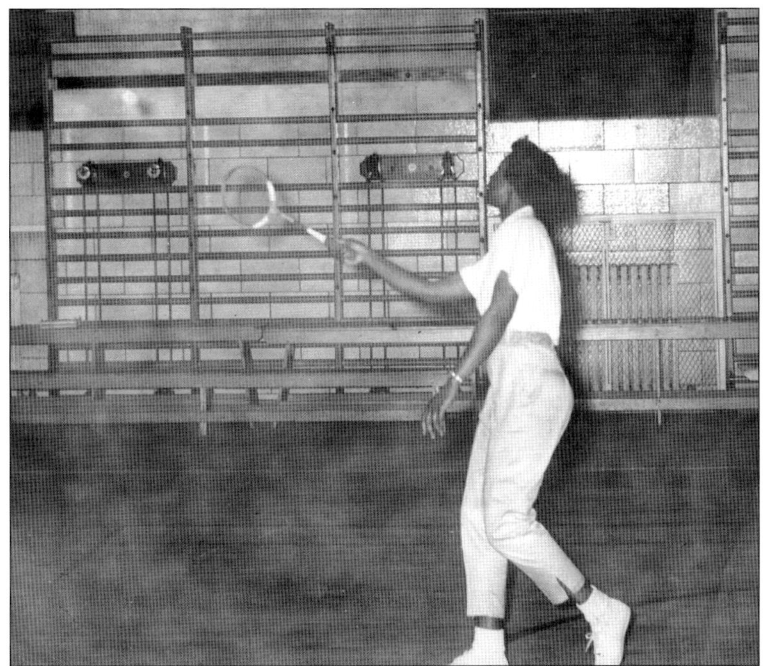

There were a variety of sports activities offered at Walnut Street. This photograph shows a woman playing badminton. (Courtesy of Dolores Washam and Lynn Clayton Jones.)

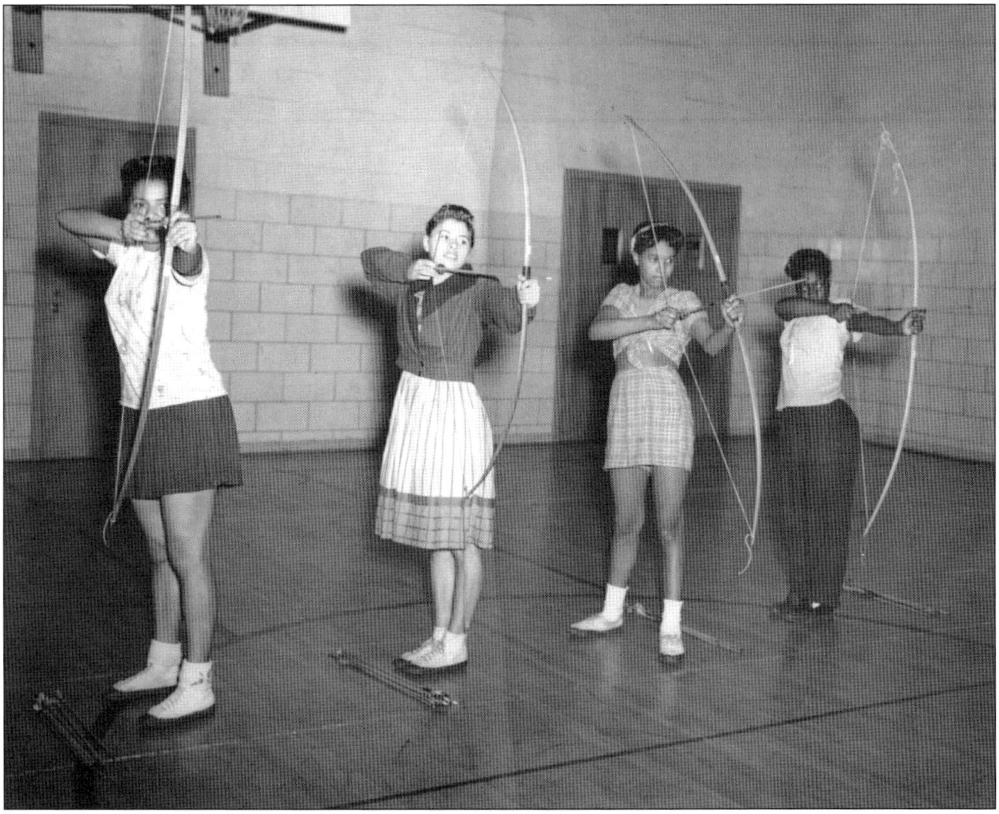

This 1948 photograph shows young women engaged in the sport of archery. (Courtesy of Dolores Washam and Lynn Clayton Jones.)

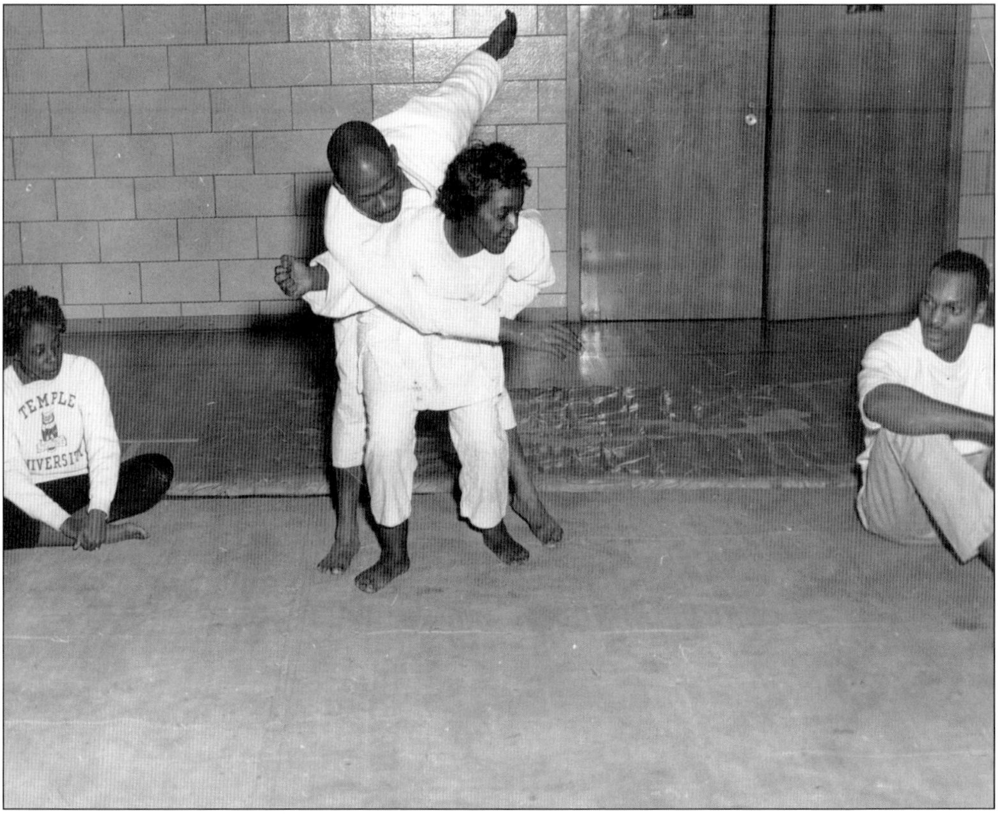

In the 1960s, coed judo classes were offered. The classes were part of the adult physical education program. (Courtesy of Barbara Washam and Lynn Clayton Jones.)

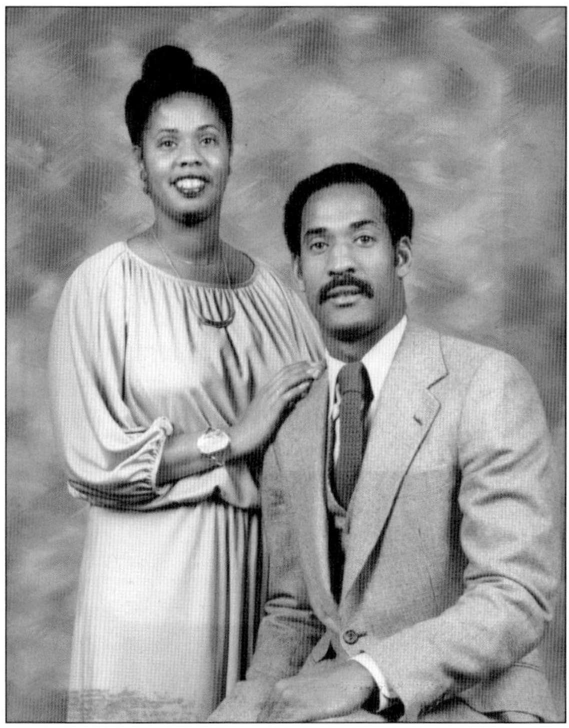

Sheryll Jackson Slade and Gilbert Jackson III participated in numerous Walnut Street programs. Both of their parents, Gilbert Jackson Sr. and Ruth Jackson, started their professional careers at the Y. They later entered careers in education. Sheryll learned to swim at the Y and, in the 1980s, became a swimming instructor herself at Walnut Street. Her brother Gilbert also learned to swim at the Y but he gravitated to itty-bitty basketball and became a high school and college basketball star. He later was an outstanding basketball coach at both high schools and colleges. (Courtesy of Sheryll Jackson Slade and Gilbert Jackson III.)

Eight

The YWCA

The YWCA originally had a building on Tatnall Street before moving to the Walnut Street location. The organization was highly structured and offered numerous programs for young girls and women. The staff and volunteers were successful women who created outstanding opportunities for African American girls and adults. This is the first edition of the *Y Echoes* newsletter, which was published after the organization moved to the Walnut Street facility. (Courtesy of the Delaware Historical Society.)

"Y" ECHOES

NEWS OF THE WALNUT STREET YOUNG WOMEN'S CHRISTIAN ASSOCIATION

VOL. I — WILMINGTON, DELAWARE — NO. 1

"That they may have life and that they might have it more abundantly"

Annual Spring Luncheon Announces Membership Drive

Membership Committee Brings Outstanding Speaker

Mrs. Sadie Mossell Alexander, Attorney At Law, Philadelphia, Penna., addressed 361 women relative to membership and its meaning in ever-changing times, such as the present. Each member was charged with the responsibility of interpreting our Christian purpose as it relates to the field of Public Affairs. Special emphasis was placed upon Civil Rights as being our rightful heritage, and the most widely discussed issue of today.

Having served on President Truman's Committee on Civic Rights, Mrs. Alexander was in a position to bring to us authentic facts pertaining to the work of that group.

Activities of Committees

The Branch Committee is the policy making and steering committee of the Walnut Street YWCA. Its chairman, Mrs. John H. Woodlen, has done an excellent job in promoting improvements of standards and work relationships between the agency and community.

Other members of the committee are Mrs. John Boston, Miss Pauline Coleman, Mrs. Robert Fleming, Mrs. Abner Fletcher, Mrs. Beauford Hall, Mrs. A. E. Henry, Miss Gertrude Henry, Mrs. Archibald Holland, Mrs. Leonard Lee, Miss Geneva Mauney, Mrs. James W. Peaco, Mrs. Harvey Peterson, Mrs. George Sykes, Mrs. Isaac Thornton, Miss Caroline B. Williams and Mrs. Echols Young.

The Public Relations Committee had its inception four years ago and its purpose is to interpret the YWCA program and give information as to its activities.

The year's outstanding project is the distribution of a kit containing the yearly calendar of events and a bibliography of materials that are of interest to volunteers and members.

Continued on Page 4

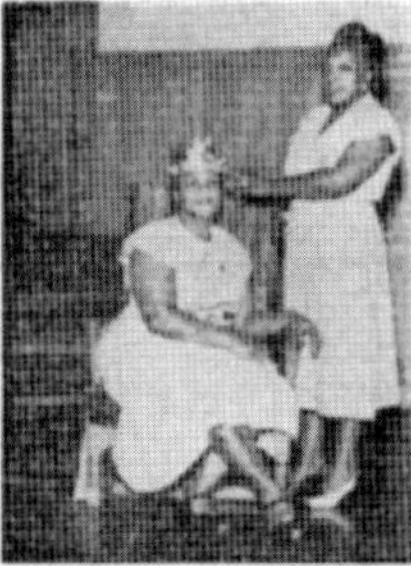

Mrs. Clara Mitchell, Captain of Falcons Team, crowned Miss YWCA by Mrs. Harvey Peterson, Chairman of Membership

The organizational structure for the membership drive took the form of a Softball League with Mrs. Harvey Peterson and Mrs. Abner Fletcher as co-managers. There were six teams managed by 33 captains.

Other winners were Mrs. Lakewood Baylor, Miss Bonita Rouselle, Mrs. Beauford Hall, Miss Geneva Mauney, Miss Delores Washam, Mrs. Octavia Raney and Mrs. John Boston.

As a result of the drive 188 new memberships and 204 renewals were reported, bringing the total membership to 1300.

Community Pride

The Pals' Club, an organization of 13 active, community-interested young women, has as its goal, the presentation of an organ to the Young Women's Christian Association. This is an out-

Continued on Page 4

NEWS BITS

Y-Teen Department

Younger sisters of the YWCA family make up the Y-Teen Department. Through the various activities of the clubs, the physical and the mental sides of a girl's life are developed . . . . Activities are centered around the needs of our Y-Teens . . . . Holidays, too, have their place on our calendar of observances . . . . Mothers are honored by the Y-Teens every spring with a banquet . . . . This department was represented by Miss Bonita Rousselle, advisor, and member of the Y-Teen Committee, and Misses Gertrude Redding and Yvonne Keys at the YM-YW Conference at Abington, Penna. Miss Bonita Rousselle and Miss Ruth Stewart represented us at the YW Conference at Reading, Penna. This conference was held on the campus of Albright College . . . . Realizing that all girls want to be charming, a course in three sessions was offered to our girls and boys, too . . . . The Y-Teen Officers Training and Setting Up Conferences are a part of our annual program . . . . We are interested in co-ed activities, too. Club "202" is a co-ed club and all senior high school students are eligible . . . . A Christmas formal dance is the feature event of this group . . . . The above mentioned activities come under the supervision of the Y-Teen Committee. The members are Miss Pauline Coleman, chairman, Miss Elsie Bryant, Miss Elsie Chippey, Mrs. Cornelia DeShields, Mrs. John Griffin, Miss Myrtle Groves, Mrs. Bernard Jones, Mrs. Edward Knotts, Mrs. Rudolph Koeller, Miss Rosemary Walley, Mrs. Catharine Smith, Mrs. Ann Stokes, Mrs. Robert Washam. Miss Ruth Dawkins, Miss Thelma Hurtt, Mrs. Roland Ross and Miss Bonita Rousselle.

Continued on Page 4

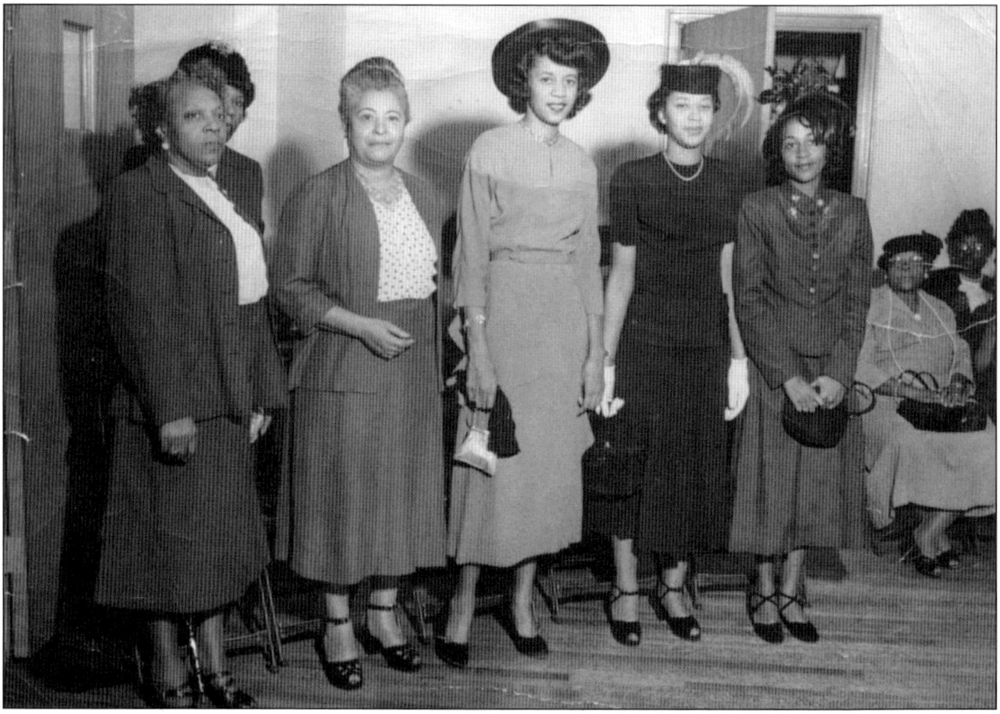

This photograph is of the 1940s staff and volunteers of the Walnut Street YWCA. Pictured from left to right are Marjorie Darrett, executive secretary; Etta Woodlin, board chair; Vivian Jackson Robinson; Ruth Jackson, physical education director; and unidentified. Marjorie Darrett became executive secretary around 1945 and remained in that position until 1955. During her tenure, she was responsible for developing many of the outstanding programs including the *Musical Hit*, the circus, the Carver Garden Club, and the Mother and Daughter Banquet. (Courtesy of Sheryll Jackson Slade and Gilbert Jackson III.)

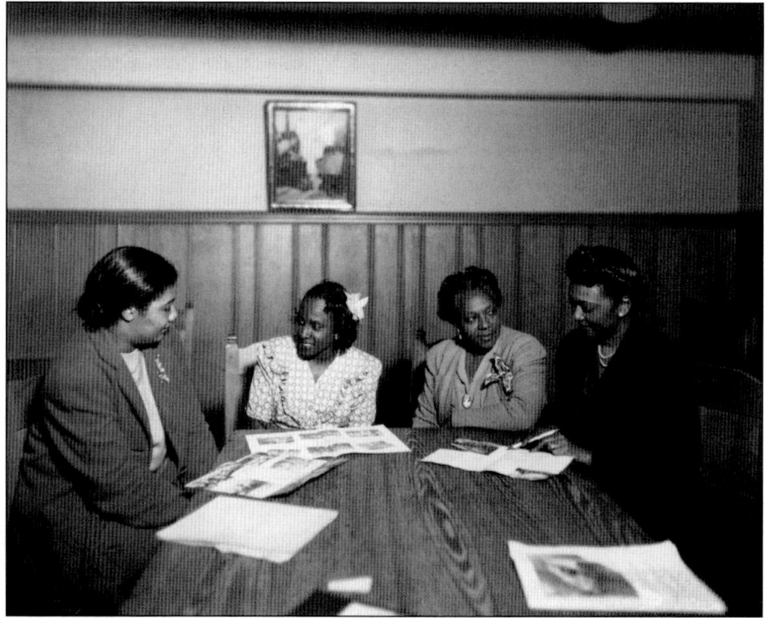

This is a meeting of volunteers and staff. From left to right are Reba Park, Marjorie Scott, Edith Hambric, and Marjorie Jackson, executive secretary. Jackson was the first executive secretary of the Walnut Street YWCA and served in that capacity until 1945. (Courtesy of the Walnut Street YMCA.)

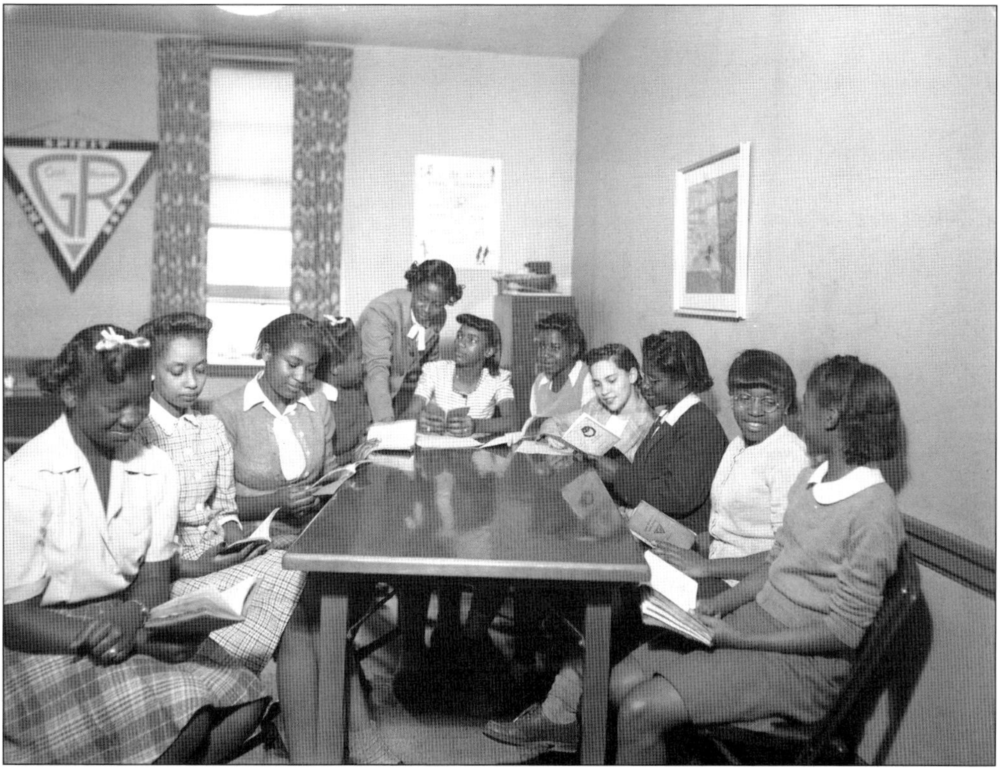

This is a 1940s photograph of the Girl Reserves. The YWCA offered many activities for young women. The group was very popular in the 1950s and 1960s and later became the Y Teens. (Courtesy of the Delaware Historical Society.)

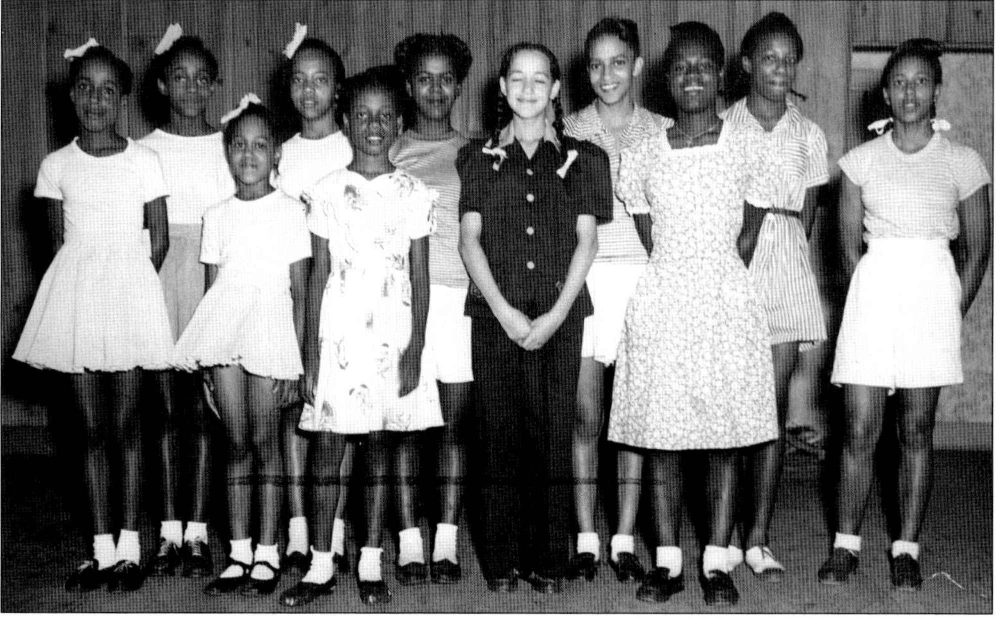

This is a 1946 photograph of the Y-Teens at the County Center Camp. The young women also had camp activities. (Courtesy of Dolores Washam and Lynn Clayton Jones.)

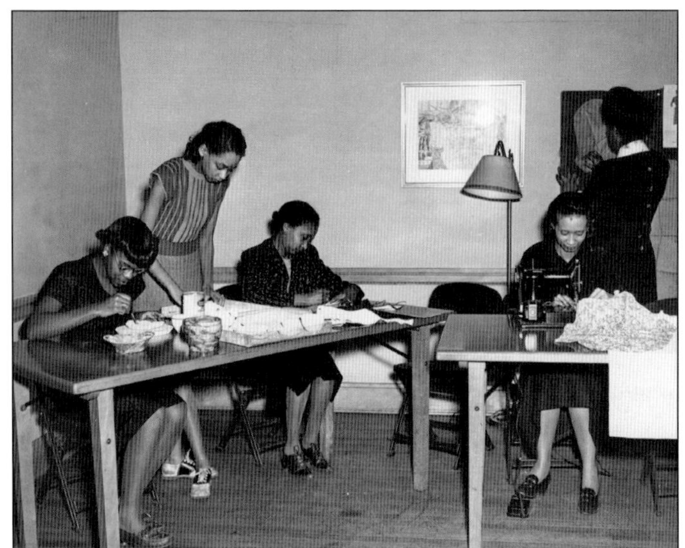

The Walnut Street YWCA offered many opportunities for women to express themselves artistically. This is a photograph of the 1940s Craft Club. Women can be seen painting, sewing, and working on craft projects. (Courtesy of the Delaware Historical Society.)

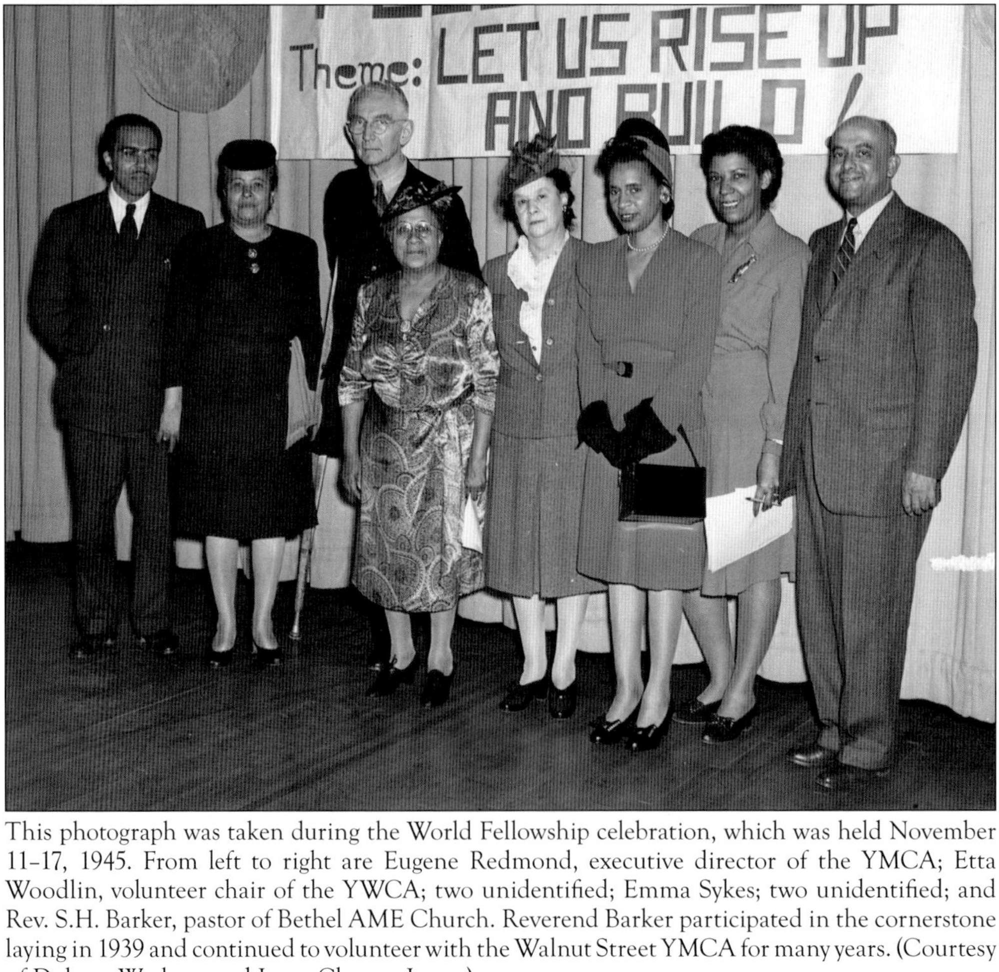

This photograph was taken during the World Fellowship celebration, which was held November 11–17, 1945. From left to right are Eugene Redmond, executive director of the YMCA; Etta Woodlin, volunteer chair of the YWCA; two unidentified; Emma Sykes; two unidentified; and Rev. S.H. Barker, pastor of Bethel AME Church. Reverend Barker participated in the cornerstone laying in 1939 and continued to volunteer with the Walnut Street YMCA for many years. (Courtesy of Dolores Washam and Lynn Clayton Jones.)

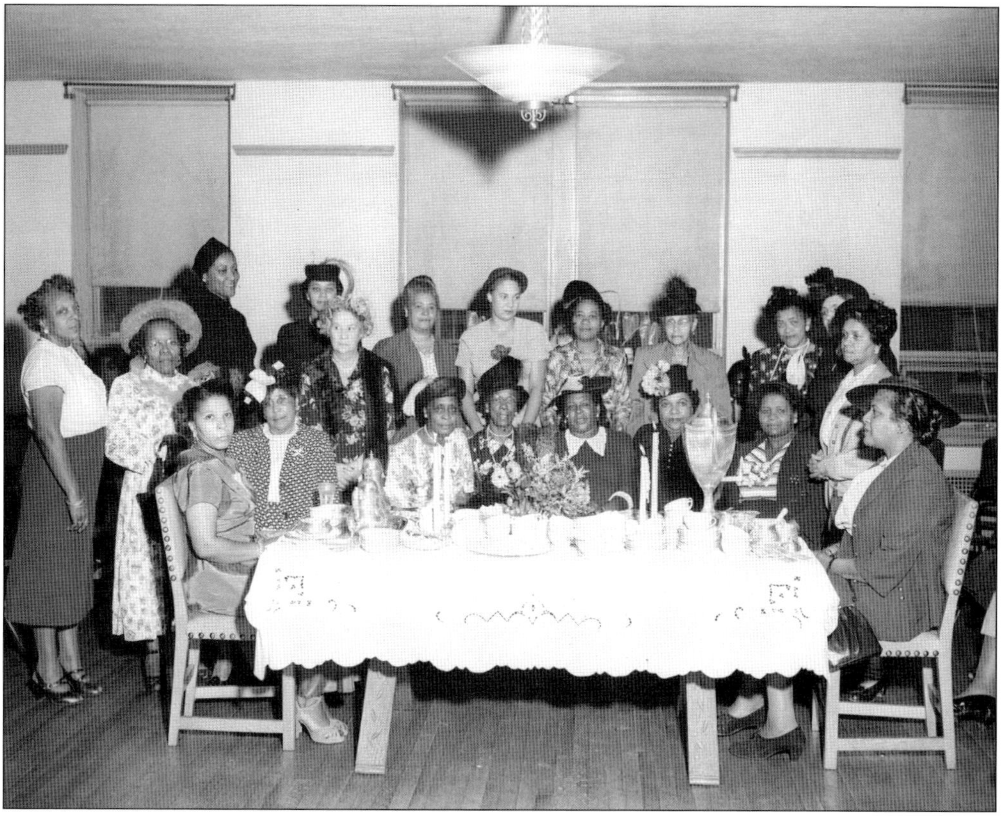

This is the 1949 Membership Tea. The Walnut Street YWCA offered many social activities for women. Early in the history of the organization, teas were quite popular. (Courtesy of Dolores Washam and Lynn Clayton Jones.)

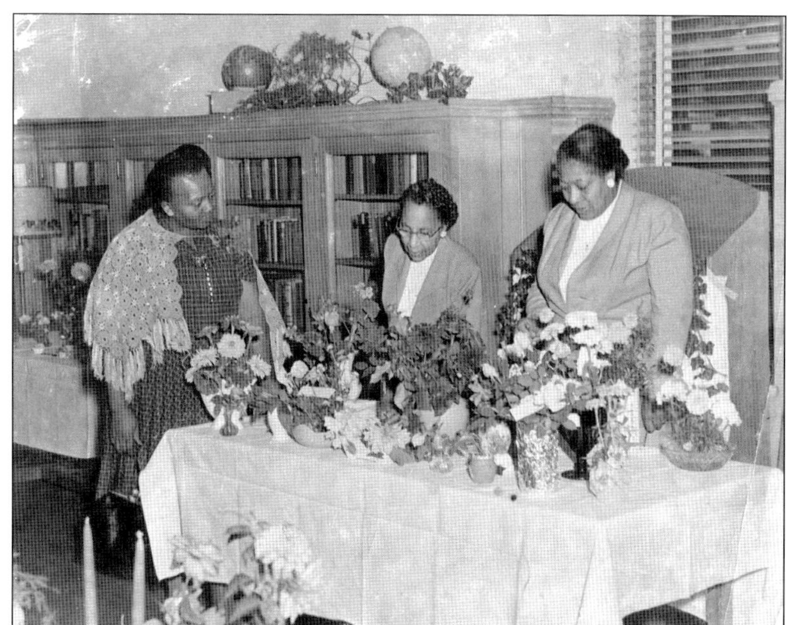

This is a 1940s photograph of the Carver Garden Club. The club was very popular and operated for many years. Pictured from left to right are Edith Hambric, unidentified, and Edith Shelton. (Courtesy of Ora Belcher.)

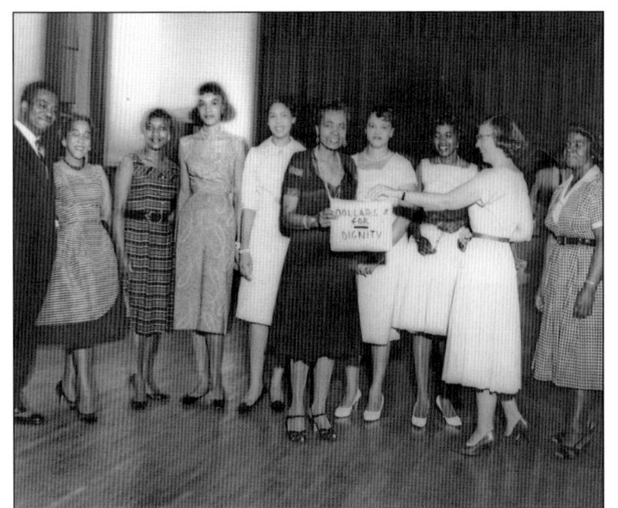

From left to right at the Dollars for Dignity event are William Young, Bessie Morgan (women's program director), unidentified, Ora Henley Belcher, Elizabeth Jordan (executive director), Joanne Church, and three unidentified. Elizabeth Jordan became executive director in 1955 after serving in that capacity in YWCAs in Omaha, Nebraska, and Roanoke, Virginia. She had degrees from Fisk University and Atlanta University. She was moved to the King Street YWCA as a program director in 1965 and retired in 1969. (Courtesy of the Walnut Street YMCA.)

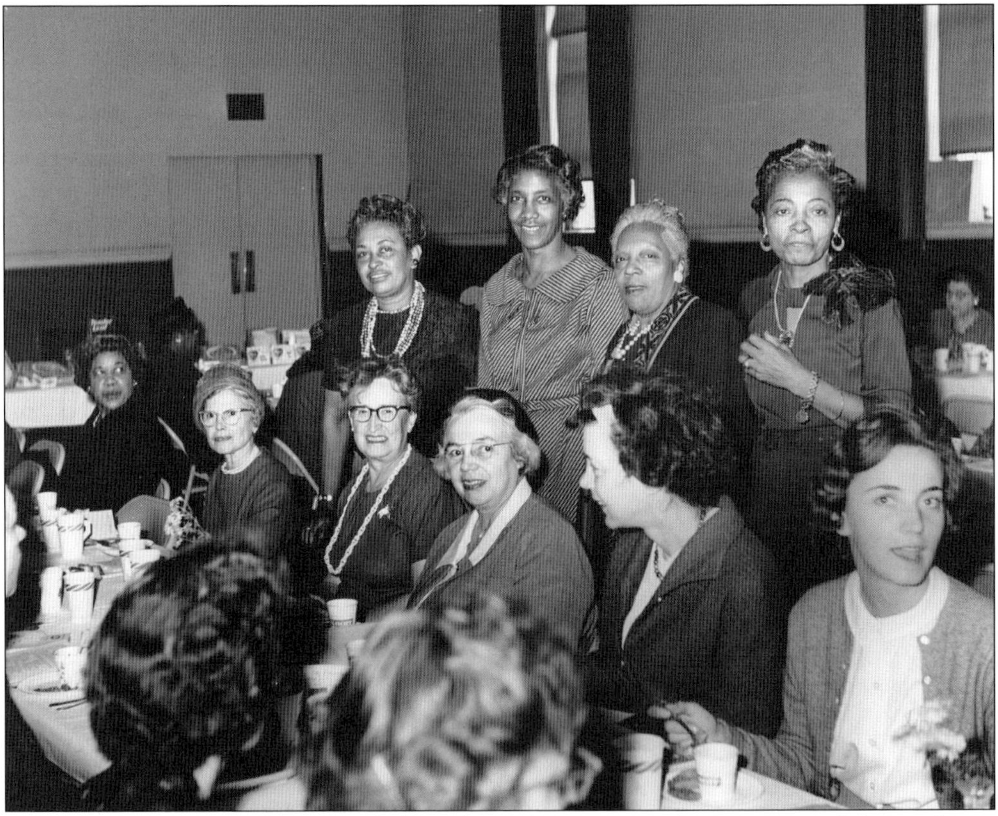

This is a 1960s YWCA event being held in the Walnut Street auditorium. From left to right are (first row) Mabel McCurdy, Gladys Jensen, unidentified, Dr. Hilda Davis, and two unidentified; (second row, standing) Tecumseh Rutledge, two unidentified, and Elizabeth Jordan (executive director). Dr. Hilda Davis was the first African American full-time professor at the University of Delaware. In 1970, she was elected to a commission, by Pres. Lyndon B. Johnson, to study the needs of African American women. (Courtesy of Dolores Washam and Lynn Clayton Jones.)

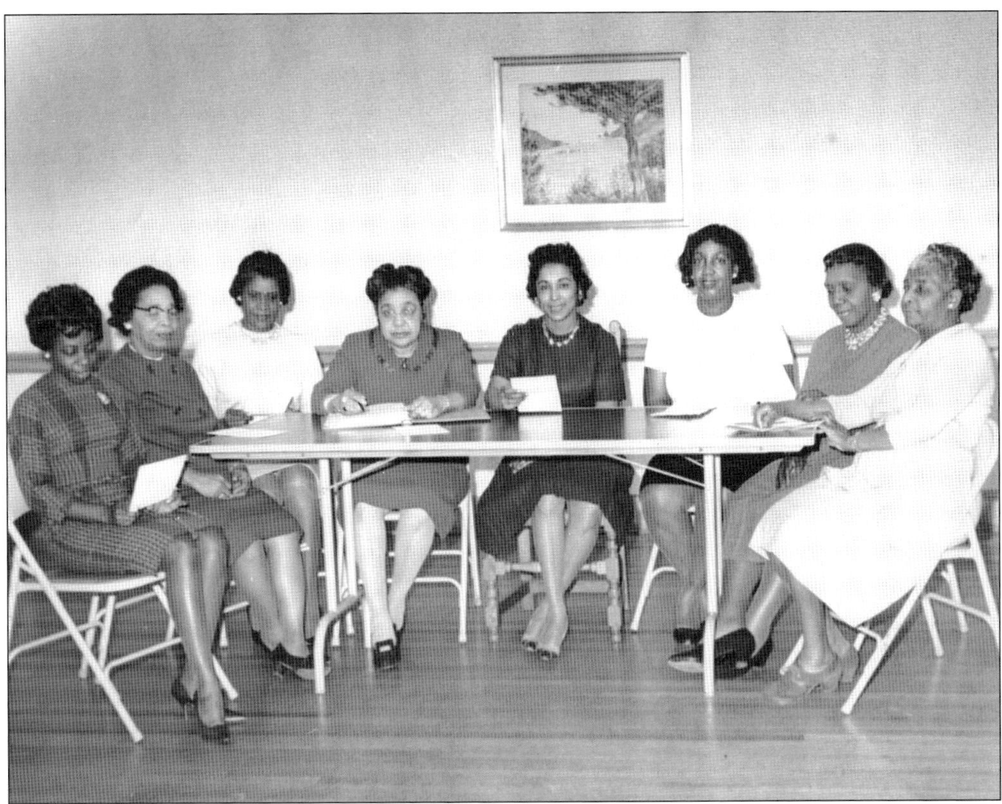

This is a meeting of Walnut Street YWCA staff and volunteers. Seated from left to right are Barbara Washam, physical education director; unidentified; Cecile Young, secretary of the YMCA; three unidentified, Hattie ?; and Alma Roberts, volunteer. (Courtesy of Dolores Washam and Lynn Clayton Jones.)

YOUNG ADULT DEPARTMENT

PUBLIC SPEAKING
Tuesday 8-10 P.M. — 12 Sessions $6.00

CHARM CLASS — Miss Wilma Schnetter
Tuesday 8-10 P.M. — 12 Sessions $6.00

SEWING, BEGINNERS — Mrs. Eva Cooper
Wednesday 8-10 P.M. — 10 Sessions $10.00

BRIDGE — Miss Magdalene Morris
Thursday 8-10 P.M. — 12 Sessions $6.00

CERAMICS
Thursday 8-10 P.M. — 12 Sessions $6.00

CLUBS AND INFORMAL RECREATION
(YWCA Membership Required)

CUP AND SAUCER CLUB
8 - 10 P. M. .... 1st and 3rd Mondays

PROFESSIONAL ART CLUB
8 - 10 P. M. .... 4th Monday

CHARM CLUB (open to graduates of YWCA Charm classes only)
8 - 10 P.M. .... 1st and 3rd Tuesdays

DRAMA GUILD
8 - 10 P. M. .... 2nd and 4th Tuesdays

I.B.M. (Interested in Business Methods)
For young business women
8 - 10 P. M. .... 2nd and 4th Wednesdays

CLUB CLIQUE — Social Club
8 - 10 P. M. .... 2nd and 4th Wednesdays

TRAVEL CLUB
8 - 10 P. M. .... (day to be announced)
Lectures and pictures of foreign lands. Plan for a trip out of the country the summer of 1960.

SPECIAL EVENTS

YOUNG ADULT CHRISTMAS TREE DECORATING PARTY
YM and YW — date to be announced
YOUNG ADULT DINNER .... Thursday, June 12, 1960
DRAMA GUILD PRESENTATION .... October 1960
YOUNG ADULT TRIP OUT OF THE COUNTRY .... July 1960

Y-TEENS CLUBS

Y-Teen Clubs are open to pre-teen and teen-age girls. General program includes — charm and good manners, choice of clothing and apparel, etiquette, family relationships, dating and boy-girl relationships, religious emphasis, choice of a career, dances, parties, trips, and splash parties in the pool.

Following is a list of clubs and place of their meetings.

Gay Teens .... Dunleith Community School
Les Sorelles .... Bancroft Jr. High
Kruse School Y-Teen Club .... Kruse School
Active Teens .... Belvidere
Howard Hi Y-Teens .... Howard High School
Teen Fun Time .... Absalom Jones School
Club Wanderlust .... Walnut Street Center
Star Queens .... Walnut Street Center

This is a schedule of events and activities of the Walnut Street YWCA. This shows the numerous activities and the cost to participate. The Y Teen outreach to communities in Dunleith and Belvedere is also listed. (Courtesy of the Delaware Historical Society.)

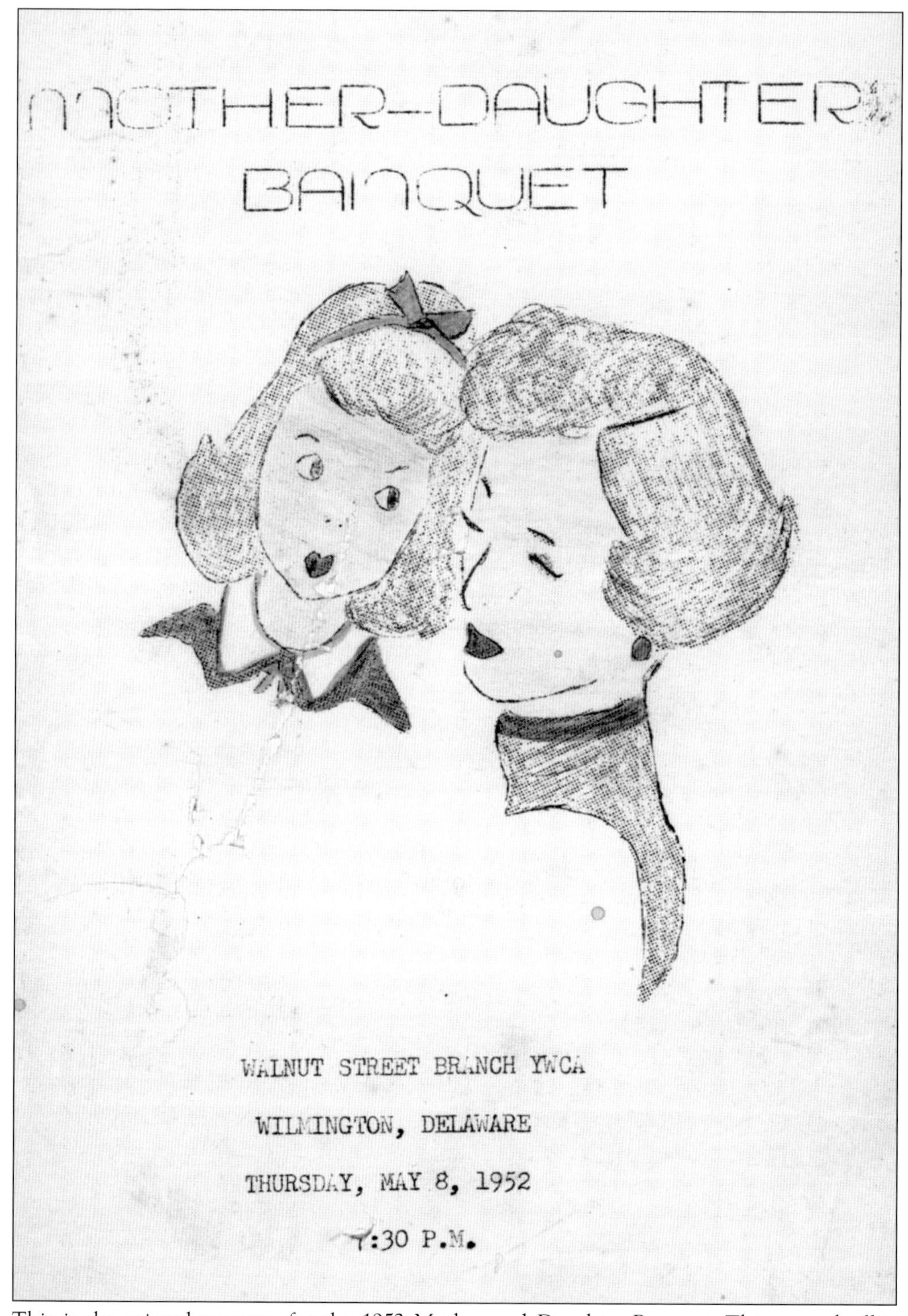

This is the printed program for the 1952 Mother and Daughter Banquet. This annual affair attracted many mothers and daughters. It was also a showcase for the talents of many teenage girls. (Courtesy of the Delaware Historical Society.)

COMMITTEE FOR TEEN-AGE PROGRAM

Miss Pauline E. Coleman, Chairman

Miss Elsie Bryant	Mrs. Irene Knotts
Miss Elsie Chippey	Miss Ann Millner
Miss Julia Christian	Mrs. Pauline Mills
Miss Bertha Coston	Mrs. Stella J. Ross
Mrs. Margie Faulkner	Miss Addie M. Turner
Miss Myrtle Graves	Mrs. Marian Washam

Mrs. Eugenia Wilson

Miss Vivian A. Jackson - Teen-Age Director

HOSTESSES

Mildred Barrett	Beatrice Starkey
Helen Benson	Alice Todd
Theresa Brown	Delores Washam

Deborah Wilson

PIANISTS

Jacqueline Dickerson	Patricia Sadler

This page of the 1952 Mother and Daughter Banquet program shows the planning committee and participants in the program. (Courtesy of the Delaware Historical Society.)

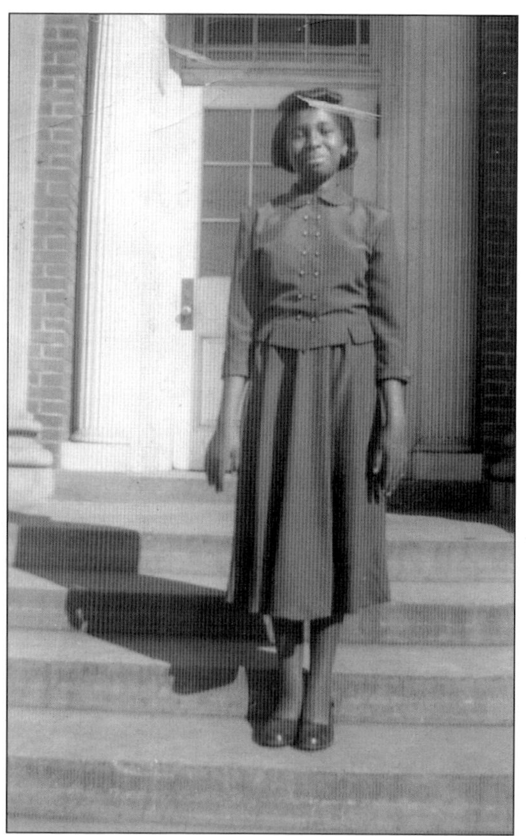

Jacqueline Dickerson Roberts was one of the high school pianists for the 1952 Mother and Daughter Banquet. Roberts started playing the piano at an early age. She then became a professional musician playing for Bethel AME Church. Later, she was a public school teacher but still continued her musical career. (Courtesy of Jacqueline Dickerson Roberts.)

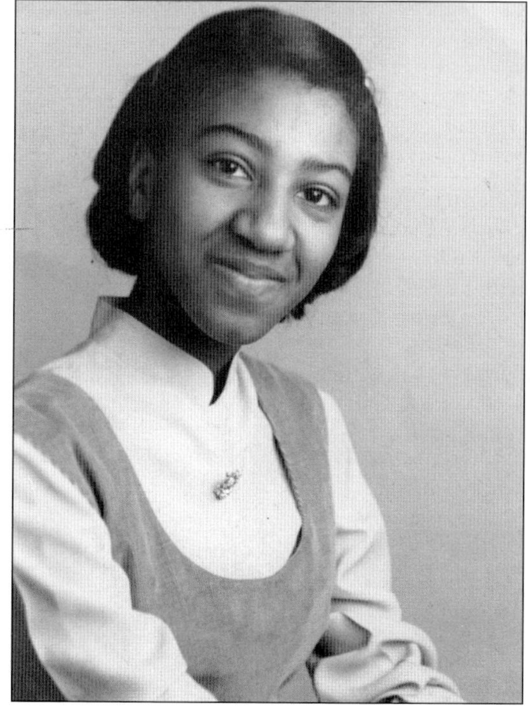

Patricia Sadler Griffin also was one of the high school pianists for the 1952 Mother and Daughter Banquet. After graduating from college, she became a teacher and, later, a school principal. (Courtesy of Patricia Sadler Griffin.)

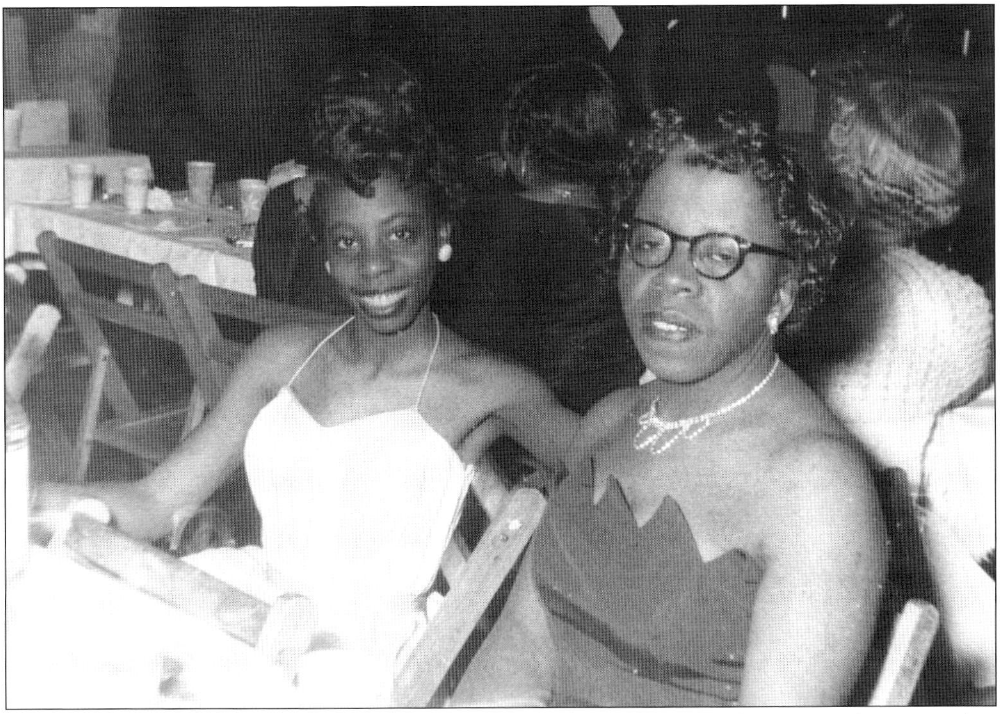

This is a photograph of Barbara Washam and her mother, Marian Washam, attending a Mother and Daughter Banquet. Barbara was the physical education director and her mother was a very active volunteer at the YWCA. Barbara's sister Dolores was also active in the organization and later became a public school teacher. (Courtesy of Dolores Washam and Lynn Clayton Jones.)

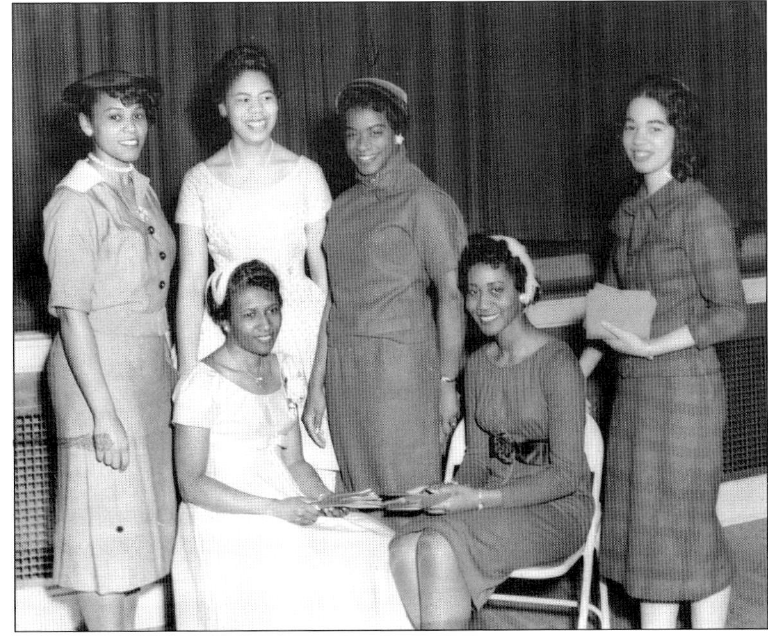

This is a photograph of the Charm Club as they are planning the Red and White Tea. The club was composed of young adult women. From left to right are (first row, seated) Doris Thomas, and Nancy Hill; (second row, standing) Ernestine Dorsey, Ora Henley Belcher, Patricia Hackett Hampton, and Cynthia Jennings. (Courtesy of Patricia Hampton.)

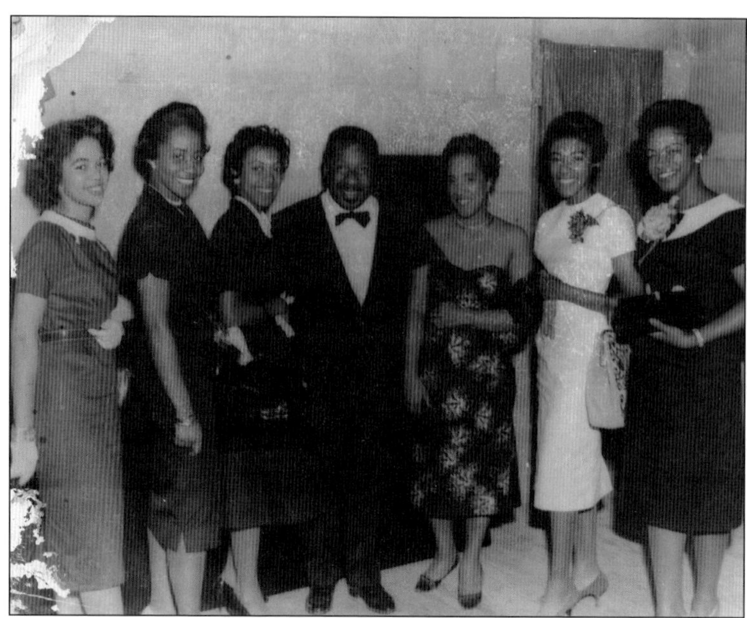

This is a photograph of the Charm Club at a social event featuring jazz musician Earl Garner. Standing from left to right are Cynthia Jennings, Nancy Hill, unidentified, Earl Garner, Bessie Morgan (program director), unidentified, and Patricia Hackett Hampton. (Courtesy of Patricia Hampton.)

YOUNG WOMEN'S CHRISTIAN ASSOCIATION

WALNUT STREET CENTER

THIS IS TO CERTIFY THAT Ora L. Henley

Has completed the Course in CHARM given by the

Young Women's Christian Association at the
Walnut Street Center
Tenth and Walnut Streets
Wilmington, Delaware

Instruction Completed March 31, 1959

Instructor

Mrs. Bessie S. Morgan
Young Adult Director

This is an example of the certificate, the participants were given at the completion of the charm course. This one belonged to Ora Henley Blecher, given to her when she finished the course in 1959. (Courtesy of Ora Henley Belcher.)

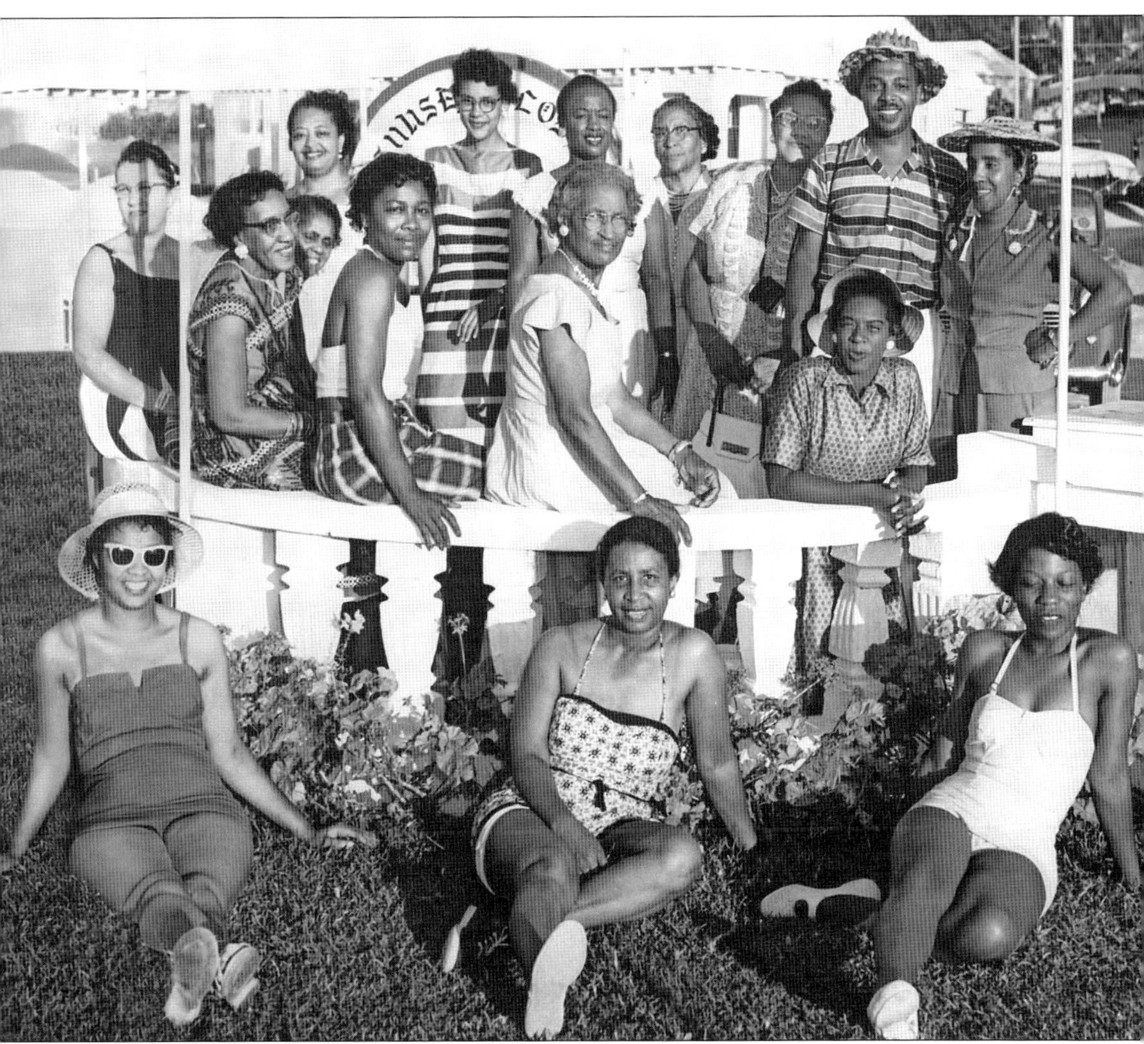

In addition to the Charm Club, Bessie Morgan created the Travel Club. This is a photograph of the group while they were in the Bahamas. From left to right are (first row, seated on the grass) Ruth Jackson, Jenny Ambrose, and Addie Mae Cole; (second row) the only identified person is the last person, Patricia Hackett Hampton, who is kneeling and leaning on the railing; (third row) unidentified, Tecumseh Rutledge, Linda Anderson, two unidentified, Thelma Young, Francis Portlock, and Bessie Morgan. Morgan graduated from New York University in fashion design. She was known for her artistic creativity which was evident in her work at the YWCA. She did set design for many of the activities. Outside of her YWCA work, Morgan was a milliner designing stunning hats for members of the community. (Courtesy of Patricia Hampton.)

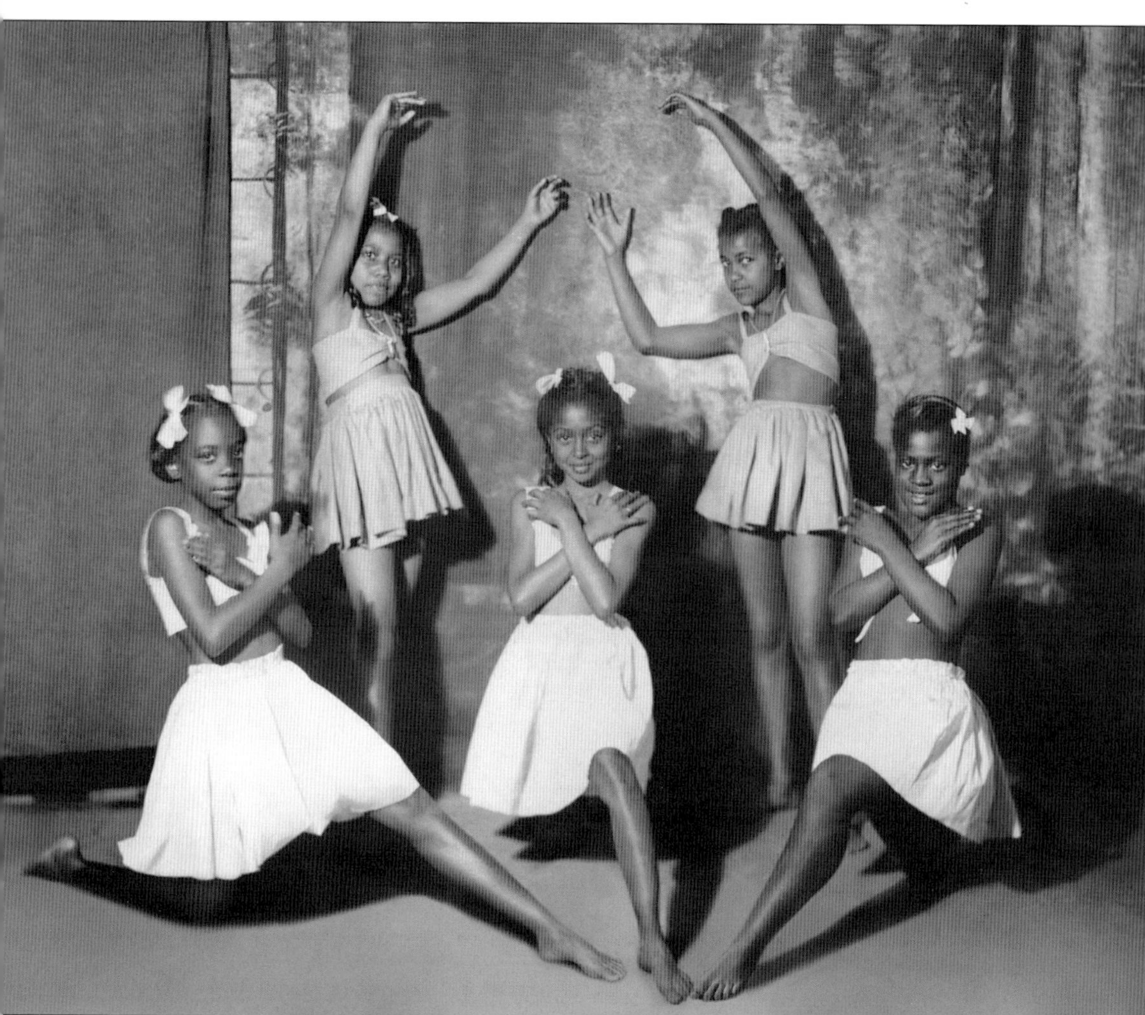

This is a 1940s ballet photograph. Pictured left to right are Barbara Washam, unidentified, Joanne Montgomery, ? Keyes, and Faith Cooper. As noted here, Washam started her connection with the Walnut Street YMCA as a young child. She then became very active as a teenager. While, a college student, she returned to Walnut Street to work in the physical education department where she established a synchronized swim team. After she graduated, Gilbert Jackson, the physical education director of the Walnut Street YMCA, recruited her to become the physical education director of the Walnut Street YWCA. The two of them expanded the swimming program and made the circus a much-anticipated event. In the 1950s and 1960s, Barbara oversaw the dance program and each Saturday collected the fees from the students and made a notation in her large ledger book. When she left Walnut Street, she continued her YWCA career at the King Street, Arden, and Newark YWCAs. (Courtesy of the Walnut Street YMCA.)

Nine

The Circus

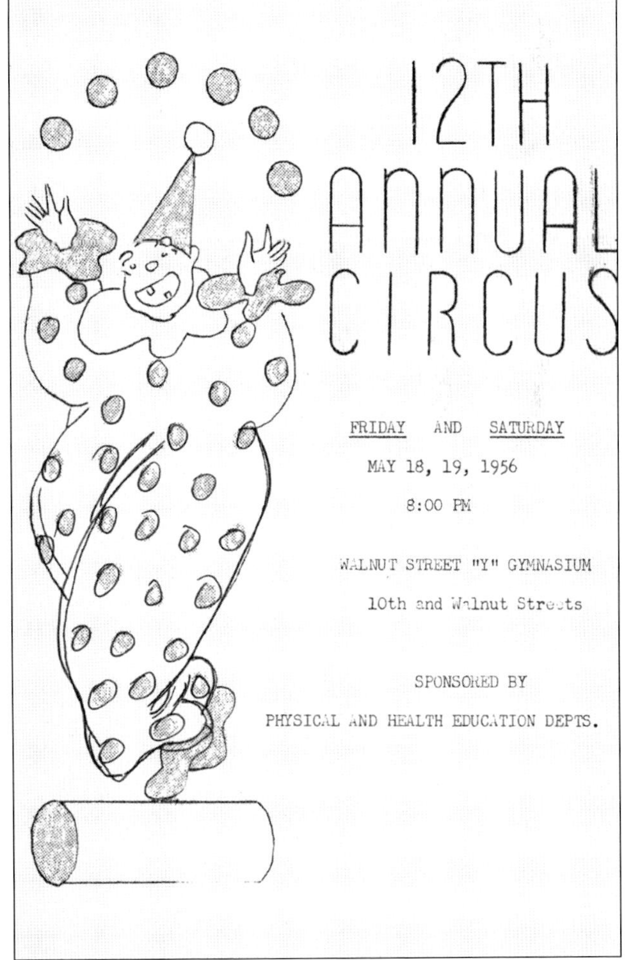

The circus was an annual event which showcased the gymnastic abilities of the young boys and girls. It started in the 1940s but became much more refined in the 1950s and 1960s. The gymnasium was decorated with crepe paper streamers, construction paper cutouts, and cardboard details. There were clowns, acrobats, tumblers, trampoline artists, and dancers. Parents and friends watched from their chairs. It was fun for all. This is the cover of the program of the 12th annual circus in 1956. The circus is documented to have continued for at least 17 years. (Courtesy of the Delaware Historical Society.)

CIRCUS PROGRAM

GRAND MARCH

DUMB-BELL DRILL-YMCA

SKATER

CLOWN SKIT

YWCA TUMBELLETS

YMCA TUMBLERS

WEIGHT LIFTING

I N T E R M I S S I O N

THE APPLE JACKERS

COMMANDO'S DRILL TEAM

PERFECTION IN BALANCE

DELICATE OPERATION

MODERN DANCE

YWCA PYRAMIDS

YMCA GYMNASTIC TEAM

YM-YWCA TRAMPOLINE DEMONSTRATION
AND SPECIAL ATTRACTION
Mr. Henry Etheridge

FINALE

RING MASTER RAYMOND TATE

* * * * * * * * * * * *

This is the program of the 1956 circus. It highlights the various acts. (Courtesy of the Delaware Historical Society.)

PARTICIPANTS

Dwight Harold
Tyrone Maxfield
Gilbert H. Jackson, 111
Frank Floyd
Spencer Henry
James Bell
Lafayette Jackson
Willard Cephas
Wayne Trader
Charles Naylor
Cornilius Naylor
Henry Lee
Marion Norwood
Freddie Johnson
William Pinkett
Lorenzo Roberts
Larry Furrowh
Herschell James
Harvey Woolfolk
Darryl Copper
Jepther Pollard
Lennell Shepherd
Stephen Dryden
Walter Faulkner
Ernest Jackson
Melvin Tingle
Fred Baynard
George Harris
Eugene Calloway
Joseph Reed
Thomas Cephas
Raymond Cephas
Richard Cephas
Harrison Cephas
Arthur Redding
Quinton Sterling
James Butler
Tyrone Furrowh
Frankie Ward
Gerald Woolfolk
William Short
Raymond Tate
Donald Patterson
Elbert Dutton
David Clover

Ann Waters
Sylvia Davis
Diana Brothers
Alice Brown
Linda Johnson
Pearl Wright
Jane Dyton
Judith McManus
Judy Gupton
Cheryll Jackson
Joan Dyson
Bonita Gordon
Adalyn Wilson
Sandra Dyton
Barbara Brown
Vivian Perkins

GUEST ARTISTS

Henry Etheridge - Former Captain of Springfield College Gymnastic Team
Walter & Whitey - Out-Standing Perfection in Balance Act
Kenneth Walker - Skating Performer

There were at least 65 participants in the 1956 circus, as indicated in this list. Many of the young people listed eventually became outstanding athletes. The circus was a training ground for their public performances in the broader community. (Courtesy of the Delaware Historical Society.)

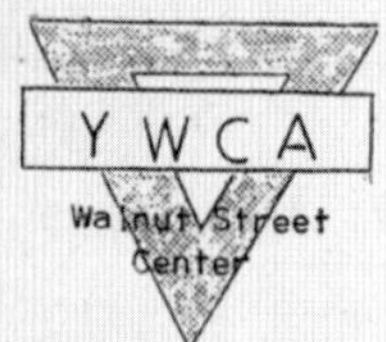

THE OPEN DOOR

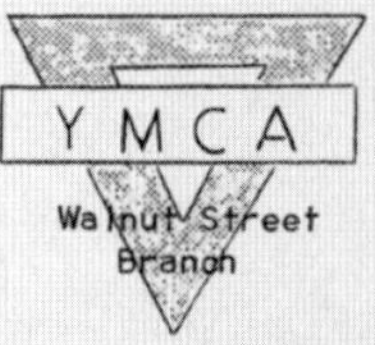

Vol. 10, No. 4 Wilmington, Delaware May, 1960

'Y' BOOSTERS CLUB STARTED IN BRANCH

The Branch Membership Committee feels that every member of the Branch is interested in having his friends participate in the activities and services of the YMCA. Further, according to Roland J. Henry, Chairman of the Committee, those members who do enroll their friends as members of the 'Y' should be recognized as "Y Boosters". The Committee has, therefore, established a "Y Boosters Club" with the only dues for membership being the enrollment of members. A "Y Boosters Club" roster will be posted in the main lobby. Every member of the YMCA should stop at the main desk or the Membership Office and pick up applications and program materials and plan to qualify right away for listing as a member of the "Y Boosters Club".

YOUTH GUIDANCE PROGRAM BROADENED

The Industrial Services Committee of the Branch has expanded the Vocational Conference which it began last year in co-operation with the guidance department of Howard High School. This year every student will be given an opportunity to discuss an occupational field of his choosing with a consultant in this field. This feature should add tremendously to the value to the students.

In preparation for the program Frederick T. Marston, President of the Kaumagraph Co. and a member of the committee, spoke to an assembly of Howard High and 9th grade students from Bancroft Jr. High School on May 17th.

Other members of the Planning Comm. are Mrs. Madeline C. Burton and Dr. Leroy M. Christophe of Howard School, Anson B. Nixon and Wesley J. Marshall.

ANNUAL CIRCUS PROVES POPULAR SUCCESS

The 16th Annual Circus sponsored by the Health and Physical Education Departments of the YM and YWCA was held on Friday and Saturday, May 6th and 7th. The many parents and friends who were in attendance were treated to a very fine performance. A new feature of the 1960 Circus was the introduction of the Side-Shows which were held before the main tent and during intermission. Over 100 of our members participating in the Circus and members of the committees and many of our friends helped to put over the program.

James Johnson, Manual Brunswick and Willard Cephas were winners and outstanding in the tumbling tournment held at the Central Branch YMCA.

Two large groups of our younger boys have passed their Jr. Life Saving requirements and also completed beginners and swimmers tests. Members of the Physical Leaders Corps gave very fine assistance in training and preparation of persons for the annual circus and also in the completion of each league that was conducted this winter and early spring.

QUALIFIED PERSONS NEEDED FOR JOB REFERALS

The Industrial Services Department is constantly looking for Negro men and women who are qualified for the increasing number of new job opportunities which are becoming available as a result of the work of this department. If you are qualified in a specific field, register at once as a possible placement.

The 1960 *Open Door* newsletter featured an article on the 16th annual circus. It was held for two days with over 100 participants. That year, the circus added sideshows, which were held before the main event and during intermission. The coverage also mentioned that Willard Cephas, Manual Brunswick, and James Johnson participated in the Central Branch tumbling tournament and were winners of the event. (Courtesy of the Delaware Historical Society.)

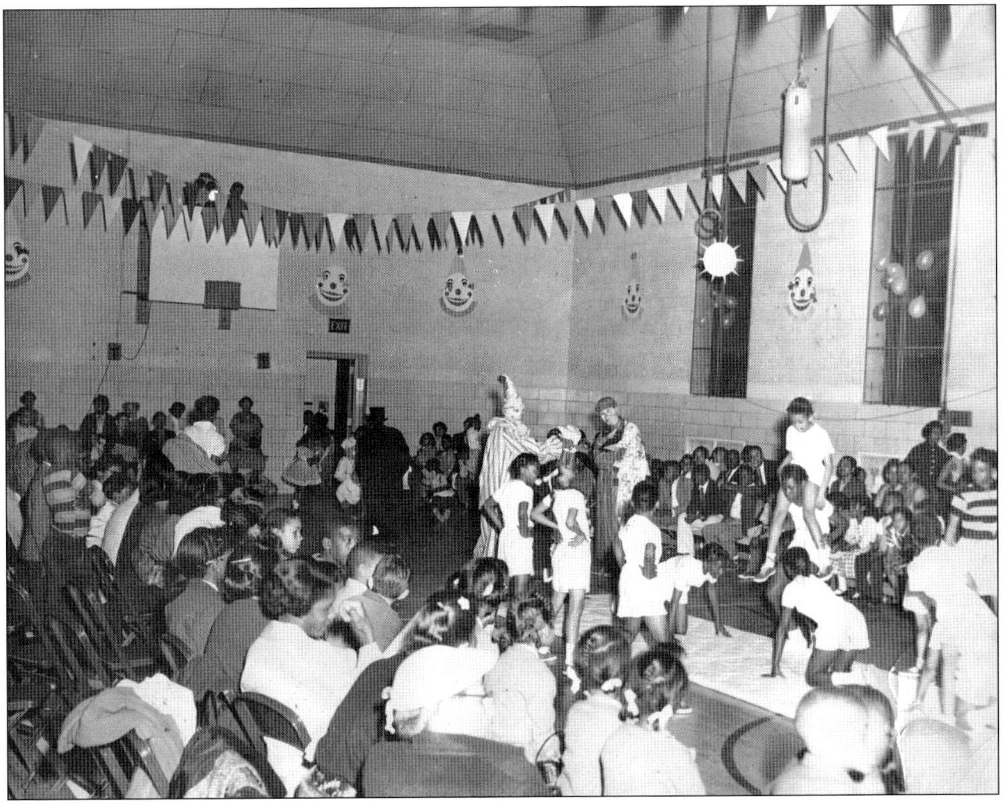

This is a wide-angle view of one of the large group circus events. It took a great deal of coordination on the part of the physical education staff to choreograph all these children. (Courtesy of Dolores Washam and Lynn Clayton Jones.)

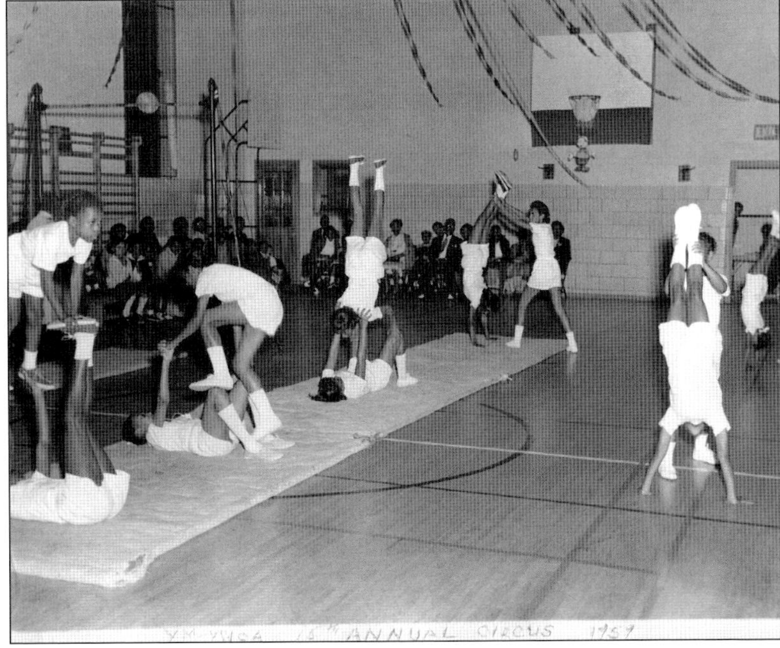

This is an example of one of the tumbling events. Tumbling was one of the skills that was always highlighted at the circus. (Courtesy of Dolores Washam and Lynn Clayton Jones.)

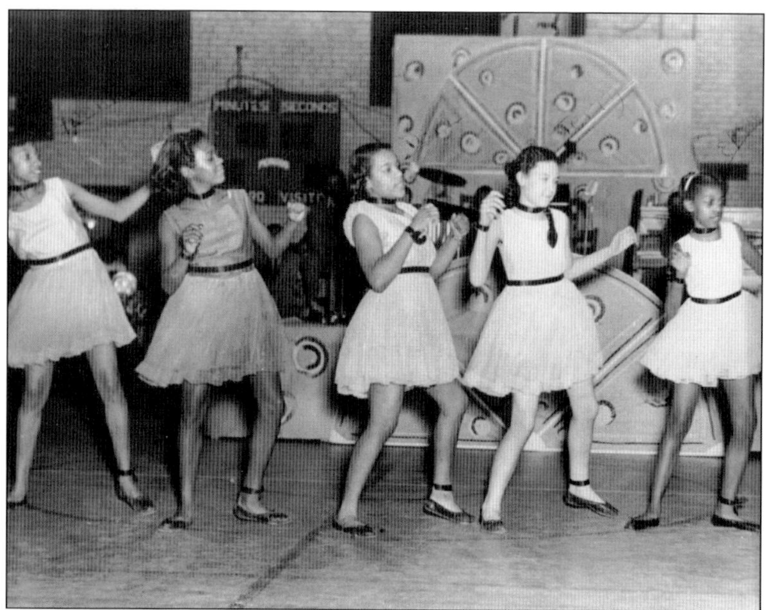

There were always dancers from the ballet classes. This image is from the very early 1950s. From left to right are Yvonne Bratcher, Pattie Harris, Doris Peaco, Terry Taylor, and Elsie Hackett. (Courtesy of the Delaware Historical Society.)

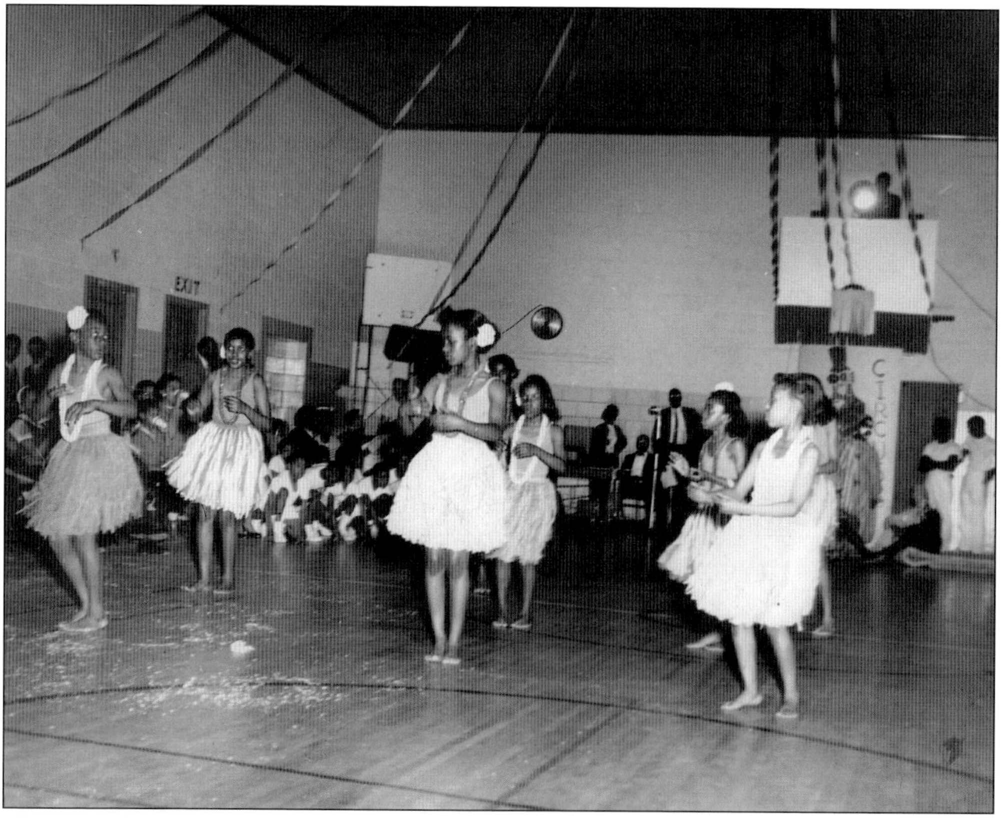

This is another group of dancers from a later circus. Dance performances were always an integral part of the circus. Many of the children also participated in the dance program. (Courtesy of Dolores Washam and Lynn Clayton Jones.)

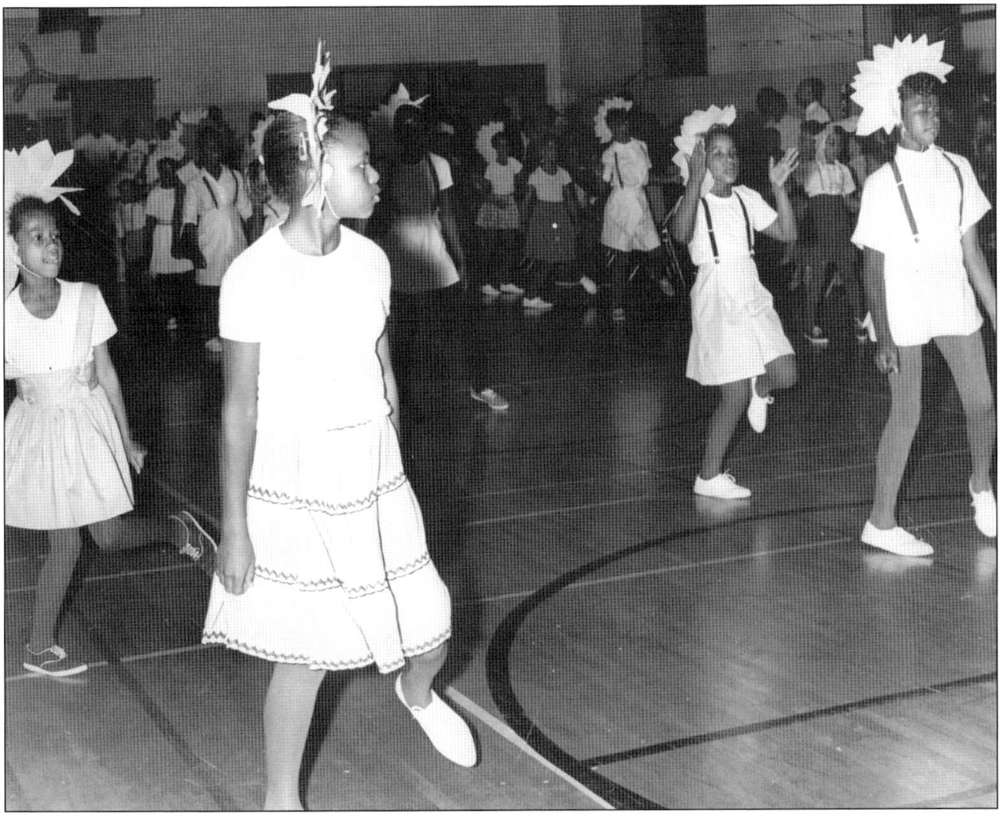

These dancers are from a late 1960s circus event. Notice their fancy headdresses. Some of the parents helped create the costumes. (Courtesy of Dolores Washam and Lynn Clayton Jones.)

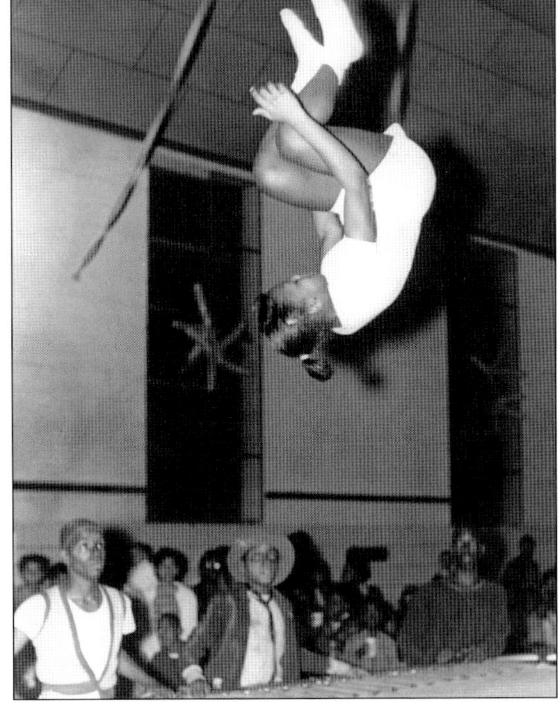

This young woman on the trampoline, Judith Gupton Wiley, was one of the outstanding female tumblers. One year, she was even paired with the award-winning gymnast Willard Cephas. (Courtesy of Dolores Washam and Lynn Clayton Jones.)

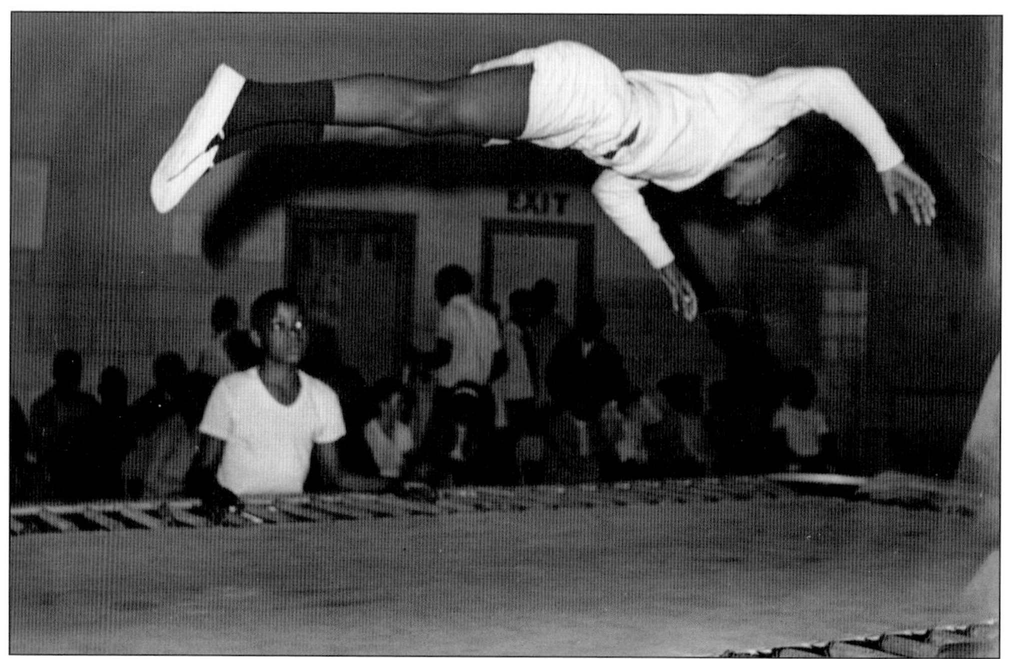

Willard Cephas was not only an outstanding swimmer but he was also an award-winning gymnast. In this photograph, he is seen as a young man performing on the trampoline. Around this time, Willard was also very active in other activities at the Y. He was the outstanding camper for two years in a row. (Courtesy of the Walnut Street YMCA.)

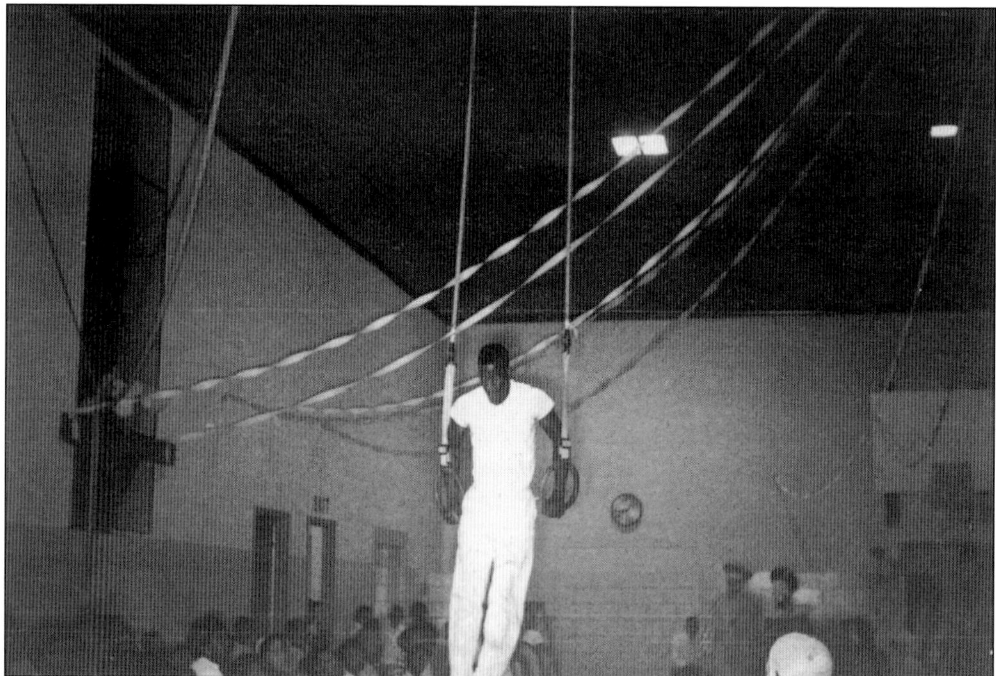

Willard Cephas is seen here as a young adult giving a special demonstration on the rings. He was also noted as being the only person able to do a triple back flip on the trampoline. Cephas was often a featured performer at the circus. (Courtesy of Willard Cephas.)

Ten

Clubs and Activities

ADULT PROGRAM
YOUNG ADULT PROGRAM
SCHEDULE

Y. M. C. A.
Y. W. C. A.

Young Adult Program
Y.W.C.A.—MRS. BESSIE MORGAN
Director

* * * *

Young Adult & Adult Program
Y.M.C.A.—MR. GEORGE H. POE, JR.
Membership-Program Secretary

* * * *

FALL - 1956

Walnut Street Christian Association
Tenth and Walnut Sts. - Wilmington, Del.
For Information Call OLympia 8-5205

In addition to swimming, sports, and athletics, there were many other activities at the Walnut Street YMCA and YWCA. This is the cover for the fall 1956 young adult program schedule for both the YMCA and YWCA. (Courtesy of the Delaware Historical Society.)

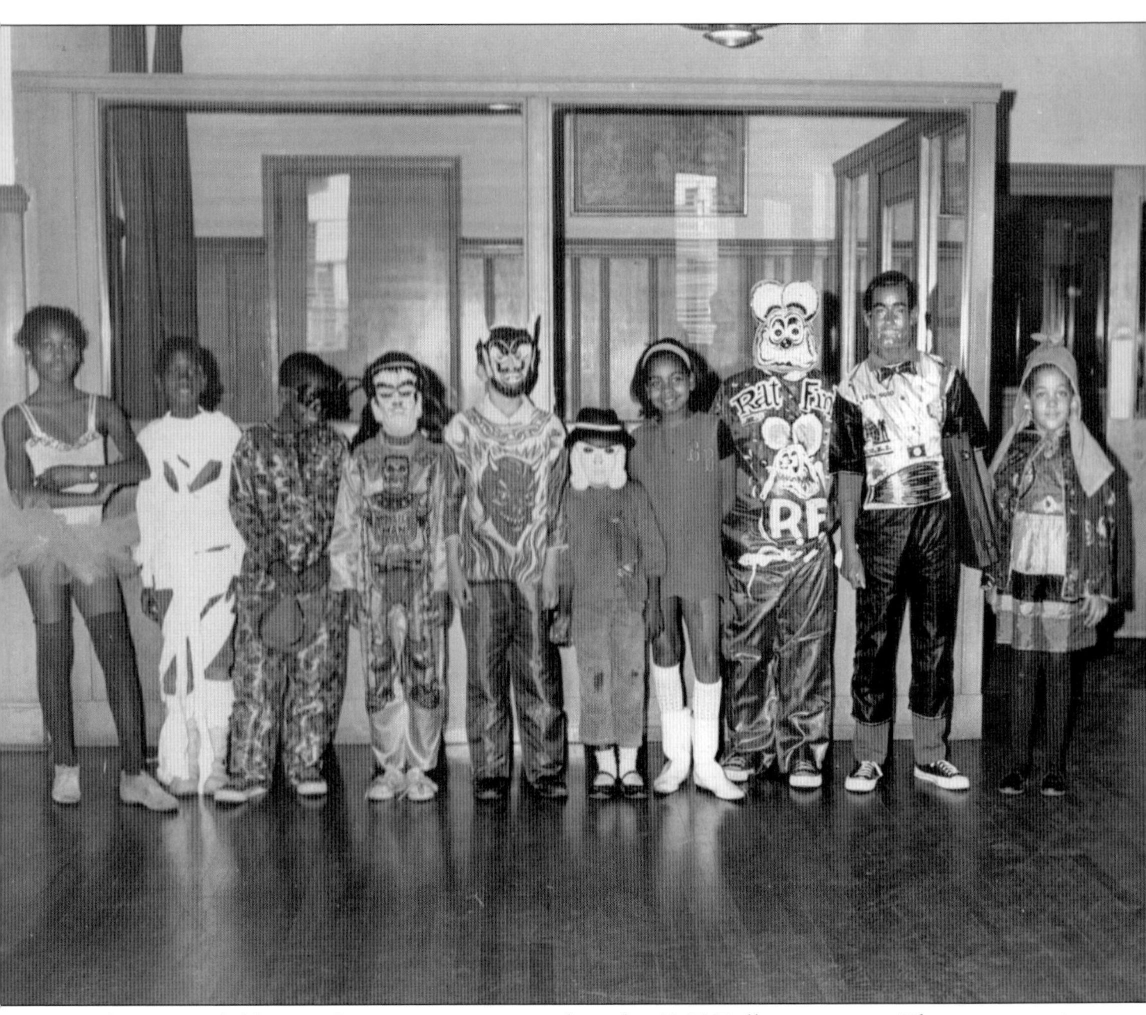

The young children in festive attire are attending the 1965 Halloween party. There was music, games, refreshments, a magic show, and a movie. Some of the children were even able to go for a swim. (Courtesy of the Walnut Street YMCA.)

Young Men's Christian Association of Wilmington and New Castle County

Walnut Street Branch

Halloween Party for Youth Department Members
Saturday, October 30, 1965
10:00 A.M.

9:15 A.M. -- Leadership for Halloween Party to meet in Room 211.

10:00 A.M. -- Members and friends assemble in auditorium -
Mr. William Ward
Mr. Arthur White
Music ---------------------------- Anthony Jackson

10:10 A.M. -- Welcome --------------------- Mr. Samuel Peterson

10:15 A.M. -- Games ------------- Mark Marconi, William Hicks, Mr. George H. Poe, Jr.

10:45 A.M. -- Prizes to members of Guessing Contest (How many Beans in Jar?) ----------------------- Mr. Thomas Roberts

10:50 A.M. -- Refreshments ------ Miss Doris Cannon, Carl Lucas, Dwight Bunting, Walter Brown, Robert Wright, Mr. Kenneth Miles, Herbert Barr

Judging of Costumes: Charles Hayward, Don Brown, Mr. Herman McKinney, Mr. William Ward , Drew Mander

11:10 A.M. -- Prizes to be presented for costumes

11:20 A.M. -- Magic ------------------------- Michael Sullivan

11:50 A.M. -- Movie ------------------------------ Adolphus Ward

(Gra-Y members - grades 3 thru 6 may remain for movie or obtain Physical Department Passes from Mr. Kenneth Miles for gym-swim program at 12 noon).

12:20 P.M. -- Adjournment

Other Responsibilities:

Main Floor --------------------------- Mr. Herman McKinney
Second Floor ------------------------- Mr. Thomas Roberts
Photographer and Name Tags ------------------ Steven Jackson
Magician ----------------------------------- Jerome Samuels

This was the program for the Halloween party. There were prizes for the best costumes, and a photographer was available to take pictures of the partygoers. (Courtesy of the Walnut Street YMCA.)

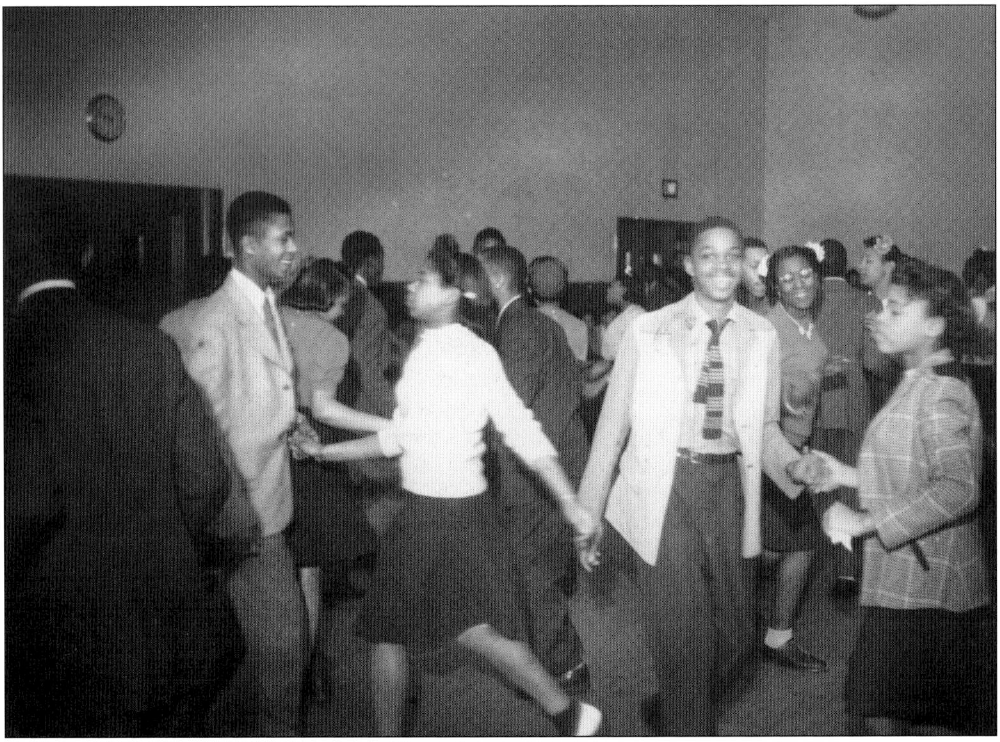

El Trocadero was the teenage dance club that was held every weekend. The group started in the 1940s and continued until the late 1960s. Here, one can see the young people enjoying themselves on the dance floor. Every year, there was a New Year's Eve party. In the 1940s, the party included one of the well-known bands in the area. (Courtesy of the Delaware Historical Society.)

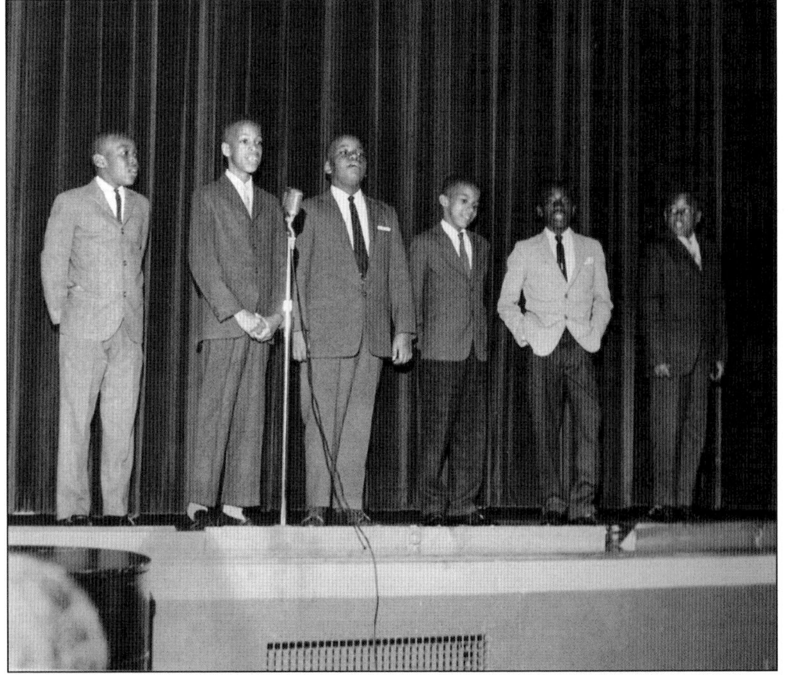

The event seen here was one of the many talent shows. One day, George Taylor noticed five young men singing. As a result, he started a boys' choir. These young men may have been some of the original singers. (Courtesy of the Walnut Street YMCA.)

The Gray-Y was a club for young boys of elementary school age. Many of the clubs were organized in local schools. This January 1969 photograph taken at the George Gray School shows Forest Dixon, the club leader, meeting with a young man. The blackboard behind him has information concerning the YMCA. (Courtesy of the Walnut Street YMCA.)

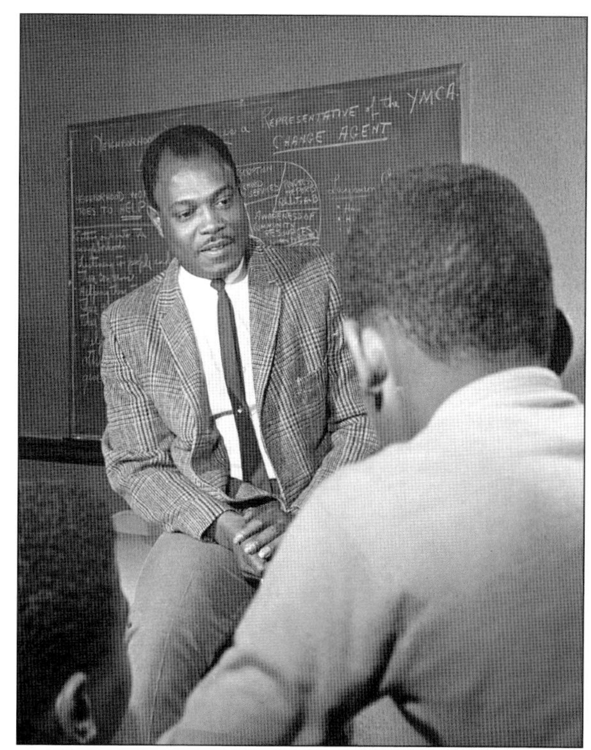

This photograph is of a breakfast in the cafe after a Gray-Y overnight bunk-in. The young men arrived on a Friday evening where they played games and went swimming. They slept overnight and had breakfast in the morning. The older young man on the right wearing glasses is William Young Jr. He was a member of the Hi-Y and was supervising the younger boys. (Courtesy of the Walnut Street YMCA.)

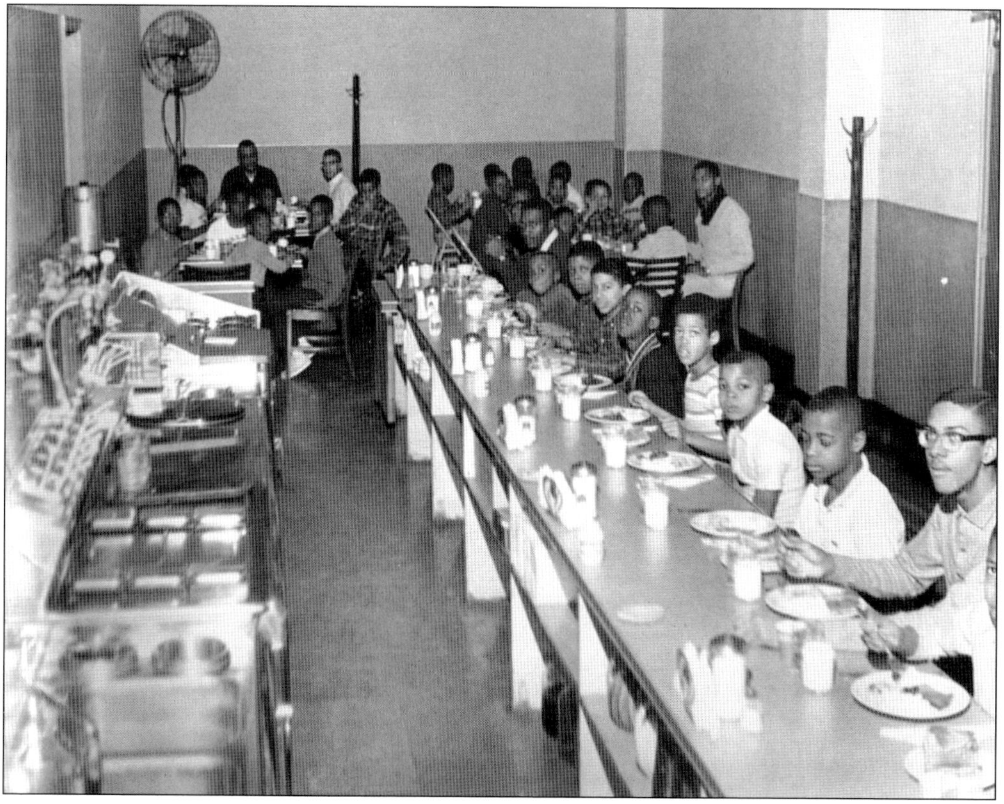

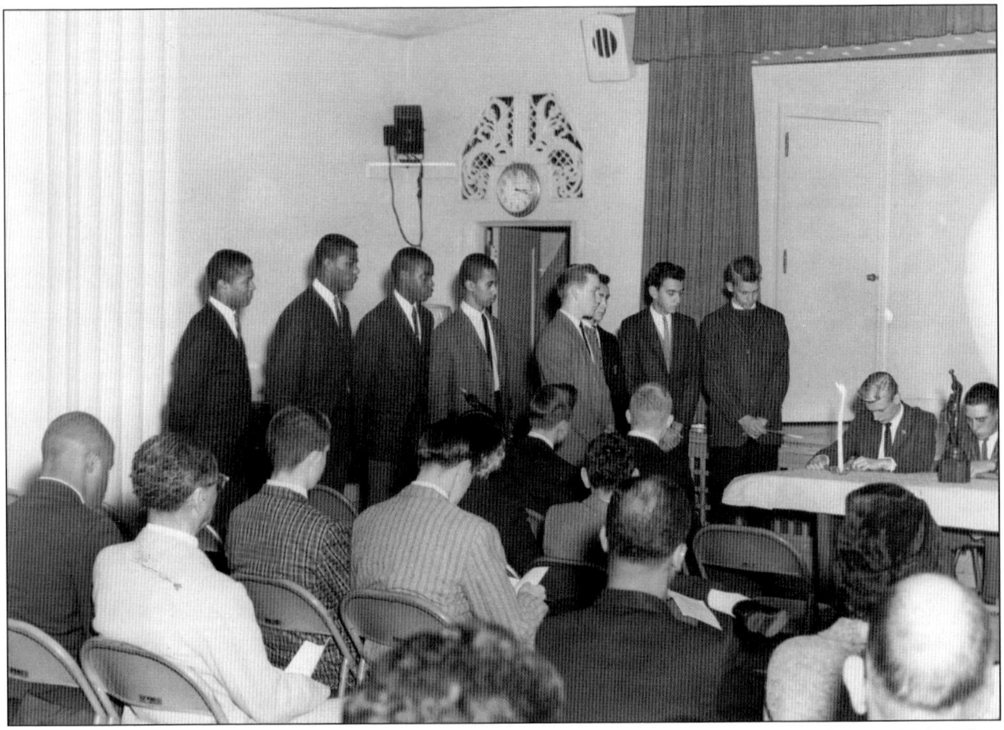

This is the Hi-Y induction, rededication, and installation service held on December 3, 1961. This photograph shows young men from both Walnut Street and the Central YMCA being inducted together. Standing from left to right are the Walnut Street members: Spencer Henry, Theodore Irving, Alan Brown, and Ronald Gibson. In addition to participating in the Hi-Y, Henry was an excellent swimmer but made history in track. He is known for anchoring the 1962 Howard High School relay team that won the Penn Relays Championship of America and for winning state titles in the 100- and 200-meter events. Henry went to Morgan State University, where he continued to gain honors in track. After graduation from college, he coached track at Wilmington High School and Dickinson High School and earned titles with those teams. He later served as principal of Dickinson High School. The Philadelphia Phillies even hired him as a running coach. (Courtesy of the Walnut Street YMCA.)

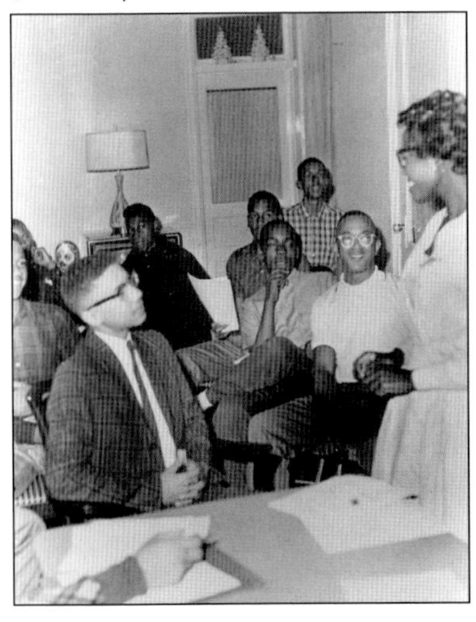

This is a meeting of the Hi-Y at the home of William Young Sr. The woman in the picture is from Ghana and is giving a talk about her country. The participants, from left to right, are Ernest Eggleston, Dan Reynolds, Robert Young, Alan Lawrence, William Young, Reggie Hill, Bruce Hall, and Clyde Knotts. (Courtesy of the estate of William S. Young Sr.)

Ralph Evans Sr. was the president of the Athenian Hi-Y at Howard High School in the 1960s. He used the leadership skills he developed to eventually become a vice president at a major paper manufacturer. (Courtesy of Beverly Evans.)

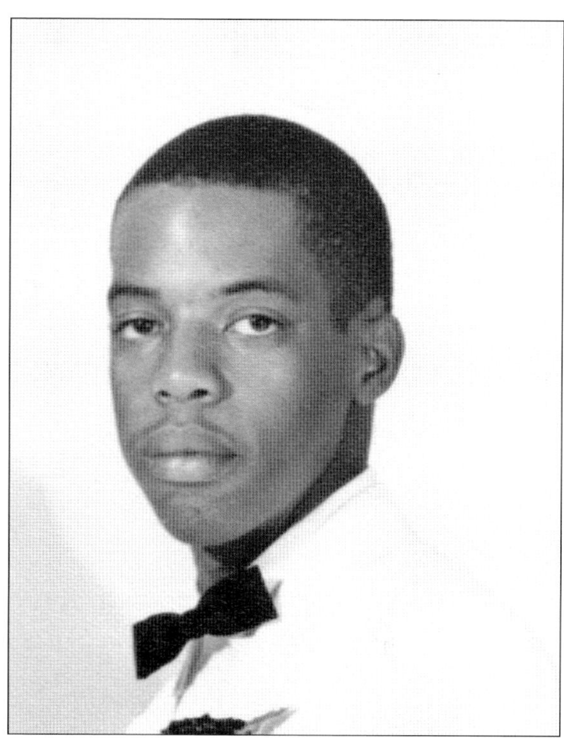

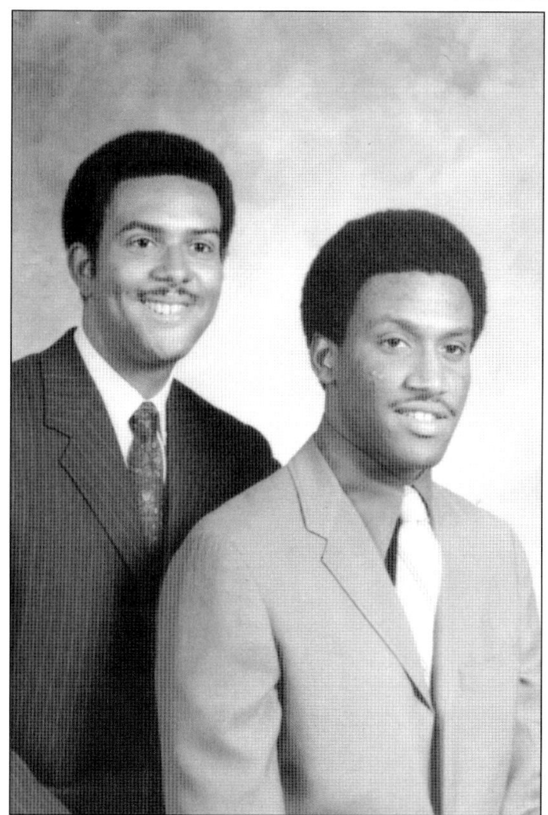

Brothers William S. Young Jr. (on the left) and Robert Young were both active in the YMCA, especially the Hi-Y. Their parents were employed at the organization and their father served most of his life as a member of the board of managers. William S. Young Jr. also served on the board of managers. (Courtesy of William and Anita Young.)

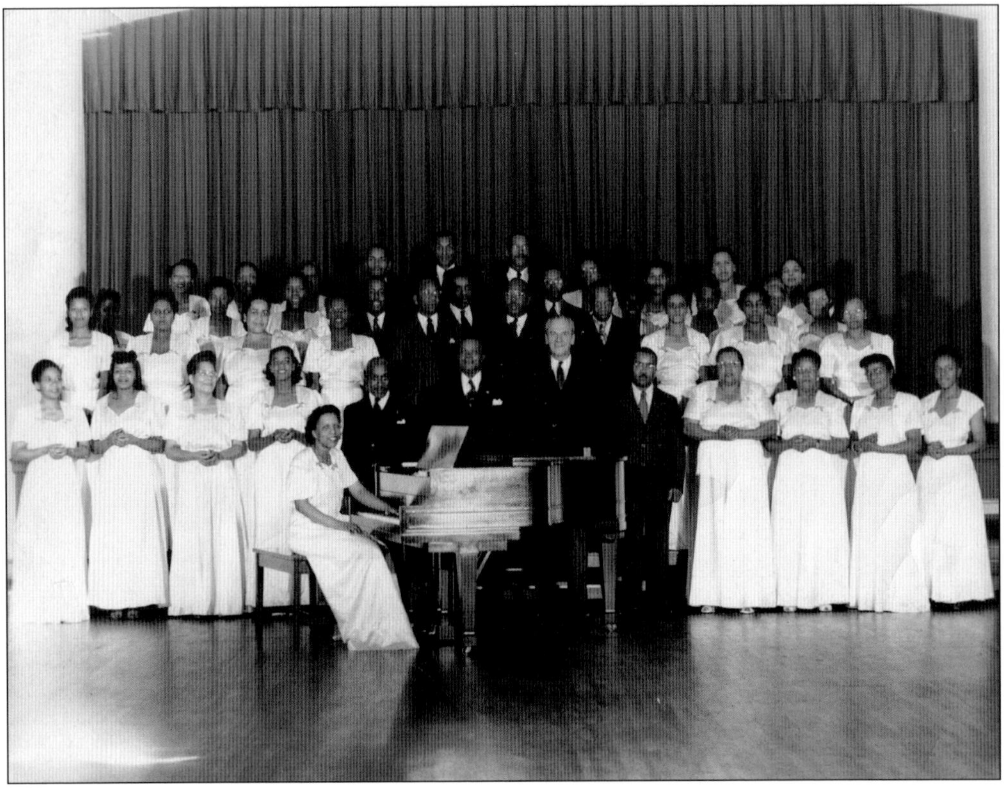

Choir Celeste was created in the late 1940s by Etta Woodlin. The first director, Daniel Boyer, is seen in the first-row center. Ventie Millis Williams, the accompanist, is seated at the piano. (Courtesy of Florence Collins Hardy.)

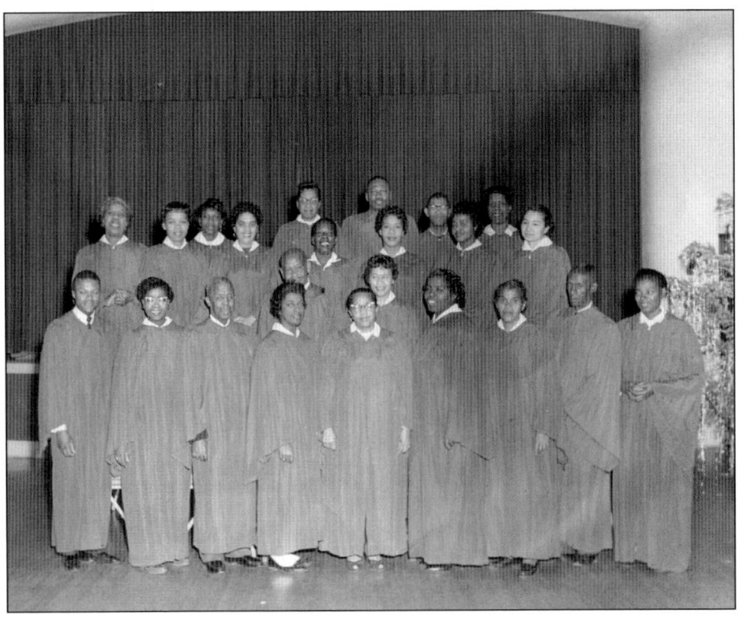

This is a later photograph of the Choir Celeste and shows them in their burgundy robes. Apparently, this is a Christmas concert because a Christmas tree can be seen in the far right of the photograph. By this time, the new accompanist is Ruth Ann Burton. She is standing in the second row, second from the left. (Courtesy of Florence Collins Hardy.)

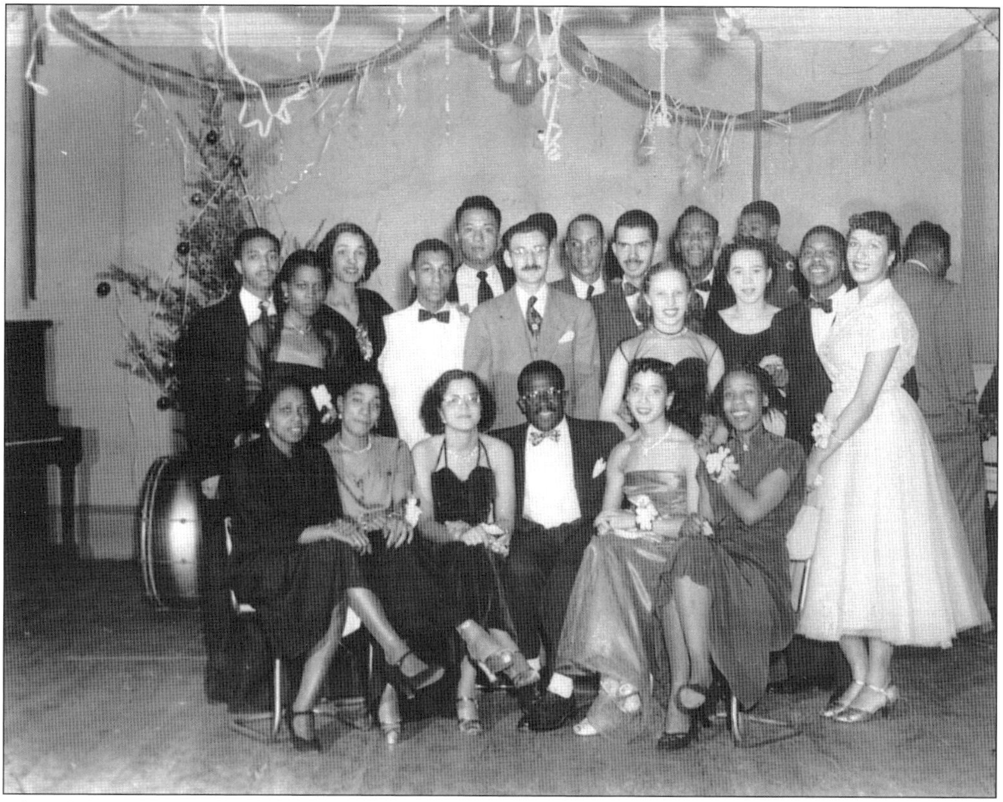

The Theater Guild performed very professional productions. The director was David Gray. Here, the group poses during their 1950 Christmas party. From left to right are (seated) unidentified, Mary Clark, Jean Anderson, Bill Myers, Luvenia Gray, and Margaret Davis; (standing) Frances Portlock, Alma Hamilton, Janice Anderson, John Russell, Ricardo Madella, Morris Levenberg, Stansbury Ferrell, Hilmar Jensen, Yvonne Jensen, David Gray, unidentified, Patsy Williams Sherman Clark, and Ariel Munce. (Courtesy of Stephanie Evans.)

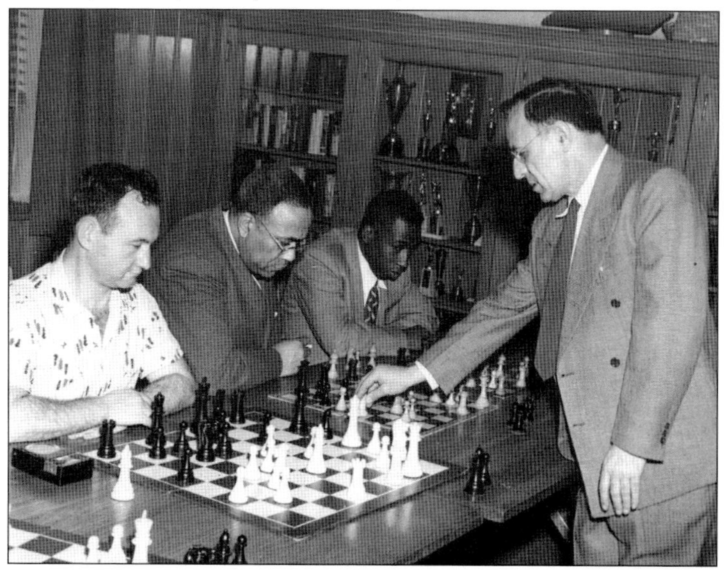

This is the Chess Club. Sitting, from left to right, are two unidentified and Walter Ransom. Ransom spent most of his adult life highly involved with the Walnut Street YMCA. He served as president of the Top Ten Social Club, chair of the Youth Work Committee, and numerous other committees. He was also cited for his volunteer service (Courtesy of the Walnut Street YMCA.)

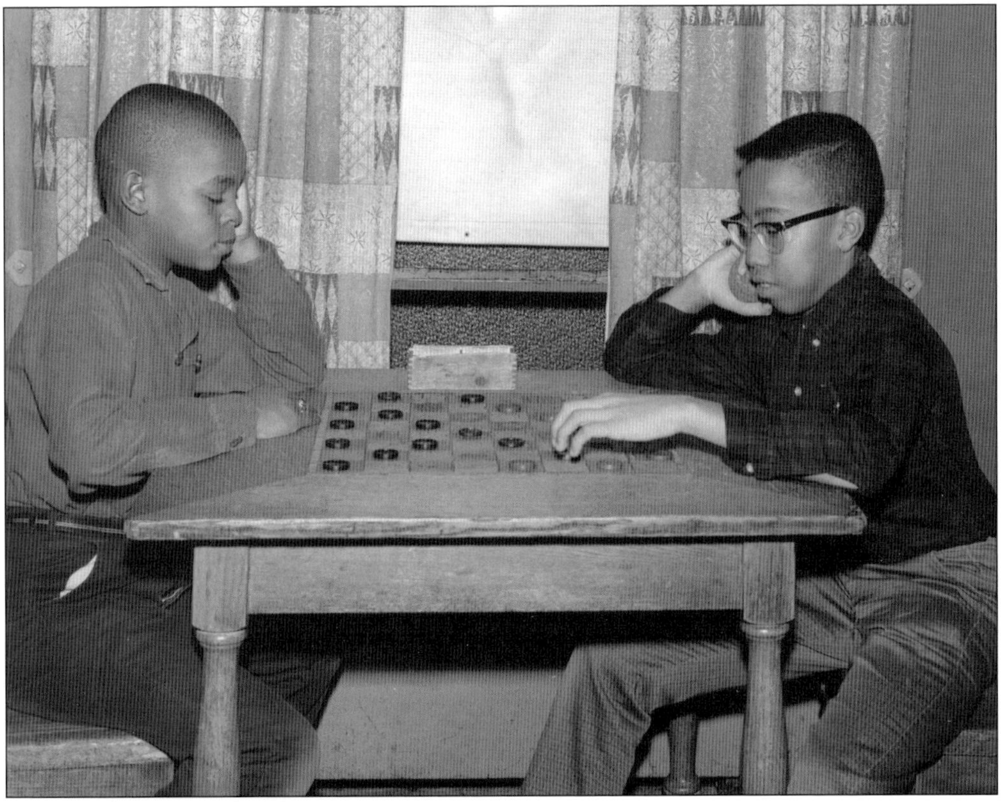

These young boys are participating in a checkers competition. There were many activities for young men at Walnut Street. In addition to athletic clubs, there were other activities such as the Checkers Club and Camera Club. Both of these clubs were sponsored by the Boys Department. (Courtesy of the Walnut Street YMCA.)

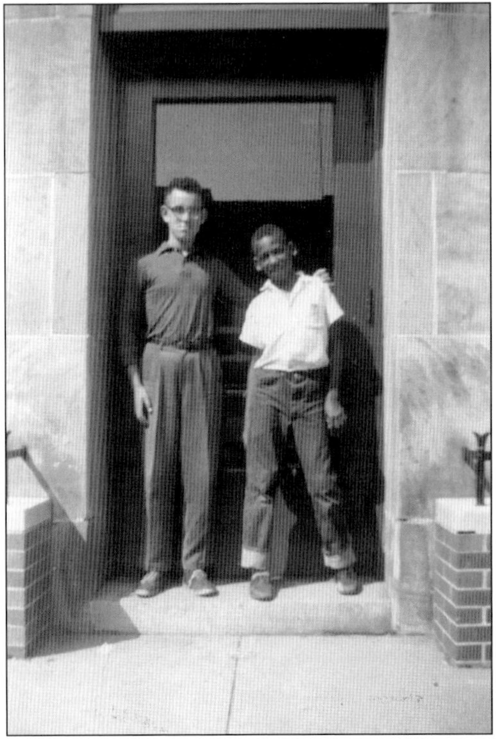

The Camera Club was created for young men to learn photography skills. These young men are part of the club and pose on the steps of the boys' entrance to the building. The advisors were Howard Cooper and James White. (Courtesy of the Walnut Street YMCA.)

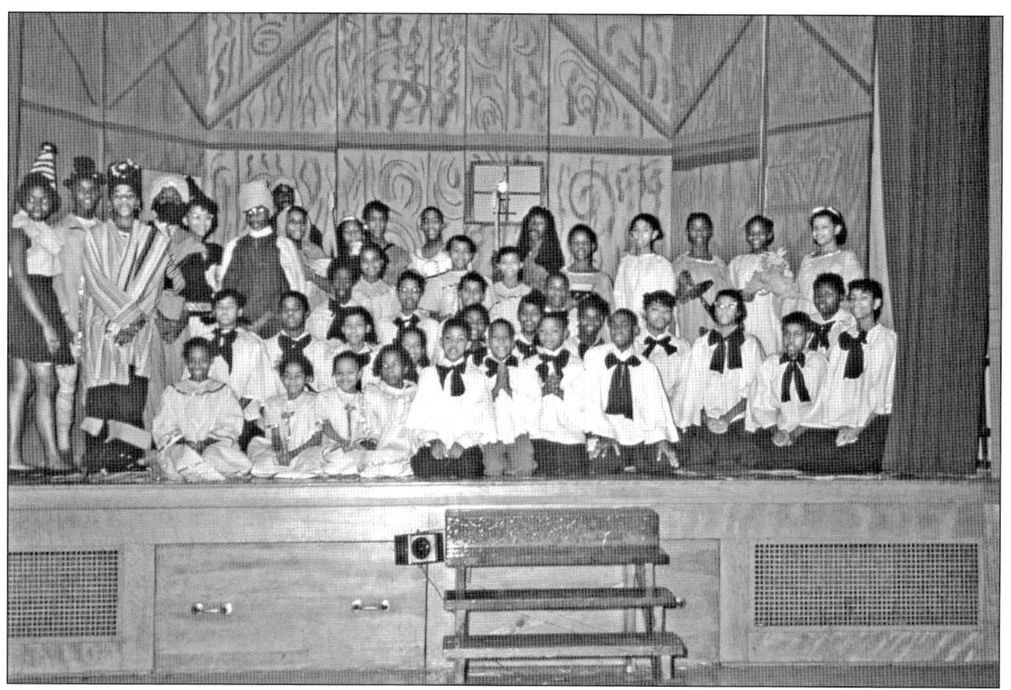

Every year, the Absalom Jones School performed a Christmas play at Walnut Street. This is the cast from a 1950s performance. The play was performed at both the school and the YMCA. (Author's collection.)

SLUM CLEARANCE - IMPLICATIONS FOR WILMINGTON

The first in a series of Public Affairs Programs will be sponsored by the Unity Club of the Walnut Street Branch Y.M.C.A. Monday, May 21, 1956 at 8 P.M. at the Walnut Street Y.M.C.A. auditorium, Tenth and Walnut Streets.

The Topic is "Slum Clearance - Implications for Wilmington."

The speakers will be Mr. William H. Burton, President of the East Side Home Owners Association and Rev. F. Raymond Baker, Chairman of the Wilmington Housing Authority. Several resource people will be present to answer questions.

The program will be moderated by Mr. Wagner D. Jackson, member of the Mayor's Urban Renewal Committee.

The program is to be presented in the public interest by the Walnut Street Branch Y.M.C.A. and is open to the public

The Walnut Street YMCA was engaged with issues of importance to the African American community. In 1956, an information session on slum clearance was held as part of the Public Affairs programming. That year, the Wilmington Housing Authority focused on the clearance of slum areas. This was of concern for the people of the East Side of Wilmington, where the Walnut Street YMCA was located. (Courtesy of the Walnut Street YMCA.)

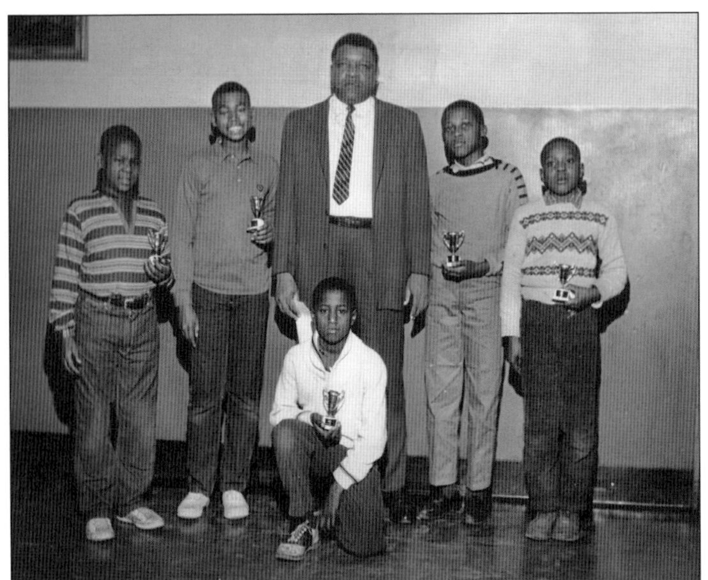

This group of young men are holding trophies, but it is not apparent which club they are representing. The young man kneeling in the front is Maurice Smith, and standing from left to right are Charles Tate, Melvin Brisco, Herman McKinney, Thurman Brown, and George Washington. McKinney was employed by the organization and was also a resident in the dormitory. He appears to be the advisor of the group. (Courtesy of the Walnut Street YMCA.)

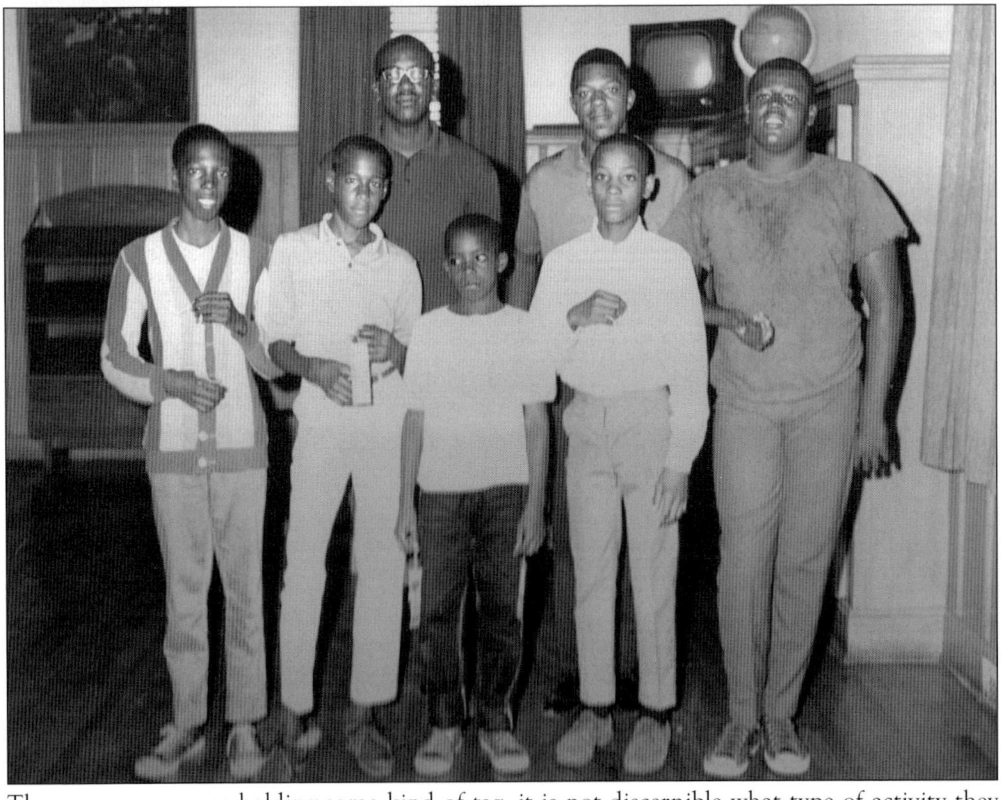

These young men are holding some kind of tag; it is not discernible what type of activity they represent. From left to right are (first row) unidentified, Billy Ward, Jay Faulkner, Vernell Jackson, and Edward Johnson; (second row) unidentified and Herman Pulliam. Johnson learned to swim at Walnut Street when he was about six years old. As a teenager, he passed the lifesaving course and became a lifeguard. Johnson also worked at the bowling alley and sometimes earned as much as $25 a week. (Courtesy of the Walnut Street YMCA.)

Enid Wallace Haley has a long history with the YMCA. She learned to swim at the Walnut Street Y and participated in other activities there. The leadership skills she honed at Walnut Street served her well in adult life. She became a highly respected professional at Delmarva Power. Wallace-Haley has won numerous awards for her community service. She is a direct descendent of Frederick Douglass. Wallace-Haley made history when she became the first African American female board chair of the YMCA of Delaware. (Courtesy of Enid Wallace Haley.)

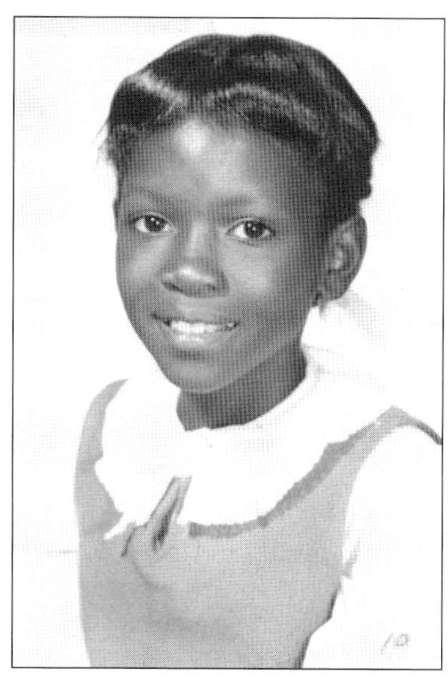

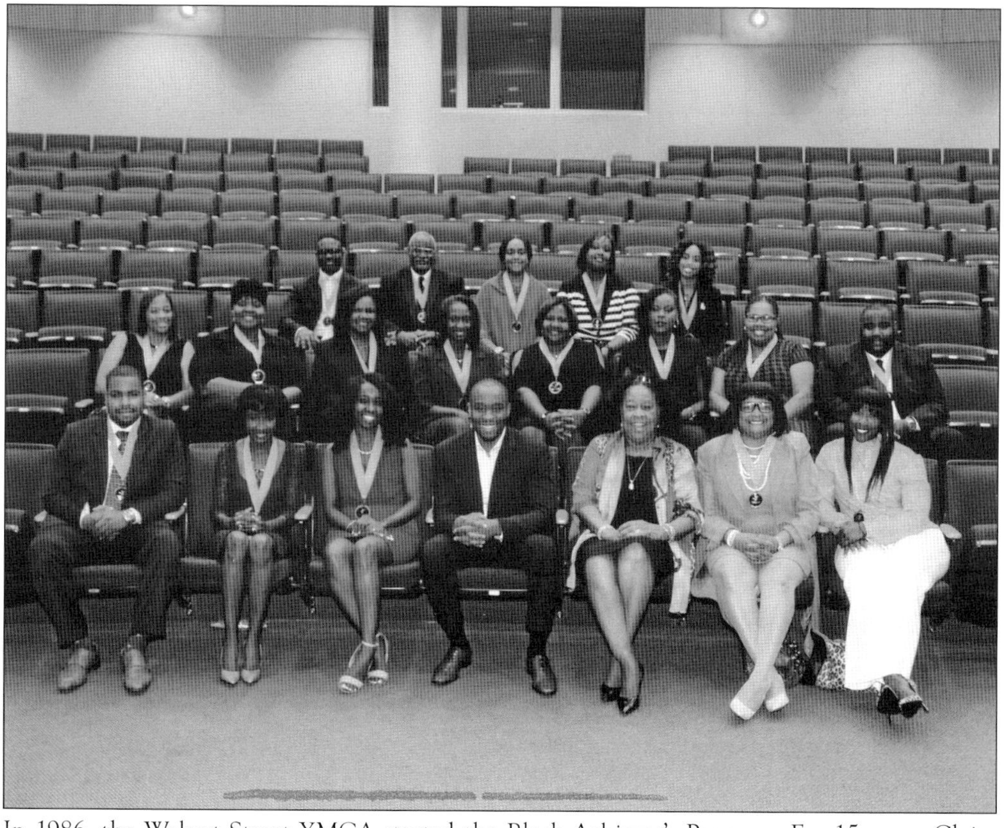

In 1986, the Walnut Street YMCA started the Black Achiever's Program. For 15 years, Claire Lamar Carey headed the program. As a tribute to her longtime contributions, an award was named in her honor. In addition to her work at Walnut Street, Carey also served as the board president of the YWCA of Delaware. From 1991 to 1997, she held a volunteer position on the national YWCA board becoming vice president. She is pictured here with one of the Black Achiever classes. Carey is the third person from the right in the first row. (Courtesy of Claire Lamar Carey.)

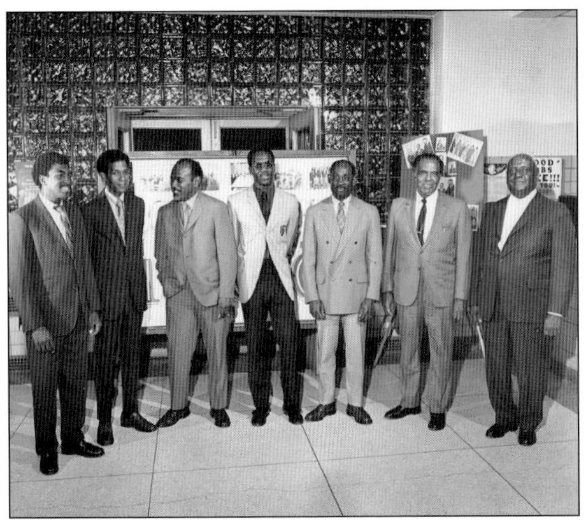

This is a photograph of the staff of the Walnut Street YMCA in what appears to be the early 1960s. From left to right are Donald Ridgeway, housing; Charles Henry, youth programs; Ernest Congo, industrial services; Darrell Clark, industrial services at the Central YMCA; Gilbert Jackson, part-time swimming instructor; John B. Redmond, executive director; and George Taylor, physical education. Jackson had left his position as physical education director for a teaching career but maintained his connection with Walnut Street as a part-swimming instructor. (Courtesy of the Walnut Street YMCA.)

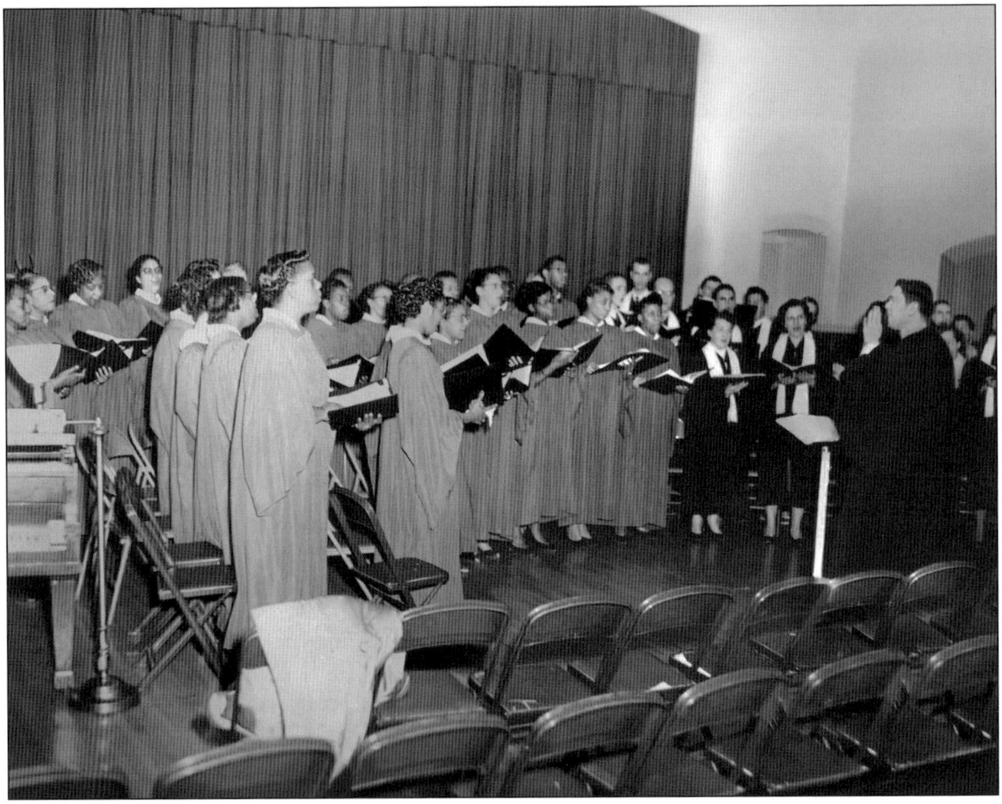

This is a 1950s photograph of what appears to be an interracial choir. There was an interracial Youth Fellowship Choir with the King Street YWCA and the Walnut Street YWCA. Since there is no identification on the image, it is not clear whether this is that group. There are two identifiable individuals in the photograph: the first woman on the left is Bernice McMicken, who was a night clerk at the Walnut Street YMCA registration desk, and almost directly in the sight of McMicken on the second row facing the front is Retha Simpson Fisher. Fisher was a member of the YWCA Youth Fellowship Choir and the Walnut Street YWCA Y-Teens. Many years later, she became noted for establishing the Food Bank of Delaware. (Courtesy of the YMCA.)

Bibliography

DeShields, Reba E. and Thelma T. Young. *The Walnut Street Branch of the Young Women's Christian Association, History 1935–1945.* Walnut Street YWCA, 1921.

Martin, Debra C. "Wilmington's Civil Rights Activism: Walnut Street YMCA 1940–Present." City of Wilmington Department of Planning and Development, www.wilmingtonde.gov/about-us/city-history/civil-rights-activism. Accessed March 27, 2023.

Young, William S. Sr. History of the Walnut Street Branch YMCA, Fiftieth Anniversary and Annual Meeting. Walnut Street YMCA, 1943.

"1940 Formal Dedication Ceremonies of New Building." *Sunday Morning Star*, September 1, 1940: 14, 16.